Embodying Aga Tausili

Embodying Aga Tausili

A Public Theology from Oceania

Mercy Ah Siu-Maliko

LEXINGTON BOOKS/FORTRESS ACADEMIC
Lanham • Boulder • New York • London

Published by Lexington Books/Fortress Academic
Lexington Books is an imprint of The Rowman & Littlefield Publishing Group, Inc.
4501 Forbes Boulevard, Suite 200, Lanham, Maryland 20706
www.rowman.com

6 Tinworth Street, London SE11 5AL, United Kingdom

Copyright © 2021 The Rowman & Littlefield Publishing Group, Inc.

All rights reserved. No part of this book may be reproduced in any form or by any electronic or mechanical means, including information storage and retrieval systems, without written permission from the publisher, except by a reviewer who may quote passages in a review.

British Library Cataloguing in Publication Information Available

Library of Congress Control Number: 2020949024

ISBN 9781978708525 (cloth) | ISBN 9781978708549 (pbk)
ISBN 9781978708532 (epub)

Contents

List of Figures and Tables — vii
Foreword by David Tombs — ix
Acknowledgments — xi

Prologue: Framing the Study — 1
1 Public Theology — 23
2 The Samoan Context — 47
3 Interwoven Strands of *Fa'asamoa* — 61
4 Listening to "the Public": A *Talanoa* Approach to Field Research — 95
5 *Talanoa* about *Aga Tausili* (Core Values) — 111
6 *Talanoa* about Public Theology — 143
7 The Contours of a Samoan Values-Centered Public Theology — 179
8 Case Study for a Samoan Public Theology: Domestic Violence — 193
Epilogue — 219

Bibliography — 225
Index — 249
About the Author — 257

List of Figures and Tables

FIGURES

Figure 4.1	Steps in the *Talanoa* Process	103
Figure 4.2	Steps in Developing a Grounded Theory	104
Figure 5.1	Values Flowing from *Alofa*	133

TABLES

Table 5.1	Core Values of Village Group	122
Table 5.2	Core Values of Nongovernmental Organizations Group	126
Table 5.3	Core Values of Church Group	127
Table 5.4	Core Values of Government Workers and Politicians Group	130

Foreword

As a Samoan theologian, Mercy Ah Siu-Maliko has been engaging in courageous conversations relating to public theology for a number of years. As is clear in her writing, she passionately believes that public theology can contribute to social transformation on the most pressing issues facing the Pacific churches. She cares deeply for the church, and for how the church can be a channel of God's truth and justice, as well as God's grace and love.

In articulating a public theology in Samoa, this book also has much to say about public theology in other parts of the world. It will be of interest to anyone who wants to know more about public theology and its central concerns. At the same time, its most obvious positive contribution is in relation to Samoa, and to the broader Oceanian region, where discussion of public theology is only just beginning. Ah Siu-Maliko shows that, above all, a credible public theology for Samoa must also be a local and contextual theology. It must speak into, and speak out from, authentic Samoan culture (*fa'asamoa*).

As the book shows, the best way to do this is to ground public theology in the Samoan context in the culture's core values (*aga tausili*), which find parallels in corresponding Christian values—these values being love, justice, reciprocal respect, selfless service, and consensual dialogue. The book weaves these values together into a bold and creative vision of a vibrant theology that is rooted in a distinctively Samoan worldview. This approach complements and extends other innovative and important books that have offered a Samoan postcolonial perspective and brought Samoan values to bear on the Bible, such as Vaitusi Nofoaiga's work *A Samoan Reading of Discipleship in Matthew* (2017).

The vision of public theology offered here is closely oriented to praxis and to social justice. Ah Siu-Maliko has worked tirelessly within the church to confront issues that many would rather pass over in silence or avoid altogether. These include the painful subject of family violence, and violence against women and girls more generally, which she discusses as a case study of her values-centered public theology in chapter 8. In Samoa, and in Samoan communities in Aotearoa New Zealand, the churches have an unparalleled social position and moral authority, which offers unrivaled potential to offer leadership on this issue. In her other writings, Ah Siu-Maliko has written about some of the challenges related to the churches' response to social issues such as violence against women, and she has offered contextual bible studies to aid in this work. In this book, she shows how such initiatives can be supported by her holistic vision of public theology. As such, the book makes a major contribution to the global conversation on public theology, and sets out her especially welcome Samoan perspective.

Professor David Tombs
Howard Paterson Chair of Theology and Public Issues
University of Otago

Acknowledgments

I remember with a thankful heart God's grace and faithfulness during my research and work toward the completion of this book. I am grateful to a number of people who have assisted me tremendously along the way, including:

The Department of Theology and Religious Studies at the University of Otago, in particular Professor Murray Rae, Professor Paul Trebilco, and Professor David Tombs of the Centre for Theology and Public Issues.

A very special thank-you from the bottom of my heart to my dearest friend and mentor Dr. Lydia Johnson for working tirelessly in proofreading and editing this manuscript into its current form.

My appreciation goes to the editorial team at Lexington Books for their assistance and support, and to Dr. Jione Havea for his very helpful comments, which have greatly strengthened the book.

I want to thank my husband and partner in ministry, Rev. Dr. Selota Maliko, and our children, Gamaliel Sialafua Latatuli, Yona Julia, and Lolomaitiga Selota, for their encouragement and support.

I give thanks to all of these God's agents, through whom God has sustained and brought me to this moment.

This book is dedicated to the memory of my parents, Lolomatauama Eddie George Ah Siu and Tagaloa Launiu Palaamo-Ah Siu.

Prologue
Framing the Study

Christianity sets no limits on the Good News of Jesus Christ, but its view of the relevance of Christian faith for the whole of society has been somewhat contested throughout its history. The history of Christianity demonstrates the complexity of the relationship between the religious and secular spheres. This is illustrated in popular culture today by, for example, debates in France about the display of religious symbols such as Muslim headscarves in public,[1] or legal battles in the United States over conservative Christians' refusal to serve homosexual customers.[2]

Some sociologists of religion contend that religion is making a comeback in the secular West that is facilitating Christian re-engagement with social issues. John Micklethwait and Adrian Wooldridge make this viewpoint clear in the title of their book *God Is Back: How the Global Revival of Faith Is Changing the World*, arguing that religious perspectives are increasingly becoming an accepted part of public discourse in Europe.[3] While the "Christian Right" in the United States has long been vociferous in its public campaigns against abortion and gay rights, proponents of the "comeback" position presumably are referring to an uptick in mainstream religious voices arguing for social justice in areas such as immigrants' rights, income inequality, and climate justice.

Other commentators, however, question any notion of a resurgence of religion (specifically Christianity) in the West, noting the steady decline in church participation.[4] The question of whether Christianity is growing or waning today is complex rather than straightforward. According to Manfred Ernst's most recent research,

1. Only about one-third of the world's population are Christians, with a slight decrease over the past 100 years. 2. The percentage of Christians

in Europe, North America, Australia and New Zealand is decreasing, as well as the percentage (to a much lower extent) in Latin America and Polynesia, while the percentage of Christians in relation to the total population has increased in Africa, Asia, Melanesia and Micronesia.[5]

Kevin Ward is among those sociologists of religion who posit that, while church involvement is declining in the West, belief in the essence of the Christian faith is holding steady, and indeed may be growing in some contexts. He contrasts "belonging" (which is declining) with "believing" (which is relatively strong).[6] In general, the older, established churches are declining, while newer churches and para-churches (often called NRMs or New Religious Movements) are growing. Ernst's research shows that the most dramatic trend in worldwide Christianity in the post–World War II era has been the "rapid growth of Pentecostal-charismatic Christianity and the concomitant emergence of thousands of independent local churches."[7] These newer churches are popular because they offer a personalistic faith that makes adherents "feel good" amid the stresses of postmodern life. However, rather than engaging with the world, they retreat from the world. They have made significant inroads in the island nations of Oceania.[8]

At the same time, ultra-conservative forms of several established religions have dramatically expanded their societal impact across the globe. Although their personal motives may be similar to those of adherents of the NRMs (finding a secure anchor against the tides of unprecedented social change), rather than retreating into personal spirituality these religious movements are very engaged with the world around them. They want to remake their societies to conform to their beliefs, and thus their religious fervor goes hand in hand with extreme forms of nationalism.

This trend can be seen in movements such as the Buddhist nationalists attempting to rid Myanmar of its Rohingya Muslim minority; Hindu nationalists attacking Muslims in India; Muslim extremists attempting to create an Islamic caliphate (super-state) across the Middle East; and the Christian Right in the United States, who want to make the United States a white Christian nation where ethnic minorities are unwelcome and the right to own guns is sacred.

What all of these contemporary religious groups have in common is that they exist in "the world." They are a part of the social fabric of their contexts, wherever those may be. Even those who seek to retreat from the world and do not overtly speak into the public sphere are having an impact on their societies. Those who identify with extreme religious nationalism, in contrast, scream loudly into the public sphere, grabbing the public's attention, but not in a way that promotes the common good.

The question for this study is not so much whether religion is waning or resurging, but rather, "What are we being called to say and do as Christians in the social contexts where we live?" This study situates that question contextually in the Pacific Islands (generally referred to in this work by the more common designation, Oceania), and specifically in the public sphere of Samoa. To answer this question, we seek a guide in the form of public theology.

PUBLIC THEOLOGY AS AN OVERARCHING FRAMEWORK

Jürgen Moltmann in *Theology of Hope* argues that theology must reflect publicly the character of God's Kingdom, which is by its very nature relational at every level, including the societal and cultural.[9] Clarence Joldersma goes a step further claiming that everyone is religious, in the sense that we all share an "ultimate concern" as human beings about life's deepest questions.[10] Expressions of this ultimate concern will inevitably take us into the public sphere.

> Everyone has a comprehensive framework of basic beliefs as answers to these ultimate concerns . . . that shape how to live and think about the world. This set of basic beliefs could be called a "basic theology." Articulating one's basic theology, critically examining it, . . . exploring how it can help clarify non-theological issues, and exploring how it can lead to human flourishing can then all be claimed as doing public theology.[11]

Elaine Graham is among those public theologians who optimistically maintain that "the re-emergence of religion in public, in areas such as politics, urbanization, social policy and law, may well turn out to be the defining characteristic of our generation."[12] However, while more religious voices may be clamoring to be heard in public, we should not naively dismiss the legacy of the privatization of Christianity. The fact that Western Christianity became increasingly privatized under the influence of the Enlightenment (also known as the Age of Reason) in the eighteenth century, which drew a line between the sacred and secular spheres, predisposed many churches not to take a public stance *as the church* on social issues, leaving such activism largely to secular actors and institutions. This at times led to the church's silent complicity in discrimination, violence, and abuse, an example being the silence of many churches on slavery in the American South in the 1800s.

There were, of course, notable exceptions to this privatizing trend. One well-known example was the Christian activist William Wilberforce's public campaign in England to end slavery in the first half of the nineteenth century.

Although he typified the common belief in his day that Christian faith was about cultivating personal morality, he believed that if enough Christians nurtured this morality it would spill over into public policies.[13] John Wesley, founder of the Methodist movement in mid-eighteenth-century England, also believed that personal sanctification (holiness) would result in public action to relieve the suffering caused by the widespread poverty and social-class disparities that were the hallmark of English society in his day.[14]

Confronted with the dire global crises impacting the world today—from the social inequalities that accompany globalization, to the growing upheavals caused by the climate crisis, to violent conflicts resulting in mass migrations—an increasing number of public theologians in the West have called for Christians to re-engage with the world.

> Writers such as Archbishop Williams, Jonathan Chaplin, Madeleine Bunting, Roger Trigg, Chris Marshall and others are saying [that] religious voices should no longer be excluded from the public domain, not only because religion is more high profile than before, but because, as Williams himself puts it, one of the consequences of religious interests being excluded from public debates is a coarsening of political discourse.[15]

Jonathan Chaplin[16] and Rowan Williams[17] in particular have pointed out that any attempt to exclude religious voices from public discourse does an injustice to the increasing numbers of religious voices desiring the right to be heard. Duncan Forrester, one of the pioneers of public theology, argues that "to withdraw . . . from public debate would result in [theology's] serious impoverishment."[18] Melissa Yates makes a more basic argument for the necessity of theology's re-engagement with the public sphere, namely that "one's basic moral/religious convictions are (partly) self-constitutive and are therefore a principal ground . . . of political deliberation and choice. To "bracket" such convictions is therefore to bracket—to annihilate—essential aspects of one's very self."[19]

These assertions are all valid, but a challenge for religious voices being taken seriously in the public sphere is that the Christian religion has been trivialized in the West (and, one could argue, this trend can also be seen in other parts of the world). Stephen Carter has examined the ways in which American popular culture has trivialized Christianity in recent decades, thereby undermining its role as a significant mediating force between the people and the state.[20] Such trivializing can be seen today in the "marketing" of churches, especially the so-called mega-churches, as religious entertainment centers that vie for "customers" with the latest in technological wizardry, rousing praise bands and self-absorbed theology (which some critics refer to as "Jesus-is-my-boyfriend" theology[21]). This dumbing-down of Christianity undercuts its ability to make meaningful contributions to the search for moral solutions to society's problems.

This is a rather confusing picture of religious impulses at times at odds with each other in the world today. A viable approach to public theology has the potential to be an antidote to this confusion. This work posits that there is a critical need for the development of an effective public theology for the particular social context of Samoa (and, by extension, other island nations in Oceania, and indeed potentially other contexts beyond Oceania).

In this study I will construct a framework for the contours of such a public theology by, first, explicating key elements of what constitutes a public theology, both from literature on public theology largely by Western theologians, and also from contributions by Pacific Islander theologians to discourse on contextual theology. I will then examine the religious, cultural, and public contexts of contemporary Samoa, where the core values of love, respect, consensual dialogue, selfless service, and justice collectively guide what Samoans describe as their *fa'asamoa* (Samoan way of life). I will show how these core values have points of convergence with corresponding Christian values, and make the claim that a public theology for Samoa must be grounded in these Samoan-Christian values. This way of doing public theology may suggest a broader appeal to a values-centric approach to public theology in other contexts.

To further support my argument for the development of a Samoan public theology, this study will provide insights from the findings of field research, gleaned from interviews with seventy-five participants living and working in different settings in Samoa—village, church, government, and non-governmental organizations. These research participants defined what they perceived to be core values for themselves and for Samoa, and what they believed a Samoan public theology might look like.

I submit that a public theology is vital for the common good and flourishing of all members of Samoan society and that the key features of this theology are the core values that undergird the Samoan culture and the Christian faith. This contextual public theology is fleshed out at the end of this work by means of a case study on a public theology response to the pertinent social issue of domestic violence.

PERSONAL ORIENTATION TO PUBLIC THEOLOGY

My initial interest in public theology began when I was researching my Master of Theology thesis at Pacific Theological College in Fiji from 1997 to 1998. My thesis drew heavily on Paulo Freire's concept of *conscientization*. Conscientization, according to Freire, is the process in which men [and women], not as recipients, but as knowing subjects, achieve a deepening awareness both of the socio-cultural reality that shapes their lives, and of their capacity to transform that reality through action upon it.[22]

This process was designed originally for the purpose of teaching illiterate peasants in Brazil to read, in order that they could then vote and become decision-makers in their communities. Conscientization was then applied to broader learning contexts for illiterate people, where there was a great disparity between the rich and the poor.[23] Freire found that education, whether formal or informal, is never neutral. It is always "political" in the sense that its objective is either to maintain the status quo or to educate for liberation.

Freire's philosophy of conscientization was subsequently adapted to liberate people from any unjust situation. It aimed to bring about radical social, political, and economic changes for the poor and oppressed of the so-called Third World[24] as they become actively engaged in bringing about their own liberation. This conscientization comes about through the cultivation of critical analysis skills regarding one's sociocultural conditioning.

In my Master's thesis, I situated the conscientization process among women in the Women's Fellowships of the Methodist Church of Samoa. This process was implemented through interactive bible studies, as a way of providing women the space to voice their concerns as they participated in their own process of empowerment. The biblical stories selected for study[25] brought to light particular social problems, such as violence and threats to neighborliness, which women were able to name and discuss openly.

In my own theological engagement with Freire, I discovered that the transforming power of the gospel can lead to an all-encompassing liberation in our relationships with one another, with society, with creation, and with God. This focus moves beyond Freire's "liberating education" to uncovering, instilling, and acting on the gospel's transformative vision in our own communities and societies.

My next exposure to public theology occurred during 2005 and 2006, when I was working for a regional ecumenical organization, the South Pacific Association of Theological Schools (SPATS), based in Fiji. SPATS' objective is to strengthen theological education in the Pacific region by developing and maintaining mutual cooperation among the region's twenty-six accredited theological schools, so as to further quality theological education and leadership training in the region.

I was the coordinator of Weavers, SPATS' advocacy program designed to promote theological education for women throughout the region. This program also addressed social issues affecting the lives of Pacific Islander women. One of the issues we targeted was violence against women. In order to raise people's consciousness on this issue, we held forums and workshops to promote dialogue and action around the problem of violence against women in Oceania. These forums included representatives from theological schools, churches, and civil society. The final product of these consultations was a coursebook about violence against women in Pacific island societies, which included recommendations regarding the role of the churches in preventing and responding to this widespread social problem.

The experiences and knowledge acquired from engaging in theological studies and working in the Pacific region raised my own awareness of the realities affecting the common good of Pacific Islanders, including those in my native Samoa. My personal conscientization led me toward my doctoral research on a contextual public theology for Samoa that would translate the message of the gospel in Samoa's public sphere, in a culturally relevant way. That research forms the backbone of this book.

DEFINING KEY CONCEPTS

In order to understand the framework and presuppositions that undergird the proposed Samoan public theology, a number of key concepts need to be explained at the outset, as they form the foundation of this study. They are described in the sub-sections below.

Public

The origin of the word *public* is the Latin *populus* or *poplicus*, which denotes a particular "mass" or population who are associated with a common interest. Alastair Hannay acknowledges the common association of "public" today with nationalities, but notes its historical evolution:

> It [public] refers to a people from within the bounds of a nation. . . . But in Roman times the term acquired chiefly political connotations, and the public were often identified as those who actually participated in national assemblies and spoke for the nation.[26]

What was public was what was collectively shared by these stakeholders and open to view.

Gabriel Vasquez and Maureen Taylor identify the *public* as a population of individuals associated with civic affairs, or affairs of state.[27] The American philosopher John Dewey defined *public* more broadly as any "group distinctive enough to require recognition and a name"[28]—that name being "the public." Here the public is any group of people who, facing a common problem, organize themselves to address it.[29]

Public may also refer to inclusivity, something freely available and open to everyone. However, there are situations where this understanding cannot be assumed due to political, economic or cultural factors. Alastair Hannay acknowledges that "not all debate on public affairs . . . [is] itself public in the sense of being open to view . . . . Public in this sense would refer to those events . . . to which the people have access as spectators."[30] The definition of *public* thus varies according to specific contexts and traditions, but I use the term in this study to refer to all Samoan citizens, as they collectively have a stake in how life is lived in the Samoan context.

Public Sphere

The origins of the concept of the *public sphere* may be traced back to Aristotle. Aristotle viewed the public sphere as public life represented in the setting of the marketplace (*agora*), where citizens gathered as equals to discuss matters of common concern.[31] Building on this historical understanding, Gurcan Kocan defines the *public sphere* as relationships "socially and politically constituted or constructed in particular times and places, with the active involvement of people sharing a set of traditions."[32]

One of the most prominent theorists of the public sphere in the past half-century is the German philosopher Jürgen Habermas. Habermas regards the public sphere as an open forum, and traces its roots to seventeenth- and eighteenth-century Europe, when new concepts of public opinion began to emerge.[33] This notion of the public sphere developed in societies where the state and market economies dominated daily life, such that a "bourgeois public sphere evolved in the tense field between state and society."[34] This notion of the public sphere is associated with specific public spaces and practices in which an informed public opinion is "shaped and maintained, resists the powers of politics and markets, and is characterized by critical discussion between equal participants, free of constraint."[35] Here private people can join together to form a public. Public theology can take place in this public sphere, when it both informs and is informed by public opinion on public issues.[36]

The American political philosopher Iris Marion Young summarizes Habermas's idea of the public sphere as "a process through which problems of the whole society are discussed, processed, and finally brought to influence the formation of . . . law and public policy."[37] For Young, the public sphere is "the primary connector between people and power. We should judge the health of a public sphere by how well it functions as a space of opposition and accountability, on the one hand, and policy influence, on the other."[38]

A word of caution is issued by the Turkish American philosopher Seyla Benhabib, who warns that, in Habermas's idea of the public sphere, the distinction between public and private can have the unintended effect of moving issues that affect women (issues of "reproduction, nurture and care for the young, the sick, and the elderly"[39]) into the private realm and out of the public sphere. She argues that if the public sphere is to be open to any discussion that affects the population, there cannot be distinctions between "what is" and "what is not" discussed.[40] This cautionary note is important in the Samoan context, where certain topics are avoided in public settings, and where certain groups (women and youth in particular) are restricted from public debate.

Samoan Public Sphere

In the Samoan context, the public sphere is often associated with the media, in the form of newspapers, television, and radio. Village councils and parliament can also be regarded as examples of the public sphere, because they are spaces where open discussions take place. But it is important to note that the rationale for a public sphere in Samoa is different from that in Western societies, where individual rights and personal freedoms are paramount. In Samoa, cultural protocols provide the criteria for one's entry into the public sphere. For example, the public sphere of the village council is open only to individuals who are *matai* (chiefs) and the untitled men who serve the *matai* (the untitled men being present to provide such service during village council meetings, but not as decision-makers). One's access into this public sphere thus depends on one's status, and it is often gender-restricted. In some villages in Samoa, women are not allowed to become *matai* or to run for parliament.

The media is ostensibly a more open public sphere in Samoa, because theoretically anyone can express his or her opinion through public comment platforms in newspapers, television, or radio. However, some individuals and families have been banished from their villages for exercising this freedom. The reality of Hannay's assertion that not all debate on public affairs is itself public, in the sense of being open to view or access, is evident in the Samoan public sphere. Cultural protocols and norms restrict some people from entering specific Samoan public spheres.

"Public" in Public Theology

Writers on public theology have pointed out that there is not just one public to which public theology relates. David Tracy describes the *public* in public theology as referring to the academy, church, and society, whereas Max Stackhouse identifies four such publics: religious, political, academic, and economic. Marion Maddox speaks of the *public* in public theology in three ways. First, it refers to "everything else" (beyond the individual), especially the arenas of the state and markets.[41] Second, it implies spaces where people can deliberate "independently of all other pressures and interests; [it is] a place that no one can colonise."[42] Third, it seeks to provide public goods accessible to all.[43]

Kenneth Himes and Michael Himes define Christians' engagement with the public as signaling a concern for all issues that affect our common life. This is a broad understanding that incorporates not only the political sphere but also the sociocultural systems of a society. In this sense, as Robert Wuthnow posits, *public* as it relates to public theology refers to "something broader than either politics or public policy, namely the ongoing discourse that takes place in any society about its collective values."[44] This suggests our collective responsibility as Christians to make constructive changes for the good of society. In support of this view, Kathryn Tanner contends that the *public* in public theology refers to "the sort of deliberation in common that shapes a responsible citizenry."[45]

According to Don Browning and Francis Schüssler Fiorenza, "Theology becomes public insofar as it enters into dialogue with many voices and diverse communities towards the transformation of the marginalized in society."[46] This notion draws on an understanding of public as referring to any group of people who are connected through their mutual interest in particular issues of concern for the common good. Members of these publics need not even be located in the same place, and may include diverse citizen groups—for instance, the electorate, civil society organizations, local community groups, lobbying groups, or churches.[47]

Common Good

The concept of the common good was first explicitly articulated over 2,000 years ago in the writings of Plato, Aristotle, and Cicero. The ethicist John Rawls has defined the *common good* as "certain general conditions that are . . . equally to everyone's advantage."[48] In the Christian tradition, the common good is summed up in the second great commandment, to "love your neighbor as yourself." Its development as a Christian concept "goes back at least as far as John Chrysostom in the fourth century, with St. Thomas Aquinas shaping it into the form in which we know it today, as he synthesized the thinking of Aristotle and Augustine in the 13th century."[49] It is thus not surprising that Roman Catholic social teachings are filled with statements equating the common good with Christians' desire that God's "will be done on earth," for which Christians pray in the Lord's Prayer.[50]

Walter Brueggemann speaks of the erosion of the common good as a crisis confronting postmodern societies—including the Christian church:

> The great crisis among us is the crisis of the 'common good,' the sense of community solidarity that binds us all in a common destiny—haves and have-nots,

the rich and the poor. We face a crisis about the common good because there are powerful forces at work among us to resist the common good, to violate community solidarity, and to deny a common destiny.⁵¹

This notion of the common good, in David Hollenbach's words, "can only be the good that exists in a community of solidarity among active, equal human beings."⁵²

Theology

The word *theology* has its origin in two Greek words, *theos* and *logos*, one meaning "god" and the other "word." Theology is thus "words (or "the Word") about God." Anselm (d. 1109 CE) famously described theology in his seminal work, *Proslogium*, as *faith seeking understanding*.⁵³ Here faith creates a desire to understand the ways of God, and thus requires believers to make active use of the gift of reason. By the Middle Ages, the term "theology" had come to be understood as systematic, disciplined reflection on the triune God.⁵⁴

In the contemporary era, Daniel Migliore has expanded on the notion of theology as "faith seeking understanding" by incorporating and engaging with theological perspectives not previously heard, particularly from the Global South and from women.⁵⁵ John Macquarrie has defined *theology* as "the study which, through participation in and reflection upon a religious faith, seeks to express the content of this faith in the clearest and most coherent language available."⁵⁶ This definition highlights three essential elements of theological discourse: participation, reflection, and expression.

But while the "discipline" of theology largely came to be associated with scholarly discourse among those viewed as professionals situated in academia, the actual boundaries of theology extend far beyond the academy. If theology is "faith seeking understanding," then the faithful are all practitioners of theology. Howard Stone and James Duke are among those who understand Christian theology as every believer's human response to the gift of faith; it is our collective "seeking after understanding—a process of thinking about life in the light of the faith that Christians engage in because of their calling."⁵⁷

For Jürgen Moltmann, theology is understood as being open to new insights emanating from particular cultures, while being rooted in scripture and tradition. It is his conviction that Christian theology must be in and for the world and receptive to the ethical demands made of it by its social situation. To speak theologically is thus to speak into the public sphere. Doing theology in this way also means engaging in an open-ended path. As Moltmann describes his own journey on this path, *the road emerged as I walked it*.⁵⁸ Along this road there are many "worldly" issues which theologians must respond to, but in addressing these issues they must also speak of God. If not, the theological dimension is lost.

Contextual Theology

Bruce Nicholls has rightly claimed that "the history of the church is a history of contextualized theologies that are varying responses to the work of the Spirit of God in particular historical contexts."[59] Contextual theology as a definable movement began with the World Council of Churches (WCC). Although elements of the contextual approach had appeared in WCC discussions in 1955, when the WCC organized the Bangalore Conference on the Indigenization of Worship, the movement began in earnest in the early 1970s.[60] The term "context" was first used in this sense at a WCC council meeting in Louvain in 1971,[61] which was shortly followed by the introduction of the term "contextualization" by the Theological Education Fund in 1972.[62]

Perhaps the most influential proponent of contextual theology is the Catholic theologian Stephen Bevans'.[63] He focuses not so much on the nature of theology as on the variety of ways in which theology interacts with socio-cultural contexts.[64] Bevans' defines contextual theology as "a way of doing theology in which one takes into account the spirit and message of the gospel; the tradition of the church; the culture in which one is theologizing; and social change within that culture, whether brought about by western technological process or the grassroots struggle for equality, justice and liberation."[65] He even goes so far as to claim that

> Doing theology contextually is not an option, nor is it something that should only interest people from the Third World, missionaries who work there, or ethnic communities within dominant cultures. The contextualization of theology—the attempt to understand Christian faith in terms of a particular context—is really a theological imperative. As we have come to understand theology today, it is a process that is part of the very nature of theology itself.[66]

Bevans' describes six models of contextual theology, which are briefly summarized below.

The Translation Model: This model of contextual theology focuses on studying a given culture for potential parallels with the Christian faith and then communicating biblical and theological insights through this cultural lens. Here, "the values and thought forms of culture and the structures of social change are understood not so much as good in themselves, but as convenient vehicles for this essential, unchanging deposit of truth."[67] The

Translation Model is probably the one most people think of when they do theology in context.⁶⁸ *Truth* is defined by the Christian faith, and the concern is to avoid corruption of the faith by culture, while acknowledging that the gospel can only take root if it is "translated" and made at home in particular cultures.⁶⁹

The Anthropological Model: This model takes what typifies a given culture and looks for God in it. It is creation-centered, focusing on the world being God's world, in contrast to redemption-centered theology which sees the world as fallen and corrupt. The anthropological model celebrates the reality of God's image and work present within every culture. The strength of this model is that it takes all peoples and cultures seriously; its weakness lies in its potential failure to critique the ways in which every culture falls short of God's designs for human wholeness.

The Praxis Model: This model is focused on the outworkings of faith in a given context. It follows a continuous cycle of action and reflection, and "regards theology not as a generally applicable, finished product that is valid for all times and all places, but as an understanding of and wrestling with God's presence in very particular situations."⁷⁰ The praxis model emphasizes the living out of the gospel as a reflective engagement with people's lived experience. Its strength lies in the imperative of living life together in Christ and belief in the transformative power of social change. The danger is that the elevation of contextual experience may end up supplanting the message of the gospel.⁷¹

The Synthetic Model: This model, "tries to preserve the importance of the gospel message and the heritage of traditional doctrinal formulations while at the same time acknowledging the vital role that context has played . . . even to the setting of the theological agenda."⁷²

It assumes that a given context has elements of both uniqueness and similarities with other contexts. The strength of this model is its assertion that every voice belongs at the theological table. The danger is that those doing theology may end up selling out to a dominant cultural narrative or avoiding confrontation with it. Along the continuum from creation-centered to redemption-centered approaches, Bevans' locates the synthetic model at "the center of the continuum, midway between emphasis on the experience of the present . . . and the experience of the past."⁷³

The Transcendental Model: In this model, "theology happens as a person struggles more adequately and authentically to articulate and appropriate [the] ongoing relationship with the divine."⁷⁴ This must happen if we are to understand God's revelation in particular contexts. This model interprets individuals' or communities' experiences in the light of God's revelatory action, which is received in specific contexts. The advantage of this model is its acknowledgment that all authentic theology emerges from within a context. Its disadvantage lies in the unanswered question of who gets to define what "authentic" means.

The Counter-Cultural Model: Bevans' acknowledges that there are practitioners of theology who believe that "some contexts are simply antithetical to the gospel and need to be challenged by the gospel's liberating and healing power; . . . the gospel represents a . . . radically alternate worldview that differs profoundly from human experiences of the world and the cultures that humans create."[75] The benefit of this approach is its critical stance toward culture, which may be lacking in some of the other models. A disadvantage is that it may alienate people who are embedded in their cultures and who may feel that Christians from elsewhere are denigrating their cultural values and worldviews.

Among Bevans' six contextual theology models, the synthetic model serves as the primary typological framework for developing a Samoan contextual public theology. The synthetic model shares many common elements with both the translation model and the praxis model. Like the former, it sees the Bible as more than a rigid hermeneutical lens through which to view experiences. Like the latter, it acknowledges that context is more than simply the concepts that are important to a given culture; the wisdom found in particular contexts must be acted on.[76]

In highlighting the importance of contextual theology, this study takes seriously the assertion of public theologian Clive Pearson, originally from New Zealand but based in Australia, that Pacific Islanders must do theology in a way that takes their context(s) seriously. New Zealander theologian Neil Darragh offers a similar challenge when he states that those who have historically been on the periphery of theological conversation must become doers of theology rather than passive recipients and consumers of ideas that have arisen elsewhere.

In response to this challenge, more Pacific Islanders are now highlighting the importance of developing theologies that emerge from within their respective contexts. This process counteracts the undermining of island cultures experienced during the process of colonization. There is a growing awareness in Oceanian contexts that uncritically accepting foreign frameworks for doing theology may subvert cherished patterns of cultural identity and even perpetuate neo-colonialism.

Public Theology in Samoa

Mataupu silisili fa'alaua'itele and *terosia fa'alaua'itele* are the two Samoan translations of public theology used interchangeably in this book. *Mataupu* is "topic or issue," and *silisili* can be translated as "significant." *Fa'alaua'itele* is "public" or "general." *Mataupu silisili fa'alaua'itele* is public theology within the Protestant tradition, while *terosia fa'alaua'itele* is public theology within the Catholic tradition. *Terosia* refers to theology. The shape of a Samoan public theology will unfold as Samoa's core cultural and Christian values are articulated and allowed to inform the praxis of public theology in Samoan society.

Values

The term *values* connotes elements of moral worth in the character of a person or group, underpinning and manifesting what a person prizes most—rather like the "pearl of great price" in Jesus's parable (Matt 13:45–46).[77] Kenneth Medhurst and James Sweeney speak of *factual values*—"the motives of the heart—social, psychological and spiritual imperatives at the roots of human action and making demands on the person."[78]

Modern theories of values in the West are largely grounded in the work of scholars such as Melvin Kohn (values and class),[79] Milton Rokeach (general value systems),[80] and Clyde Kluckholm (values at the group level).[81] They all concur that values are evident at both individual and group levels. At the individual level, values are internalized social representations of moral beliefs to which people appeal as the ultimate rationale for their actions. They are the values an individual inculcates through the process of socialization.

At the group level, values are cultural ideals held in common by members of a group; the group's "social mind" is encompassed in concepts described as values.[82] Rokeach provides a succinct explanation of how a collective value system is shaped in his comment that such values are "the result of all the cultural, institutional and personal forces that act upon a person throughout his lifetime."[83] This explanation points to the fact that values are influenced by many forms of socialization, including those of religious institutions.

Samoan Values

My translation of values as *aga tausili* has affinities with the way it is defined by the Ministry of Education, Sports, and Culture in Samoa, which reflects a holistic incorporation of beliefs and actions. Here values are "the internal beliefs and attitudes held by individuals and groups that are used in responding to everyday events."[84] My own understanding of *aga tausili* will highlight how these core values function as the moral underpinning of the *fa'asamoa*. They are the ideal moral behaviors to which Samoans aspire, defining their sense of identity as Samoans.

In this book I propose that there are five underlying core values in the *fa'asamoa*: *tautua* (selfless service), *fa'aaloalo* (reciprocal respect), *soalaupule* (consensual dialogue), *alofa* (love), and *amiotonu* (justice). They are identified as *aga tausili* through the agency of *aga-i-fanua* (customs of the land) and *fa'akerisiano* (Christian tradition and practice). All Samoans are nurtured in these values, regardless of their social location, and all of these values are interwoven threads of one overarching value system, which is *fa'asamoa*.

SIGNIFICANCE AND CHALLENGES OF THIS STUDY

This study offers an original articulation of a public theology that is grounded in a particular society's core values—in this case, Samoan society. In appropriating Samoan core values as a public theology response to social problems—fleshed out in this work by means of a case study on domestic violence—I hope to offer a contextual theological contribution that has ramifications not only for Samoan church and society but for other similar contexts as well. My assertion is that a values-centered public theology has much to offer to the relationship between the churches and public life in every social context.

The core values highlighted in this work reflect the creative interplay between the moral praxis of *fa'asamoa* and the Christian faith. The discussion of the specific social issue of domestic violence from theological, sociological, and cultural perspectives highlights the importance of an interdisciplinary approach to developing a contextual public theology.

The qualitative research undertaken in this work aims to be as representative a sampling of the Samoan public as possible, while acknowledging that qualitative research cannot be "representative" in the same way that quantitative research claims to be. This research provides a snapshot of a wide range of participants from different social settings in Samoa, but it does not include children and youth under twenty-one years of age, since the contributions of participants required the knowledge and experience associated with adulthood.

Challenges encountered during the fieldwork portion of this study included gaining access to some participants and ensuring that their participation would actually take place (especially for those with heavy work obligations), helping participants to feel comfortable talking about a serious and unfamiliar topic, and translation issues. Although my status as the wife of a pastor was helpful in gaining access to participants, it may also have occasionally acted as a barrier to free expression on the part of some participants.

Participants did not always find it easy to talk about their Samoan core values. Fanaafi Aiono-Le Tagaloa suggests that this is because of the tendency of Samoans, like other Pacific Islanders, not to interrogate their values, which are considered intrinsic and thus taken for granted.[85] Moreover, to ask a Samoan about his or her values could imply that one is questioning the integrity of that person's parents, family, and village of origin. In other words, talking about values in Samoa opens up a thickly woven web of interrelatedness, which necessitates considerable interpretive skills.

My attempt to *talanoa* (dialogue freely) with the study participants about their core values was not always an easy task for me personally. This is so because values are connected to emotions. They are a motivational construct that refers to the desirable goals people strive to attain. Talking with fellow Samoans about core values is thus not merely an academic exercise, in the way this is understood in the Western academic world. This kind of conversation involves my whole being as a Samoan, and that of my conversation partners as well.

Translation is an obvious difficulty in all cross-cultural studies. In this study, the difficulties of translation were multilayered, affecting both language translations and cultural discourse translations. Some research participants had difficulties with the Samoan language translations of public theology concepts. This was not surprising given that public theology is a specialized concept previously unknown in Samoa.

STRUCTURE OF THE STUDY

This work consists of this Prologue, eight chapters, and an Epilogue. The Prologue introduces the research topic and defines key terms used in the study. Chapter 1 provides an in-depth discussion of public theology, highlighting its core themes and characteristics. Chapter 2 introduces the Samoan context, and briefly describes the five core values of Samoan culture, noting parallels with Christian values. Chapter 3 explores the Samoan culture in greater depth, analyzing the complexities of the *fa'asamoa* in terms of their bearing on the ways in which core values are understood and enacted.

Chapter 4 provides an explanation of how the field research for this study was conducted using the *talanoa* methodology, and how data was analyzed using constructivist grounded theory. Chapters 5 and 6 bring into focus the results of the field research, highlighting participants' narratives about their core values (chapter 5) and their views on public theology (chapter 6). The findings from the field research, together with the understandings of public theology and *fa'asamoa* in earlier chapters, provide the backdrop for the articulation of a Samoan public theology.

Chapter 7 describes the contours of a values-centered Samoan public theology, reviewing its constituent elements, and the contextual factors that are critical in constructing a public theology for the Samoan context. Chapter 8 then explores ways in which such a public theology might be applied to a particular case study—the problem of domestic violence in Samoa. In constructing a public theology around this issue, Samoa's core values, resources of the Christian faith, and insights from the research participants and secular scholarship are all brought to bear. Chapter 8 presents a praxis-centered response to the research question that undergirds this work: *What might a Samoan public theology look like?*

The Epilogue recapitulates the main arguments of the study, summarizing the major insights and discoveries and the arguments for a Samoan public theology. Finally, it makes recommendations concerning ways to develop this model of public theology in the Samoan public square.

NOTES

1. Margarita Mooney, "The Catholic Bishops Conferences of the United States and France: Engaging Immigration as a Public Issue," *American Behavioral Scientist* 49, no. 11 (2006): 1457.

2. See John Corvino, "Drawing a Line in the 'Gay Wedding Cake' Case," *New York Times*, November 27, 2017, https://www.nytimes.com/2017/11/27/opinion/gay-wedding-cake.html. This concerns the famous case of a conservative Christian bakery owner who refused to bake a wedding cake for a gay couple.

3. John Micklethwait and Adrian Wooldridge, *God Is Back: How the Global Revival of Faith is Changing the World* (New York, NY: Penguin, 2009).

4. See, for example, Paul S. Peterson, *The Decline of Established Christianity in the Western World: Interpretations and Responses*, Studies in World Christianity and Interreligious Relations (London: Routledge, 2017).

5. Manfred Ernst, "Ecumenism in the Pacific Islands: A Stocktaking at the Beginning of the 21st Century—Global Developments in Christianity," in *Navigating Troubled Waters: The Ecumenical Movement in the Pacific Islands Since the 1980s*, ed. Manfred Ernst and Lydia Johnson (Suva, FJ: Pacific Theological College, 2017), 498.

6. See Kevin Ward, *Losing Our Religion? Changing Patterns of Believing and Belonging in Secular Western Societies* (Eugene, OR: Wipf & Stock Publishers, 2013). He raises the pertinent question, "If 'believing without belonging' is increasing, what does this mean for the future of churches?" (x).

7. Ernst, "Ecumenism in the Pacific Islands," 499. Ernst's research shows that the percentage of members in the historic mainline churches in Samoa has decreased from 91% in 1961 to 64.9% in 2011.

8. Ibid., 499–500. Ernst cites statistics confirming the general trend across Oceania, in which non-mainline churches and NRMs have grown significantly in the past fifty years, while the established mainline churches have declined. This has contributed to conflict and to the weakening of ecumenical cooperation.

9. Jürgen Moltmann, *God for a Secular Society: The Public Relevance of Theology* (Minneapolis, MN: Fortress Press, 1999), 5.

10. Clarence Joldersma, "Shared Praxis: A Pedagogy of Hope for Public Theology," *Journal for Peace and Justice Studies* 10, no. 1 (1999): 67–93.

11. Ibid., 68.

12. Elaine Graham, *Between a Rock and a Hard Place: Public Theology in a Post-Secular Age* (London: SCM Press, 2013), 35.

13. See Adam Hochschild, *Bury the Chains: Prophets and Rebels in the Fight to Free an Empire's Slaves* (Wilmington, DE: Mariner Books, 2006). John Piper has said of Wilberforce, "What made Wilberforce tick was a profound allegiance to what he called the 'peculiar doctrines' of Christianity. These, he said, give rise, in turn, to true affections—what we might call 'passions'—for spiritual things, which, in turn, would lead to transformed morals, which, in turn, would lead to the political welfare of the nation." John Piper, "Peculiar Doctrines, Public Morals, and the Political Welfare," *Public Lecture, Bethlehem Conference for Pastors*, Bethlehem, PA, February 2, 2002, https://www.desiringgod.org/messages/peculiar-doctrines-public-morals-and-the-political-welfare.

14. For an exposition of what we might call Wesley's 'public theology,' see Richard P. Heitzenrater, *Wesley and the People Called Methodists*, 2nd edition (Nashville, TN: Abingdon Press, 2013).

15. Andrew Bradstock, "In Search of a Good Society: Theology, Secularism and the Importance of Vision," *Public Lecture*, Ephesus Centre, Timaru, NZ, July 14, 2013.

16. Jonathan Chaplin, *Talking God: The Legitimacy of Religious Public Reasoning* (London: Theos, 2008).

17. Rowan Williams, "Rome Lecture: Secularism, Faith and Freedom," *Keynote Address*, Pontifical Academy of Social Sciences, Rome, November 23, 2006.

18. Duncan B. Forrester, *On Human Worth: A Christian Vindication of Equality* (London: SCM Press, 2001), 72–73.

19. Melissa Yates, "Rawls and Habermas on Religion in the Public Sphere," *Philosophy and Social Criticism* 33, no. 7 (2007): 883.

20. Stephen L. Carter, *The Culture of Disbelief: How American Law and Politics Trivialize Religious Devotion* (New York, NY: Basic Books, 1993), 23–43.

21. See "Jesus Is My Boyfriend, and Other Things You Should Keep to Yourself," *The Pocket Scroll*, August 13, 2013, https://thepocketscroll.wordpress.com/2013/08/07/.

22. Paulo Freire, *Cultural Action for Freedom* (Cambridge, MA: Harvard University, 1972), 27.

23. Mercy Ah Siu-Maliko, "Conscientization and Pacific Women," *Pacific Journal of Theology* II, no. 41 (2009): 64–84.

24. The term 'Third World' was first coined by the French anthropologist and historian Alfred Sauvy in 1952, in "Trois Mondes, Une Planète (Three Worlds, One Planet)," *L'Observateur* (August 1952): 14–17. *Third World* was the common designation in the latter half of the twentieth century for countries outside the then two dominant global spheres of influence—the *First World* (the developed 'West' [North America, Europe, and nations such as Australia and New Zealand]), and the *Second World* (the Soviet Union and those nations in its orbit). Since the break-up of the Soviet

Union, it has become more commonplace to refer to what used to be called the Third World as the 'developing nations,' 'least developed nations,' or 'the Global South.'

25. For example, The Woman at the Well in Jn 4:7–29, and the Parable of the Good Samaritan in Lk 10:33–37.

26. Alastair Hannay, *On the Public: Thinking in Action* (New York, NY: Routledge, 2005), 10.

27. Gabriel M. Vasquez and Maureen Taylor, "Research Perspectives on 'the Public'," in *Handbook of Public Relations*, ed. Robert Lawrence Heath and Gabriel M. Vasquez (London: Sage Publications, 2000), 10.

28. Cited in Hannay, *On the Public*, 23.

29. See John Dewey, *The Public and its Problems: An Essay in Political Inquiry*, rev. edition, ed. Melvin L. Rogers (University Park, PA: Penn State University Press, 2012 [1927]).

30. Hannay, *On the Public*, 11.

31. See Gurcan Kocan, *Models of the Public Sphere in Political Philosophy*, Eurosphere Online Working Paper Series #2 (Istanbul: Istanbul Technical University, 2008).

32. Ibid., 1.

33. This notion of the public sphere, according to Habermas, evolved as the private sphere of the family expanded outward to what he calls the 'literary public sphere.' This was a setting in which collective discussions of art and literature became possible in a new way. By the eighteenth century, such conversations were extending beyond the universities into new types of publications and new venues. These exchanges, through the proliferation of periodicals and debates held in coffee houses and salons, came to be seen as the expression of the informed public opinion of the society as a whole. See Jürgen Habermas, *The Structural Transformation of the Public Sphere: An Inquiry into a Category of Bourgeois Society* (Cambridge, MA and London: MIT Press, 1991), 231. See also Charles Taylor, *Modern Social Imaginaries* (Durham, NC: Duke University Press, 2004), 83–84.

34. Habermas, *Structural Transformation of the Public Sphere*, 141.

35. Ibid. See also Dirk Smit, "Notions of the Public and Doing Theology," *International Journal of Public Theology* 13, no. 4 (2007): 432–33.

36. Ibid.

37. Iris Marion Young, *Inclusion and Democracy* (Oxford: Oxford University Press, 2000), 170.

38. Ibid., 173–74.

39. Seyla Benhabib, "Models of Public Space: Hannah Arendt, the Liberal Tradition, and Jürgen Habermas," in *Habermas and the Public Sphere*, ed. Craig Calhoun (Cambridge, MA: MIT Press, 1992), 89–90.

40. Ibid., 89.

41. Marion Maddox, "Religion, Secularism and the Promise of Public Theology," *International Journal of Public Theology* 1, no. 1 (2007): 92.

42. Ibid.

43. Marion Maddox, "A Case for Public Theology in Secular Contexts," *Annual Lecture in Public Theology*, School of Theology, University of Auckland, July 2006.

44. Robert Wuthnow, *Christianity in the Twenty-first Century* (New York, NY: Oxford University Press, 1993), 171.

45. Kathryn Tanner, "Public Theology and the Character of Public Debate: Observations on the Ramifications of Christian Beliefs, Symbols and Doctrines for Socio-Economic and Political Issues," *Annual of the Society of Christian Ethics* 16 (1996): 80.

46. Ibid.

47. Vincent Price, "The Public and Public Opinion in Political Theories," in *The Sage Handbook of Public Opinion Research*, ed. Wolfgang Donsbach and Michael W. Traugott (London: Sage Publications, 2008), 11–24.

48. Claire Andre, Manuel Velasquez, Thomas Shanks, and Michael J. Meyer, "The Common Good," Last modified August 2, 2014, http://www.scu.edu/ethics/practicing/decision/common good.html.

49. Andrew Bradstock, "Recovering the Common Good: The Key to a Truly Prosperous Society?," *Public Lecture*, Centre for Theology and Public Issues, University of Otago, January 21, 2013.

50. Ibid.

51. Walter Brueggemann, *Journey to the Common Good* (Louisville, KY: Westminster John Knox Press, 2010), 1.

52. David Hollenbach, "Public Theology in America: Some Questions for Catholicism after John Courtney Murray," *Theological Studies* 37, no. 2 (June 1976): 290–303.

53. See Brian Davies and G. R. Evans, eds., *Anselm of Canterbury: The Major Works* (Oxford: Oxford University Press, 1998). Before Anselm, Augustine (d. 430) had coined a similar description of theology, *crede ut intelligas*, or "believe that you may understand."

54. See Gerhard Ebeling, *s v Theologie: Begriffgeschichtlich*, Religion in Geschichte und Gegenwart, Vol. 1, ed. Kurt Galling (Tubingen: Mohr [Paul Siebeck], 1957), col. 754; and Ferdinand Deist, *A Concise Dictionary of Theological Terms, with an English-Afrikaans and Afrikaans-English List* (Pretoria: Van Schalk, 1984), 172.

55. See Daniel L. Migliore, *Faith Seeking Understanding: An Introduction to Christian Theology*, 2nd edition (Grand Rapids, MI: William B. Eerdmans, 2004).

56. John Macquarrie, *Principles of Christian Theology* (London: SCM Press, 1997), 1.

57. Howard D. Stone and James O. Duke, *How to Think Theologically*, 3rd edition (Minneapolis, MN: Fortress Press, 2013), 3.

58. Jürgen Moltmann, *Experiences in Theology: Ways and Forms of Christian Theology* (Philadelphia, PA: Fortress Press, 2000), xv. Italics in original.

59. Bruce Nicholls, *Contextualization: A Theology of Gospel and Culture* (Downers Grove, IL: InterVarsity Press, 1979), 54.

60. See Bruce Fleming, *Contextualization of Theology: An Evangelical Assessment* (Pasadena, CA: William Carey Library, 1980), 33–51; and Harvie M. Conn, "Contextualization: Where Do We Begin?," in *Evangelicals and Liberation*, ed. Carl E. Armerding (Phillipsburg, NJ: Presbyterian and Reformed Publishing, 1977), 90–119.

61. Petros Von Vassiliadis, "Orthodoxie Und Kontextuele Theologie," *Okumenische Rundschau* 42 (October 1993): 452.

62. Fleming, *Contextualization of Theology*, xi.

63. Robert Schreiter, another prominent figure in contextual theology, prefers to use the term 'local theology.' He identifies three approaches (translation, adaptation and contextualization) as models for engaging in local theology. See Robert J. Schreiter, *Constructing Local Theologies* (Maryknoll, NY: Orbis Books, 1985).

64. Paul Duane Matheny, *Contextual Theology: The Drama of Our Times* (Eugene, OR: Pickwick Publications, 2011), 29.

65. Stephen Bevans, *Models of Contextual Theology*, rev. and exp. (Maryknoll, NY: Orbis Books, 2002 [1997] [1992]), 1.

66. Ibid., 3.

67. Ibid., 37.

68. Ibid.

69. Matheny, *Contextual Theology*, 35.

70. Ibid., 78.

71. David J. Bosch, *Transforming Mission: Paradigm Shifts in Theology of Mission* (Maryknoll, NY: Orbis Books, 1991), 428–32.

72. Bevans, *Models of Contextual Theology*, 89.

73. Ibid., 88, 90.

74. Ibid., 105.

75. Ibid., 118.

76. Marc Cortez, *Models, Metaphors, and Multivalent Contextualizations: Religious Language and the Nature of Contextual Theology* (MTh Thesis, Western Theological Seminary, 2004), 68.

77. James Ian H. McDonald, *Christian Values: Theory and Practice in Christian Ethics Today* (Edinburgh: T&T Clark, 1995), xvii.

78. Kenneth Medhurst and James Sweeney, "Public Theology and Changing Social Values," *Studies in Christian Ethics* 17, no. 2 (2004): 122.

79. See, for example, Melvin Kohn, *Class and Conformity: A Study in Values* (Chicago, IL: University of Chicago Press, 1989).

80. See, for example, Milton Rokeach, *Understanding Human Values* (New York, NY: Free Press, 2000).

81. See, for example, Clyde Kluckholm, *Mirror for Man: The Relation of Anthropology to Modern Life* (New York, NY: Books on Demand, 1985).

82. Daphna Oyserman, "Values, Psychology of," in *International Encyclopedia of the Social & Behavioural Sciences*, Vol. 25, ed. James D. Wright (Oxford: Pergamon/Elsevior, 2015), 16151.

83. Milton Rokeach, *The Nature of Human Values* (New York, NY: The Free Press, 1973), 23.

84. Alastair Hannay, *On the Public* (New York, NY: Routledge, 2005).

85. See Fanaafi Aiono-Le Tagaloa, *Tapuai: Samoan Worship* (BA Hons Thesis, University of Otago, 2001).

Chapter 1

Public Theology

The concept of *public theology* has become increasingly prominent in recent theological scholarship. This is evident in the wide range of publications, academic programs, conferences, and centers established to enhance various societies' awareness of the relationship between theology and public issues. Those who engage in public theology often draw on the contributions of disciplines such as sociology, philosophy, social ethics, religious studies, and cultural studies.[1]

Ongoing discussions on public theology tend to focus on issues that are also relevant for theological ethics, "questions concerning their sources, methods, and goals, the intended persons and groups to whom theological ethics has been and should be addressed, and the relationship between Christian churches, institutions and individuals and the larger societies in which they live, work, and worship."[2] The diversity of issues addressed in these discussions reflects a range of concerns among those who write about public theology regarding what it is, what its boundaries are, and the appropriateness and usefulness of public theology, both as an analytical concept and as a method of doing theology and ethics.[3]

This chapter begins with an overview of salient literature on public theology. It is not exhaustive but, rather, representative. This is followed by a summary of perspectives on the nature and characteristics of public theology, and reflections on the importance of context in pursuing the main purpose of this study, which is a public theology for Samoa.

Extensive scholarship exists on the subject of public theology from Europe and North America, and also a growing volume of literature emerging from Asia, Africa, Australia, and New Zealand. In Samoa, the focus of this study, there are no published writings on public theology. However, there is literature which refers to issues and arguments central to public theology, mostly in the form of contextual theology. These texts emerge within the disciplines of systematic theology, biblical studies, and pastoral theology. In some of these writings, specific aspects of Samoan culture are highlighted to represent the ways Samoan people relate to God, while others seek to discover points of convergence between biblical and cultural metaphors.

Hence, although the term *public theology* is not used in Samoan theological discourse, Samoan theologians[4] do utilize certain principles of public theology, such as reflecting on the issues of the day by gleaning insights from scripture and various theological schools of thought. With increasing numbers of Samoans engaging in the field of theology, it is anticipated that new literature will emerge in the near future that brings the insights of public theology to bear in theological discourse in Samoa.

AN OVERVIEW OF PUBLIC THEOLOGY

Terms of Reference

The American theologian Martin Marty was the first theologian to intentionally use the term *public theology* to describe the activity of Christians who engage actively in social affairs, although he fully acknowledged the influence of Reinhold Niebuhr on his own understanding of public theology.[5] In adopting this term, Marty argued that the church is obligated to be present and active in the public sphere, focusing on the notion of the *public church* as a "specifically Christian polity and witness" extending to the diverse communities and social institutions with whom the church is engaged.[6]

The public church, according to Marty, describes those persons of a deeply committed Christian faith who are willing to join with others to work for the common good. More specifically, "it is a communion of communions—a family of apostolic churches with Jesus Christ at the center, churches which are especially sensitive to the *res publica*, the public order that surrounds and includes people of faith."[7] When the public church examines and critiques existing social practices and cultural understandings in the light of its deepest religious insights about justice and the common good, it does public theology.[8]

The foundation laid by Marty has had a significant impact on other theologians' articulations of public theology. Some have followed his line of thinking directly, such as the Christian ethicist David Hollenbach, who argues for the need for a public theology that addresses "the urgent moral questions of our time through explicit use of the great symbols and doctrines of the Christian faith."[9] In *The Analogical Imagination*, David Tracy defends the need to speak to such "urgent moral questions" through a public theology that articulates religious truth claims as a response to these questions.[10]

In these works, public theology is deemed to be a necessity. This is so because it is a witness to values which Christians believe are essential for the common good. The necessity of such public witness has gained traction because of a growing concern about Christianity's privatization in modernity and postmodernity, a concern noted in the Prologue. Public theology is a response to this concern; and if theology must be public, then it must speak in ways that are accessible to others and touch the deepest existential human experiences. It must also speak in the public arena as the church, not just as individual Christian citizens.

Public theology starts from the premise, then, that the church has a theological warrant for public witness. This witness is derived from the essential core of the gospel and the nature of the church. Duncan Forrester understands public theology as being responsive to the demands of scripture and the traditions of faith while attempting to discern and respond to the "signs of the times" in the light of the gospel.[11] The theological foundation of public theology is the belief that Christian principles of love and justice are both necessary and pertinent for all of God's creation, and that they should be made available to all of humanity.

The term *civil religion* has at times been associated with public theology. It was coined by Robert Bellah with reference to the American context. Civil religion, according to Bellah, consists of a basic set of religious values, communally shared and ritually celebrated to some extent by most members of a society. It is "a common public religion in society, different from and transcending particular faiths."[12] Bellah maintains that there is an underlying civil religion which is often referenced in American political discourse. It emphasizes the role of religion in supporting the nation and its people in their public life and social responsibilities.[13]

In Bellah's view, American civil religion emerged from the underlying worldview of the nation's so-called Founding Fathers. They did not typically make overt reference to Jesus Christ or to Christianity, even at a time when practically all Americans (other than Native Americans) were Christians. But the founders did speak of God.[14] When they occasionally made reference to biblical teachings, this was mostly influenced by Old Testament concepts, such that America was seen as having affinities with ancient Israel, God's Chosen People. This association fostered the notion of American exceptionalism.

Those who follow Bellah tend to think of the two concepts (civil religion and public theology) as different names for the same thing. However, considering their different origins and emphases, I concur with Harold Breitenberg, who is among those who make a strong case that the two are not the same.

He notes, for example, that "Public theology does not place emphasis on public and civic ritual celebrations that support and sustain public life, and is not primarily advanced through them."[15] Public theology's prophetic stance vis-á-vis the "powers and principalities" that control the state clearly differs from Bellah's civil religion, where Christians and the state are essentially on the same page.

The term *public ethics* has also at times been conflated with public theology. However, although the two share certain goals, and may be complementary or in dialogue around common areas of concern, they are not identical. Public ethics is concerned with putting forward a compelling set of moral values that can be applied to public policies, but these are not necessarily faith-based. Unlike public theology, public ethics does not have an explicitly religious dimension.[16]

Biblical Roots of Public Theology

Public theology is a relatively new term, but it represents what Christians have always been called to practice. This calling is clearly enunciated in scripture. For example, Lv 19:18 says, "Do not seek revenge or bear a grudge against anyone among your people, but love your neighbor as yourself."[17] The New Testament echoes this call to "love the Lord your God with all your heart, and with all your soul, and with all your strength, and with all your mind; and your neighbor as yourself" (Lk 10:27).

One could argue that the tradition of Christian public theology began with Jesus himself. As Edward Farley notes, Jesus "publicly narrated parables about the nature of God's reign and its in-breaking in human history" (Mt 13:11–17).[18] At the heart of Jesus's teachings was a concern that all might have "abundant life," as illustrated in his parables and his acts of ministry. Jesus defined his *mission* as public when he announced at the commencement of his ministry, "The spirit of the Lord is upon me, because he has anointed me to bring good news to the poor. He has sent me to proclaim release to the captives and recovery of sight to the blind, to let the oppressed go free, to proclaim the year of the Lord's favor" (Lk 4:18–19).

Richard Horsley offers one of the most comprehensive critical analyses of how Jesus became a significant public figure. Horsley makes a strong case that Jesus was an active player in the politics of first-century Palestine. Drawing on anthropological studies of peasant resistance movements in Jesus's sociopolitical context, Horsley concludes that Jesus, as a prophetic leader, "generated a movement for renewal in Israel that was focused on village communities."[19] Jesus interacted with and at times confronted public figures, and much of his ministry took place in public places. In the end, his witness of liberation, justice, and love for "the least of these" was too much for the "powers and principalities," and it was in the public sphere that his earthly witness came to its searing conclusion.

Historical Precursors of Public Theology

Even though public theology per se is a fairly recent development, there are solid examples in church history which support the claim that its fundamental purposes are firmly rooted in Christian theological traditions. Drawing on his Catholic tradition, Edward Farley highlights a number of figures in church history who might be considered public theologians. These include Ambrose (d. 165 CE), who "carried on public debates with emperors . . . about the protection of church rights"; Thomas á Becket (d. 1170), who "continuously clashed with Henry II on relations between church and state, culminating . . . in his martyrdom"; and Bartolomé de las Casas (d. 1566), who engaged in a "decades-long struggle on both sides of the Atlantic to put an end to the slavery of the indigenous peoples of the Americas."[20]

In Protestant church history, I would highlight three theologians in particular who may be considered to have engaged in some form of public theology—Martin Luther, John Calvin, and Dietrich Bonhoeffer. October 31, 1517, is still remembered in church history as the date when Martin Luther hammered his ninety-five theses to the door of the castle church in Wittenberg.[21] This could be described as an act of public theology. It was a proclamation that the gospel revealed in Jesus Christ, and the freedom of Christians to respond to the gospel, are not purely private affairs: the gospel "wants to take shape in the world; it wants to change society."[22]

Luther developed his "two kingdoms" doctrine (the spiritual and the temporal) as a "response to a question unique to his context . . . a faith question which was the consequence of honest self-reflection by Christians who held political office."[23] Luther was in many ways in agreement with Augustine's doctrine of the "two cities."[24] Augustine's City of God has parallels with Luther's Kingdom of God, and his City of Man has affinities with Luther's worldly Kingdom.

Luther believed the state was needed because not everyone can live according to godly ideals. For this reason, the state is needed as God's agent in restraining sin; if everyone lived according to God's desires, there would be no need for the state. At the same time, Luther saw the function of the state as that of controlling political matters but not spiritual matters. Unlike the state, "The spiritual government . . . is based exclusively on the Gospel; it can be seen as the ideal form of government which can only be promoted wherever it is possible. Thus, it is a government based on the orientations Jesus gives us in the Sermon on the Mount; . . . it includes love of enemy . . . and the promotion of others' well-being as the first priority."[25]

Luther's contribution to theology is noteworthy because it is a reminder of the public responsibility of the church. In his theological framework, church leaders must "go public with a clear message; congregations must become caring communities and individual members must act as Christians in their secular contexts."[26] Heinrich Bedford-Strohm thus argues that "even though Luther was not confronted with the modern publics of today, he can be called one of the most impressive public theologians of church history, making advocacy for the poor one of his top priorities."[27] However, it must also be acknowledged that Luther was not able to rise above the anti-Semitism which was endemic in his society. When his campaign to convert Jews to Protestant Christianity failed, he actively called for their persecution.[28]

Unlike Luther, the other preeminent early Protestant reformer, John Calvin, did not see a problem with the state's enforcement of religious uniformity. Calvin's political influence was seen in the city of Geneva, which went through a series of civil and religious reforms under his guidance. Calvin claimed that all authority comes from God, whether civil or spiritual; because of this, church and state should work together and help each other to "do well what God has called each to do."[29]

In Romans 13, Calvin found legitimation for his belief that governments and their officials are ordained by God for the purpose of promoting the common good. There is thus a warrant for obedience to civil authorities as part of a Christian's obedience to God.[30] He saw anyone who attempted to overturn God's ordained social order as in fact resisting God. At the same time, Calvin acknowledged that "dictatorships and unjust authorities are not ordained governments; they are not God's original intention."[31]

In the context of the twentieth-century Protestant German church, theologians such as Karl Barth and Dietrich Bonhoeffer felt the necessity to dig deeply into scripture and church tradition to find resources adequate to the challenges of the twentieth century, particularly the rise of Nazism.[32] This is clearly demonstrated in the Barmen Declaration of 1934 drafted by Barth. There Barth insisted that "the Christian contribution to public life and public debate should be firmly rooted in the heart of the Christian faith, that it should be confessional, a way of proclaiming the Gospel rather than a commentary on current affairs from a Christian standpoint."[33]

Bonhoeffer believed that Luther's separation of the two realms "deeply contradicts both biblical and Reformation thought," because "there are not two realities but only one reality, and that is God's reality revealed in Christ in the reality of the world."[34] Bonhoeffer's public theology was anchored in his conviction that Christians are obligated to engage with the societies in which they live *as believers*, and that they must do so through an "open process of questioning and response."[35] Frits de Lange describes Bonhoeffer's public theology in this way:

Dietrich Bonhoeffer delivered his most important contribution to public theology while he was locked-up behind a prison door and wrote personal letters, which had to be smuggled out secretly.... His *Letters and Papers from Prison*[36] represented the kind of theology that most of today's practitioners of public theology should like to develop, because it was (1) an *authentic* theology, not abstracted from the concrete personal life of the one who was doing it, but rooted in a powerful Christian engagement; it was (2) a *dialogical* theology, not an isolated product of the interior monologue of an academic theologian..., but the experimental and fragmentary result of an open process of questioning and response; and, above all, it was (3) a theology that spoke of God in the midst of life, not at its borders. It was a theology that asked believers to live a *worldly* life without reservations and without the escape into what Bonhoeffer called: "religion."[37]

Two twentieth-century theological traditions are noteworthy as historical precedents for public theology. The first is the Social Gospel movement, which came to prominence in the early twentieth century in the United States and Canada. Influenced by Walter Rauschenbusch's "Kingdom of God" theology,[38] this largely Protestant movement sought to apply Christian ethics to social problems, especially economic inequality, poverty, the suffering of immigrants, racism, and militarism. Rauschenbusch's call to the church to focus on systemic or social evil (rather than only on personal sin) relied on a notion of the Kingdom of God which "can test and correct the church; is a prophetic, future-focused ideology; and a revolutionary social and political force that understands all creation to be sacred, and can help save the sinful social order."[39]

Finally, a significant theological tradition that has influenced public theology is liberation theology. It emerged initially in the 1960s out of situations of extreme poverty and political oppression in Latin America, and has since spread to many other contexts around the world. It has affinities with public theology in its exploration of the relationship between Christian theology and political activism, particularly in struggles for social justice, human rights, and the alleviation of poverty.[40] In taking as its starting point the voices of the poor and marginalized themselves, liberation theology also resonates with public theology's insistence that "the public" are the subjects and practitioners of theology, and that Jesus came as a liberator for all who are oppressed. Liberation theology has deeply influenced a number of public theologians, especially Forrester[41] and Moltmann.[42]

All of these historical influences have helped to shape public theology today. The inspiration of those with vision and courage who have led the way in advocating for the public role of theology have aimed to bring about transformations in both the purpose and the method of doing theology, for the well-being of their societies.

Public Theology as a Western Construct

Public theology has developed mostly in secular Eurocentric[43] societies, where the separation between church and state has been most evident, and it would appear that an increasing number of theologians from the West[44] identify with some form of public theology. In the most general sense, public theology emanating from the West is systematic reflection on issues relating to public life, carried out in the light of theological conviction and with the support of theological disciplines. This reflection usually involves drawing out a faith community's interpretations of religious traditions and texts in relation to critical social concerns in particular societies.

In this sense, as the British public theologian Elaine Graham maintains, public theology is "concerned with the church's relationship to the world, to political powers, to economic problems, to governance, to moral questions, to citizenship and national identity, which figure consistently throughout church history."[45] Following Mary Doak, Graham writes that public theology has two main objectives: "defining and defending a public role for theological discourse in a religiously pluralistic society," over against the privatization of religious belief; and promoting a "societal commitment to maintain the quality of our public life and to pursue the common good."[46] This is a concise summary of how public theology tends to be construed in the "pluralistic societies" of the West.

In attempting to characterize public theology in these pluralistic societies, one must acknowledge that theology no longer has a privileged place in the secular societies of the West, as it did during the era of Christendom when its values and meta-narratives were uniformly embraced. Theology is now just one among many competing voices in the West. Theological insights must therefore be explained in ways that nonreligious people can understand. Public theology's contributions must be constructive and not merely abstract discourses employing traditional theological language.

Public theology in these settings also draws upon reputable work from other disciplines in order to make a well-informed contribution in the public square. If public theology practitioners are to be taken seriously in the secular arena, they must be well-versed in the relevant factors impinging on the social concern under consideration.[47] This underlines the interdisciplinary nature of public theology, in whatever context it exists. Public theology must be open to the wisdom of other disciplines so that its own contribution will be appropriately nuanced.

Public Theology's Fluid Boundaries

While there has been fairly broad consensus on what constitutes the public good, delineating clear boundaries for the discipline of public theology has proven much more difficult. Public theology is both words and actions. In many respects it overlaps with practical theology[48] and with contextual theology.[49] Such complexities have contributed to the ongoing difficulties experienced by public theologians in agreeing on a precise definition of the parameters of public theology. As Breitenberg points out, the term can "refer to a body of literature, a form of discourse, a way of doing theology and ethics, a tradition within the Christian church, and a field of study."[50]

In reality, such boundaries and categories are assumed to overlap in places of common interest. Breitenberg therefore concludes that the features mentioned above dovetail or intersect in such a way as to make it possible to construct a consensus in which public theology is marked by several key features.[51] Here "public theology involves inputting constructively to contemporary discourse in the public square, drawing upon the insights of the faith which it offers as "gift" to the secular world."[52]

Charles Mathewes prefers to speak of a *theology of public life* rather than public theology, because he believes that the so-called public theologies risk becoming "self-destructively accommodationist," thereby allowing "the "larger" secular world's self-understanding to set the terms, and then ask how religious faith contributes to the purposes of public life."[53] Defining the parameters of "public life," Mathewes writes,

> Public life includes everything concerned with the public good—everything from patently political actions such as voting, campaigning for a candidate, or running for office, to less directly political activities such as serving on a school board or planning commission, volunteering in a soup kitchen, and speaking in a civic forum, and to arguably non-political behaviors, such as simply talking to one's family, friends, co-workers, or strangers about public matters of common concern.[54]

Mathewes wants the theological agenda set in such a way that it encourages a "faithful Christian citizenship," which will then engage with public life. Such citizenship is a training ground for Christians' "fundamental vocation as citizens of the kingdom of heaven."[55]

From the South African context, John de Gruchy proposes a set of principles for public theology praxis which provide much-needed clarity in the face of public theology's perceived "indistinct boundaries":

> The first thesis is that good public theological praxis does not seek to preference Christianity but to witness to values that Christians believe are important for the common good. The second thesis argues that good public theological praxis requires the development of a language that is accessible to people outside the Christian tradition, and is convincing in its own right; but it also needs

to address Christian congregations in a language whereby public debates are related to the traditions of faith. The third thesis states that good public theological praxis requires an informed knowledge of public policy and issues, grasping the implications of what is at stake, and subjecting this to sharp analytical evaluation and theological critique. The fourth thesis insists that good public theological praxis requires doing theology in a way that is interdisciplinary in character and uses a methodology in which content and process are intertwined. In the fifth thesis, good public theological praxis gives priority to the perspectives of victims and survivors, and to the restoration of justice; it sides with the powerless against the powerful, and seeks to speak truth to power drawing its inspiration from the prophetic trajectory in the Bible. The sixth thesis contends that good public theological praxis requires congregations that are consciously nurtured and informed by biblical and theological reflection and a rich life of worship in relation to the context within which they are situated.... Finally, the seventh thesis suggests that good public theological praxis requires a spirituality which enables a lived experience of God, with people and with creation, fed by a longing for justice and wholeness.[56]

"Christian" in Public Theology

Like theology in general, for public theology to be authentic it must draw on insights from scripture and Christian tradition. Max Stackhouse affirms that "public theology points toward a wider and deeper strand of theological reflection rooted in the interaction of biblical insight, philosophical analysis, historical discernment and social formation."[57] While this is a distinctively *Christian* public theology, it must also be comprehensible and open for all to view and interpret. It is not an elite discourse, but one that contributes the resources of the Christian faith for the common good of society by bringing these resources into public conversations about social concerns. This is especially important in relation to issues which the public tends to avoid.

Duncan Forrester's way of articulating his understanding of the significance of the "Christian" in public theology prioritizes the interests of the public over those of the church. In his view, a Christian public theology "seeks the welfare of the city before protecting the interests of the church. Accordingly, public theology often takes the world's agenda, or parts of it, as its own agenda, and seeks to offer constructive insights from the treasury of faith"[58] to help in the building of a just society. In taking on the world's agenda, Christians offer something that is distinctive, and that is the gospel. For Forrester,

> The primary concern of Christians doing public theology is not individual subjectivity, nor discussion within the church about doctrine and sacraments,

though these matters are important. . . . Public theology has less to do with preaching to the world about its need for repentance and conversion and more about seeking the good of the city, contributing Christian insight to discussion of public issues and seeking reconciliation between those who are alienated from each other in the public arena.[59]

One of the great influences in Forrester's life was the challenge presented by liberation theology. "Liberation" provides metaphors, in the scriptural narratives of exodus, exile, and deliverance, for a theology that challenges unjust social structures. While liberation theology emerged out of struggles for justice in Latin American societies, public theology arose primarily as a challenge to injustices in Eurocentric societies. In response to these injustices, Forrester sought to include in theological dialogue those excluded from Christian social reflection in the past and those who have the greatest interest in reform, such as individuals and communities living in poverty or economic insecurity, or those unjustly convicted by the criminal justice system.

Forrester also struggled with the difficult question concerning how Christians can make a contribution to these public conversations in a way that can be heard by those who have no interest or stake in the Christian faith. In addressing this problem, Forrester adopted Alasdair MacIntyre's analysis of the postmodern era as one in which authoritative narratives have been effectively shattered.[60] Forrester thus speaks of offering "precious fragments of the Christian tradition that might yet be illuminating, instructive or provocative,"[61] and which can be brought to bear productively in public debate.

In a broader framework, Robert Benne defines *Christian public theology* as "the engagement of a living religious tradition with its public environment—the economic, political, and cultural spheres of our common life."[62] Christians' "living religious tradition" finds clues for transformative action in the ultimate truths associated with God's way of relating to the world, culminating in the Incarnation, and applies them to concrete issues of social concern. Benne's framework for a Christian public theology is based on four themes:

> 1) the qualitative distinction between God's salvation and all human efforts; 2) the paradox of human nature with its capacity for love and justice that is used for small or evil ends and yet that can be directed by the Spirit to care for others; 3) the two-fold action of God in the world through law and gospel; and 4) recognition of the penultimate character of human history in which God acts but human efforts cannot achieve God's reign.[63]

Benne believes that Christian theology can play a crucial role in empowering oppressed peoples to make significant contributions to their societies.

This view of public theology is based on the conviction that there is a valid and valuable Christian voice to bring to public debate and decision-making in the societies of which Christians are a part.[64] Benne also insists that Christian contributions to public debate must be based on reason and intelligible to ordinary people. This concern is echoed by the biblical scholar Paul Hanson, who calls on Christians to "develop an interpretive process that enables scriptural meaning to be conveyed in such a way that it relates responsibly, as well as relevantly, to current political, social and economic concerns."[65]

Incorporating many of these perspectives, Clive Pearson, a public theologian in the Australian context, names several of its defining characteristics. In his view, a distinctively Christian public theology

- [has] public relevance to issues of the day;
- offers intellectual rigor in support of the Church's practical engagement, seeing itself as a resourcing initiative which
- does not confine God's interests to the purely ecclesial, personal and salvific, but
- addresses theology's "three publics," namely the society, the academy and the church, with a willingness to use the language of secular discourses (e.g., human rights), [and]
- recognizes the non-privileged status of its voice in the post-modern marketplace of ideas.[66]

Building on this last point, the Australian public theologian Marion Maddox insists that "In a secular and plural society, public theology, if it is to be public in any meaningful sense, surely needs to be concerned with developing theological goods which are accessible to all, not just, say, to Christians."[67] Pearson and Maddox are taking into account the pluralistic and secular nature of Australia and New Zealand (having taught theology in both contexts), where only a minority of the population are practicing Christians.

Maddox presents an interesting metaphor for thinking about public theology's relationship to secular society—as *gift*.[68] She suggests that one model of public theology as *gift* to the public sphere can be found in the language and practices of conflict resolution and reconciliation.[69] A recent historic example is the reconciling role played by Archbishop Desmond Tutu as Chair of South Africa's Truth and Reconciliation Commission in the mid-1990s, following the end of apartheid. His appeal to Christian principles and practices of reconciliation during the life of the TRC (although not couched in explicitly Christian language) was received as *gift* and elicited respect and openness to forgiveness and restorative justice on both sides of that horrific legacy of racism.

In the Pacific region, reconciliation efforts following the 1987 military coup in Fiji, which incorporated the indigenous approach to dialogue known as *talanoa*,[70] were led by church leaders such as the Anglican bishop Winston Halapua.[71] Independence movements in Pacific island nations such as Vanuatu were also spearheaded by clergy,[72] and an Anglican lay religious order known as the Melanesian Brotherhood was the most effective and trusted agent of reconciliation during the period of ethnic unrest in the Solomon Islands between 1998 and 2003.[73]

Public Theologians

One way of identifying public theologians is in relation to their roles and social locations. While some are situated in church hierarchies and the academy, others are more praxis-based, such as church pastors and ministers-in-training in theological schools. Malcolm Brown writes that those in church hierarchies and the academy "often write for an informed audience which is . . . deeply engaged in political, missional or public life. They . . . write to influence public life, as well as the church."[74]

However, I would concur with Forrester's claim that public theology is too important a matter to be left to professionally trained theologians. Such theologians need to be involved, but only alongside other people with varied skills and experience in addressing specific social concerns,[75] including those who are recipients or victims of the policies under discussion. Forrester suggests that public theologians are those who keep alive a vision of the ending of human despair, and who speak in public deliberations in ways that are prophetic, impassioned, and yet obtainable. He also describes public theologians as those who "work hard and humbly in the quarry of the rich resources of the Bible; follow the Christian tradition; and produce the fragments of insights, challenges and the truth that may help to pave the way for the coming of God's reign."[76]

Andries van Aarde's description of the public theologian identifies Christians with specific roles in society who are committed to the common good. These could be any socially conscious Christians whose work takes them into the public sphere, such as artists, writers, nurses, teachers, or civil servants.[77] A public theologian may sometimes simply be a person who fearlessly brings the gospel to bear in public discourse about how to create a more just society. The primary social location of public theologians is not the university campus, but rather the public square, wherever it may be situated—in the village marketplace, the town council, the parliamentary public hearing, or other settings where members of "the public" gather to seek the common good in relation to a matter of shared concern.[78]

Given this broad definition of the public theologian, it should be possible to identify such persons in our own societies. Christian activists who are reflectively bringing their faith to bear on situations of injustice in their societies today may be, for example, environmentalists engaging in civil disobedience because of their understanding of God's call for "creation care" in the face of the climate crisis. Young Christian environmental activists started the *Pray For Our Pacific* movement in Samoa in 2016, urging Christians from across Oceania to pray and network to campaign for climate justice in the Pacific island nations which are on the frontlines of the climate crisis.[79] They may be thought of as public theologians.

In North America, activists from Native American tribes known as Water Protectors are drawing on their own indigenous religious traditions to protest the damaging oil and natural gas pipelines being laid under their lands and rivers.[80] An African American pastor, Rev. William Barber, started the Moral Mondays movement,[81] bringing together people from all walks of life to protest unjust laws every Monday in front of a state capitol building; this evolved into a nationwide revival of Martin Luther King Jr's Poor Peoples' Campaign. All of these activists may be considered public theologians.

CENTRAL CLAIMS OF PUBLIC THEOLOGY

Works on public theology[82] are often influenced by the unique experiences and contexts of the authors themselves. Nevertheless, there are a number of shared convictions concerning the constituent elements of public theology. I will draw especially on the account of public theology given by Sebastian Kim[83] and supported by other public theologians. Kim makes these assertions about the foundational claims of public theology:

- that theology is inherently public;
- that the dichotomy of public and private is not helpful in defining public theology;
- that, in order to establish a healthy public theology, theologians need to convince the Christian community of the public relevance of theology and, at the same time, persuade the general public of the necessity of utilizing theological insights in public discussion; and finally,
- that, in order to ensure the authentic and sustainable engagement of the church in the public sphere, it must guard against the temptation to embrace pragmatism to the point of attempting to "measure" the results of ministries in terms of statistics or external appearances. Instead, the church must develop a public theology suited to pertinent issues and relevant to the given context.[84]

In relation to the first argument, that theology is inherently public, David Tracy makes an important contribution in support of this claim by arguing that "all theology is public discourse," and that every theologian should address three publics or "distinct and related social realities": the wider society, the academy, and the church.[85] Nico Koopman follows a similar line of thinking in his assertion that a public theology unavoidably addresses three sets of questions: "firstly, the inherent nature, scope and *telos* of Christian faith; secondly, the public rationality, intelligibility, inner coherence, consistency, logic and reasonability of Christian faith; and thirdly, the impact upon, and significance, meaning and implications of Christian faith for public life."[86]

In Koopman's view, the inherently public nature of Christian convictions helps us to guard against "self-secularization" and to rediscover the wealth that the Christian tradition has to offer to the challenges of being social beings.[87] He goes on to explain that God's love "is a love for the cosmos, for humans in all walks of life—families, circles of friends, culture, work, church, society (which includes political life, economic life, ecological life, civil society, public discourse)—and for all of creation."[88] If God's love does indeed encompass every aspect of life, then clearly all theology is public theology, or has ramifications for the public sphere.[89]

Following Kim, I argue that any artificial separation between public and private is not helpful in the task of doing theology. The Christian faith is very personal but it is not private. It is both individual and communal.[90] Bonhoeffer was correct to insist that theology cannot be concentrated only on the private life of the believer, but must encompass "God's transformative presence at the crossroads of our common human life"; he saw private theology as a form of escapism which is "in direct opposition to the spirit of the gospel."[91] If theology is not interpreted and enacted with a view to its public dimensions, it is not a viable theology.

Kim's third argument, regarding the public relevance of theology, is well articulated in the works of Jürgen Moltmann and Duncan Forrester. For Moltmann, public theology "becomes political in the name of the poor and the marginalized in a given society."[92] It is therefore a form of activism rather than being limited to a description of the social function of the church.

In Moltmann's *Theology of Hope*, he challenges Christians to embody Christ's Kingdom in the world, as a way of affirming the sovereignty of God over every human activity. Indeed, Moltmann's focus on the public relevance of theology has at its core a concern for the coming of God's Kingdom in human history.[93] Scott Paeth writes that Moltmann's "Kingdom of God theology intervenes critically and prophetically in the public affairs of a given society, and draws public attention, not to the church's own interests, but to God's kingdom, God's commandments, and God's righteousness."[94]

For Ronald Thiemann, the central claim of public theology is that it is "faith seeking to understand the relation between Christian convictions and the broader social and cultural context in which the Christian community lives."⁹⁵ While it is true that Christians in Western contexts today must acknowledge that they are only one voice among others (both religious and nonreligious) in the public square,⁹⁶ Thiemann strongly emphasizes the necessity for a uniquely Christian public theology praxis, which takes as its starting point the community of faith that relies on its faith to understand and respond to the political and social order. As he concludes,

> Our challenge is to develop a public theology that remains based in the particularities of Christian faith while genuinely addressing issues of public significance. Too often, theologies that seek to address a broad secular culture lose touch with the distinctive beliefs and practices of the Christian tradition. . . . In the process, the distinctive prophetic "bite" of the Christian witness is undermined.⁹⁷

Kim's final public theology claim underscores the role of the church as engaging in issues that are germane to the needs of particular communities and the wider public. This call to the church runs counter to the conservative nature of many churches today and their propensity to evaluate their effectiveness in terms of their numbers of adherents and other institutional measurements of success, rather than in terms of their engagement with the societies in which they find themselves.

Embracing the public setting for the church's calling is also an antidote to the church's tendency to support the societal status quo. Especially in religiously oriented societies, but even to a degree in secular societies, people look to the church as the conscience of society, particularly in times of hardship. It is commonplace for people to expect the church to speak and act in situations of crisis. Yet the task of public theology is to speak and act not just in times of crisis, but in situations of everyday life that have an impact on the well-being of communities or society as a whole.

In Samoan society, where virtually the entire population self-identifies as Christians, the church should theoretically have no problem speaking and acting on issues affecting the welfare of the people. Unfortunately, this is not the case, because the church does not have the courage to speak in the Samoan public square. The government dominates the church, since those in government also occupy influential positions in the church. This has had the effect of diluting the church's prophetic witness in the Samoan public sphere, because of the influence of power, wealth, and prestige.

However, given the church's pastoral calling to offer compassion and justice to all, it has no option but to challenge whatever stands in the way of compassion and justice in society. It is called to proclaim the Good News of the gospel, affirm the justice of God, and to be an advocate for the vulnerable and the voiceless. The church does not exist to defend its own institutional interests, but to speak and act for the common good.

FINAL THOUGHTS

This chapter has provided an overview of public theology as a way of doing theology that addresses problems in particular social contexts through the lens of the liberating and reconciling thrust of the gospel. The characteristics of public theology have been elaborated according to the criteria provided by Sebastian Kim. This discussion has presented a variety of perspectives regarding the essential elements of public theology and the ways in which it may be shaped and enacted. It is clear that public theology flourishes when there is open dialogue among all stakeholders involved in struggles for social justice and well-being, especially those whose voices are often silenced or unheard.

The features of public theology discussed in this chapter have highlighted some of the key themes in the literature on public theology. These themes will have relevance in the process of developing a Samoan public theology. At the same time, an appropriate public theology for Samoa cannot be captive to any foreign vision of the common good, as it was foreign theologies and worldviews that, however well-meaning, domesticated Samoans in the past. Instead, a Samoan public theology must be a discourse based on the core values of Samoan culture as they align with the Christian gospel. These values can contribute significantly to an authentic process for defining a public theology for Samoa.

NOTES

1. Examples may be seen in works such as Peter Berger, *The Desecularization of the World: Resurgent Religion and World Politics* (Grand Rapids, MI: William B. Eerdmans, 1999), and his classic, *The Sacred Canopy: Elements of a Sociological Theory of Religion* (New York, NY: Anchor, 1990); Jacques Derrida, *Sovereignties in Question: The Poetics of Paul Celan* (New York, NY: Fordham University Press, 2005), and *Acts of Religion* (London: Routledge, 2001); Charles Taylor, *A Secular Age* (Cambridge, MA: Belknap Press, 2007); and Kathryn Tanner, *Theories of Culture: A New Agenda for Theology* (Minneapolis, MN: Fortress Press, 1997).

2. Eugene Harold Breitenberg, *The Comprehensive Public Theology of Max L. Stackhouse: Theological Ethics, Society, and Theological Education* (Richmond, VA: Union Theological Seminary and Presbyterian School of Christian Education, 2004), 1.

3. Ibid.

4. See, for example, Lalomilu Kamu, *The Samoan Culture and the Christian Gospel* (Suva, FJ: Donna Lou Kamu, 1996); Ama'amalele Tofaeono, *Eco-Theology: Aiga—The Household of Life: A Perspective from Living Myths and Traditions of Samoa* (Erlanger: Verlag fur Mission and Oikumene, 2000); Fa'alepo A. Tuisuga, *O*

Le Tofa Liliu a Samoa: A Hermeneutical Critical Analysis of the Cultural-Theological Praxis of the Samoan Context (PhD Thesis, Melbourne University of Divinity, 2010); Upolu L. Vaai, *Faaaloalo: A Theological Reinterpretation of the Doctrine of the Trinity from a Samoan Perspective* (PhD Thesis, Griffith University, 2006); Gataivai Nepo, *A Theological Study of 'Tautua' (Service) in the Light of the Christian Faith: With Special Reference to the Ministry of the Congregational Church in Samoa* (BD Thesis, Pacific Theological College, 1990); and Frank Smith, *The Johannine Jesus from a Samoan Perspective: Toward an Intercultural Reading of the Fourth Gospel* (PhD Thesis, University of Auckland, 2010).

5. See, for example, Martin Marty, "Reinhold Niebuhr: Public Theology and the American Experience," *The Journal of Religion* 54, no. 4 (October 1974): 32–45, where he depicts Niebuhr as the 'essential public theologian' who "offered a paradigm for a public theology, a model which his successors have only begun to develop and realize" (35).

6. Martin Marty, *The Public Church* (New York, NY: Crossroad, 1981), 16. See also Martin Marty, *Religion and Republic: The American Circumstance* (Boston, MA: Beacon Press, 1987). For a more recent discussion of public theology in the American context, see Steven Tipton, "Public Theology," in *The Encyclopedia of Politics and Religion*, Vol. 2, ed. Robert Wuthnow (New York, NY: Routledge, 2013), 164.

7. Marty, *The Public Church*, 16.

8. James R. Kelly, "Sociology and Public Theology: A Case Study of Pro-Choice/Profile Common Ground," *Sociology of Religion* 60, no. 2 (1999): 102. See also Michael J. Himes and Kenneth R. Himes, *Fullness of Faith: The Public Significance of Theology* (New York, NY: Paulist Press, 1993), 2, who write that the public church's "advocates do not fear an age without faith, but an age without social meaning."

9. David Hollenbach, "Public Theology in America: Some Questions for Catholicism after John Courtney Murray," *Theological Studies* 37, no. 2 (June 1976): 299.

10. David Tracy, *The Analogical Imagination: Christian Theology and the Culture of Pluralism* (New York, NY: Crossroad Publishing, 1981).

11. William F. Storrar and Andrew R. Morton, eds., *Public Theology for the Twenty-first Century: Essays in Honour of Duncan B. Forrester* (London and New York, NY: T&T Clark, 2004), 1.

12. Robert N. Bellah, "Civil Religion in America," *Daedalus* 96, no. 1 (1967): 1–21.

13. Sebastian Kim, *Theology in the Public Sphere: Public Theology as a Catalyst for Open Debate* (London: SCM Press, 2011), 4.

14. See Bellah, "Civil Religion in America."

15. Eugene Harold Breitenberg, "What Is Public Theology?," in *Public Theology for a Global Society: Essays in Honor of Max L. Stackhouse*, ed. Deidre King Hainsworth and Scott R. Paeth (Grand Rapids, MI: William B. Eerdmans, 2010), 16.

16. See Albert J. Jonsen and Lewis H. Butler, "Public Ethics and Policy Making," *The Hastings Center Report* 5, no. 4 (1975): 19–31.

17. Unless otherwise noted, all quotations from scripture in this work are from the New Revised Standard Version (NRSV).

18. Edward Farley, "Worship as Public Theology," *New Theology Review* 22, no. 1 (February 2009): 71.

19. "*Jesus and the Politics of Roman Palestine*, by Richard A. Horsley," *Press Release*, University of South Carolina Press, Last modified July 2018, https://www.sc.edu/uscpress/books/2013/7293.html. See also Richard A. Horsley, "Jesus and the Politics of Roman Palestine," *Journal for the Study of the Historical Jesus* 8, no. 2 (2010): 99.

20. Farley, "Worship as Public Theology," 72.

21. Heinrich Bedford-Strohm, "Poverty and Public Theology: Advocacy of the Church in Pluralistic Society," *International Journal of Public Theology* 2, no. 2 (2008): 51.

22. Ibid., 51–52.

23. Heinrich Bedford-Strohm, "Public Theology and Political Ethics," *International Journal of Public Theology* 6, no. 3 (2012): 275.

24. In Augustine's understanding, the City of Man consists of those who place their interests above those of God, while the City of God consists of those who place God above their own interests.

25. Martin Luther, *Lectures on Romans*, *Luther's Works*, Vol. 25, ed. Hilton C. Oswald, trans. Jacob A. O. Preus (St. Louis, MO: Concordia Publishing House, 1972), 470.

26. Klaus Nürnberger, *Martin Luther's Message for Us Today: A Perspective from the South* (Pietermaritzburg, SA: Cluster Publications, 2005), 298. One can see this concern for the poor in Luther's exegesis of Rom 13:8–10, where he calls for a practice of love that seeks the good of the neighbor. See Luther, *Lectures on Romans*, 475–77.

27. Heinrich Bedford-Strohm, *Liberation Theology for a Democratic Society: Essays in Public Theology* (Zurich: Lit Verlag GmbH & Co., 2018), 161.

28. See Robert Michael, "Luther, Luther Scholars, and the Jews," *Encounter* 46, no. 4 (Autumn 1985): 339–70. Although Luther initially called for tolerance toward Jews, he later vociferously supported their persecution. See Martin Luther, *On the Jews and their Lies, Luther's Works*, Vol. 47, ed. Helmut T. Lehmann, trans. Martin H. Bertram (Philadelphia, PA: Fortress Press, 1971).

29. Cited in Greg Forster, *The Contested Public Square* (Downers Grove, IL: InterVarsity Press, 2008), 133–34.

30. John Calvin, *Calvin's New Testament Commentaries: Romans and Thessalonians*, ed. Thomas F. Torrance and David W. Torrance, trans. Ross Mackenzie (Milton Keynes, UK: Paternoster Press, 1960), 281–83.

31. Ibid., 281.

32. Duncan B. Forrester, "The Scope of Public Theology," *Studies in Christian Ethics* 17, no. 2 (2004): 8.

33. Ibid.

34. Dietrich Bonhoeffer, *Ethics* (New York, NY: Touchstone, 1995), 58.

35. Frits de Lange, "Against Escapism: Dietrich Bonhoeffer's Contribution to Public Theology," in *Christian in Public: Aims, Methodologies and Issues in Public Theology*, Vol. 3, ed. Len Hans, Beyers Naudé Centre Series on Public Theology #3 (Stellenbosch, SA: Sun Press, 2008), 141. See also Clifford J. Green, "Bonhoeffer's 'Non-Religious Christianity' as Public Theology," *Dialog* 26 (Fall 1987): 275–80.

36. Dietrich Bonhoeffer, *Letters and Papers from Prison*, abridged edition, ed. Eberhard Bethge (London: SCM Press, 1953).

37. de Lange, "Against Escapism," 141.

38. See Walter Rauschenbusch, *A Theology for the Social Gospel* (New York, NY: Abingdon Press, 1917).

39. "Social Gospel Movement," accessed June 1, 2015, http://www.theopedia.com/SocialGospel. For an updated assessment of the Social Gospel movement, see Pierre Jacobs, "The Social Gospel Movement Revisited: Consequences for the Church," *HTS Teologiese Studies/Theological Studies* 71, no. 3 (2015): 1–8.

40. Key pioneering Latin American liberation theologians include Gustavo Gutierrez, Leonardo and Clodovis Boff, José Miguez Bonino, and Juan Luis Segundo. See seminal texts such as: Leonardo and Clodovis Boff, *Introducing Liberation Theology* (Maryknoll, NY: Orbis Books, 1987); José Miguez Bonino, *Toward a Christian Political Ethics* (Minneapolis, MN: Fortress Press, 1983); Gustavo Gutierrez, *A Theology of Liberation: History, Politics, and Salvation*, 15th anniversary ed. with new Introduction, trans. Caridad Inda and John Eagleson (Maryknoll, NY: Orbis Books, 1988); and Juan Luis Segundo, *Liberation of Theology* (Maryknoll, NY: Orbis Books, 1985). A number of feminist theologians are also considered liberation theologians, such as Ada-Maria Isasi-Diaz, Letty Russell and Rosemary Ruether. Some expressions of Asian, African and African American theologies are also considered liberation theologies.

41. For an elaboration of the influence of liberation theology on Forrester's thought, see Duncan Forrester, *Theology and Politics* (Oxford: Blackwell Publishers, 1988), especially chapters 3–6.

42. Moltmann's understanding of liberation theology emerged from his conviction that God suffers with the oppressed, who find hope through the resurrection. This vision is developed in Jürgen Moltmann, *Theology of Hope* (Philadelphia, PA: Fortress Press, 1993), and has been recently updated in his *Spirit of Hope: Theology for a World in Peril* (Louisville, KY: Westminster John Knox Press, 2019). Moltmann's orientation to liberation theology is also addressed in Geiko Müller-Fahrenholz, *The Kingdom and the Power: The Theology of Jürgen Moltmann* (Philadelphia, PA: Augsburg Fortress Press, 2001).

43. Eurocentrism is the worldview associated with Western cultures. Originally used mainly to refer to Western Europe, it includes North America and other Caucasian-dominated nations. It appeals to the values of personal initiative, individual rights and democracy, but has also been associated with Western imperialism. The term was coined in the 1970s by the Egyptian economist Samir Amin to describe the ideology of 'white exceptionalism.' See John Hobson, *The Eurocentric Conception of World Politics: Western International Theory, 1760–2010* (New York, NY: Cambridge University Press, 2012).

44. For example, Max Stackhouse, William Storrar, Andrew Morton, David Tombs, Andrew Bradstock, Elaine Graham, David Neville, Heather Thomson, John Atherton, Katie Day, John de Gruchy, Alison Elliott, David Ford, Esther McIntosh, and others mentioned in this study.

45. Graham, *Between a Rock and a Hard Place*, 72.

46. Mary Doak, *Reclaiming Narrative for Public Theology* (Albany, NY: SUNY Press, 2004), 9. Cited in Graham, *Between a Rock and a Hard Place*, 70.

47. Ibid.

48. The term *practical theology*, first used by the theologian Friedrich Schleiermacher in the eighteenth century, referred to 'rules of art' for Christian life and ministry. A working definition that came out of the twentieth century described practical theology as theological reflection grounded in the life of the church, the society and the individual, which both "critically recovers the theology of the past and constructively develops for the future." See "Practical Theology," accessed May 10, 2016, http//:theoblogy.blogspot.co.nz/2005/02/what-is-practical-theology-part-1.html.

49. See Bevans, *Models of Contextual Theology*. Bevans argues that contextual theology takes seriously both the experience of the past (recorded in Scripture and preserved in tradition) and the experience of the present—that is, context.

50. Eugene H. Breitenberg, "To Tell the Truth: Will the Real Public Theology Please Stand Up?," *Journal of the Society of Christian Ethics* 23, no. 2 (2003): 55–96.

51. Breitenberg, "What Is Public Theology?," 4.

52. Cited in Andrew Bradstock, "Public Theology? No Thanks, I'll Stick with the Normal Kind," *Public Lecture*, Centre for Theology and Public Issues, University of Otago, June 2, 2010.

53. Charles Mathewes, *A Theology of Public Life* (Cambridge: Cambridge University Press, 2007), 1.

54. Ibid. Also cited in Clive Pearson, "The Purpose and Practice of a Public Theology in a Time of Climate Change," *International Journal of Public Theology* 4, no. 3 (2010): 357.

55. Mathewes, *A Theology of Public Life*, 2.

56. John W. de Gruchy, "Public Theology as Christian Witness: Exploring the Genre," *International Journal of Public Theology* 1, no. 1 (2007): 40.

57. Eugene Harold Breitenberg, *The Comprehensive Public Theology of Max L. Stackhouse: Theological Ethics, Society, and Theological Education* (Richmond, VA: Union Theological Seminary and Presbyterian School of Christian Education, 2004), 11.

58. Duncan Forrester, "The Scope of Public Theology: What is Public Theology,?" in *Forrester on Christian Ethics and Practical Theology: Collected Writings on Christianity, India, and the Social Order*, Ashgate Contemporary Thinkers on Religion: Collected Works, ed. John R. Hinnells (Farnham, UK: Ashgate Publishing Ltd., 2010), 141.

59. Ibid.

60. Alasdair MacIntyre, *After Virtue: A Study in Moral Theory* (London: Duckworth, 1981).

61. Duncan B. Forrester, "Violence and Non-Violence in Conflict Resolution: Some Theological Reflections," *Studies in Christian Ethics* 16, no. 2 (2003): 64–79.

62. Robert Benne, *The Paradoxical Vision: A Public Theology for the Twenty-First Century* (Minneapolis, MN: Fortress Press, 1995), 4.

63. Ibid.

64. Darren Cronshaw, "The Shaping of Public Theology in Emerging Churches," Paper Presented, *Australian Association of Mission Studies and Public and Contextual*

Theology Conference, Australian Centre for Christianity and Culture, Canberra, October 4, 2008.

65. Paul Hanson, *Political Engagement as Biblical Mandate* (Eugene, OR: Cascade Books, 2010), 35–41.

66. Clive Pearson, "What Is Public Theology?," *The Council of Societies for the Study of Religion Bulletin* 47, no. 2 (2008): 92–95, accessed November 2015, www.csu.edu.au/faculty/arts/theology/pact/documents/what_is_public_theology.pdf.

67. Ibid., 93.

68. Ibid., 94.

69. Ibid.

70. *Talanoa*, the Pacific Islands style of open-ended dialogue, is defined in chapter 4, with particular reference to its usefulness as an indigenous Pacific Islands approach to qualitative research.

71. The Tongan theologian and church leader Winston Halapua was formerly Bishop of Polynesia, and later became Archbishop of New Zealand & Primate of the Anglican Church in Aotearoa New Zealand and Polynesia. During his many years based in Suva, Fiji, he was a prominent voice for reconciliation within Fiji's racially divided society. He is the author of a number of books, including *Living on the Fringe: Melanesians in Fiji* (Suva: Institute of Pacific Studies, University of the South Pacific, 2001), and *The Role of Militarism in the Politics of Fiji* (Saarbrucken: VDM Verlag Dr. Müller, 2010).

72. The Anglican priest Fr. Walter Lini was an instrumental figure in the lead-up to Vanuatu's independence in 1980, and was the country's first prime minister. Under his leadership, the French and English divisions of Vanuatu became more united, Vanuatu supported the Kanak indigenous liberation movement in New Caledonia, and was the only Pacific nation to support East Timor's struggle for independence from Indonesia.

73. The Melanesian Brotherhood, a lay Anglican religious order whose members take vows of poverty, chastity and obedience for three-year renewable terms, became well known and respected around the world as the most trusted arbiter of peace and reconciliation during the Solomon Islands' period of armed unrest between 1998 and 2003, known as the 'ethnic tension.'

74. Malcolm Brown, Stephen Pattison, and Graeme Smith, "The Possibility of Citizen Theology: Public Theology after Christendom and the Enlightenment," *International Journal of Public Theology* 6, no. 2 (2012): 185.

75. Forrester, "The Scope of Public Theology," 12.

76. Duncan B. Forrester, "Working in the Quarry: A Response to the Colloquium," in *Public Theology for the Twenty-first Century*, ed. William F. Storrer and Andrew R. Morton (London and New York, NY: T&T Clark, 2004), 437.

77. Andries Van Aarde, "What is 'Theology' in 'Public Theology' and What is 'Public' about 'Public Theology'?," *Hervormde Teologiese/Theological Studies* 64, no. 3 (2008): 123–34.

78. Ibid., 126.

79. See "How 'Pray for our Pacific' is Strengthening the Pacific Climate Movement," *350 Pacific*, accessed September 30, 2016, https://350pacific.org/.

80. For an account of the Standing Rock Sioux tribe's Water Protectors who tried to save their land and water from the Dakota Access Oil Pipeline, see Kelly Hayes, "Standing Rock and the Power and Determination of Indigenous Americans," *Pacific Standard*, March 13, 2018, https://psmag.com/magazine/standing-rock-still-rising. During their months-long riverside encampment, protesting the damage to their water and ancient burial sites by the pipeline company, they were joined by hundreds of other indigenous tribes, not only from North America but from around the world. Some were brutally beaten or arrested, and the pipeline was constructed in the end, but the Water Protectors' reliance on their indigenous nonviolent spiritual principles has inspired other environmental movements around the world.

81. The Moral Mondays movement has been described as being led by 'Christian progressives,' and is characterized by acts of civil disobedience that have led to changes in some unjust laws. In 2018 the movement evolved into a revival of Martin Luther King's Poor People's Campaign, a long-term movement to combat racism, poverty and climate change through activism in local communities across the United States. See William Barber, "America's Moral Malady and a New Poor People's Campaign," *The Atlantic*, February 2018, https://www.the atlantic.com/magazine/arc hive/2018/02/a-new-poor-peoples-campaign/552503/.

82. For example, David Tracy, Jürgen Moltmann, Max L. Stackhouse, Martin Marty, Michael and Kenneth Himes, Duncan Forrester, Vincent Bacote, Ronald Thiemann, Robert Benne, Marion Maddox, Stanley Hauerwas, John de Gruchy, Clive Pearson, and Andrew Bradstock.

83. Kim, *Theology in the Public Sphere*, 10.

84. Ibid.

85. Tracy, *The Analogical Imagination*, 3–5.

86. Nico Koopman, "Churches and Public Policy Discourse in South Africa," accessed June 2015, http://www.csu.edu.au/faculty/arts/theology/pact/documents/C hurches.

87. Nico Koopman, "A Public Theology of Global Transformation in Challenging Times?," *Unpublished Paper*, Beyers Naudé Centre for Public Theology, Stellenbosch University, South Africa, 2012, 3.

88. Ibid.

89. Nico Koopman, "Some Contours for Public Theology in South Africa," *International Journal of Practical Theology* 14, no. 1 (2010): 133–34.

90. Koopman, "A Public Theology of Global Transformation," 4.

91. de Lange, "Against Escapism," 141.

92. Storrar and Morton, "Introduction," 2.

93. Jürgen Moltmann, *Theology of Hope*, trans. J. W. Leitch (London: SCM Press, 1967), 5–23.

94. Scott R. Paeth, "Jürgen Moltmann's Public Theology," *Political Theology* 6, no. 2 (2005): 232.

95. Thiemann, *Constructing a Public Theology*, 39.

96. Ibid.

97. Ibid., 19.

Chapter 2

The Samoan Context

Concurring with John de Gruchy's claim that "all public theology is contextual," this chapter describes key aspects of the context which is the primary focus of this study—Samoa. Before exploring the contours of a Samoan contextual public theology, it is important to understand what we mean by *context*. Context is crucial in theology because it embraces the totality of circumstances, historical narratives, and communal values that shape every framework for doing theology.

Context refers to the social setting from which theology emerges. While Christian theology relies on the gospel of Jesus Christ, the traditions arising from the Jesus story in first-century Palestine were themselves mediated by culture, and the message of the gospel corresponds with God who is present in every culture. Context influences both the content and the method of our theologizing. It determines the questions we ask and highlights the things we see as important. At the same time, context cannot be the only decisive or final factor in the process of doing theology.

The first contextual observation that has relevance for a public theology in Samoa is that there is not a need for any overt religious revival or turn away from secularism, as the Christian religion is already a central focus of Samoan life. Almost 100 percent of Samoans self-identify as Christians, and the churches that are the most prominent landmarks in every village are routinely filled with worshippers. Instead, the challenge is to focus on what public theology has to offer to Samoan society, bringing analogous cultural and Christian values to bear in public discourse on social issues that are impacting Samoan society. Since the Samoan context is one which amalgamated Christianity into Samoan culture, this fusion will be important for our understanding of what a Samoan public theology looks like and why it is important.

A key contextual question thus becomes: *How do we articulate and utilize a contextual framework that is rooted in the Samoan cultural context and, at the same time, is in line with the Christian faith?* I wish to present a framework for a Samoan public theology that is grounded in the Samoan core values of love, justice, selfless service, consensual dialogue, and respect. These core values are embedded not only in the *fa'asamoa* (Samoan way of life) (see chapter 3) but also in the Christian faith, and are acknowledged publicly as reflective of the Samoan way of life. It is for this reason that these values are introduced in this chapter alongside parallels found in scripture.

In examining the Samoan context through the lens of these core values, Bevans' insights on contextual theology are helpful. Focusing specifically on the creation-centered nature of most of the models of contextual theology in Bevans' framework, the underlying assumption is that culture is a gift to be appreciated—an assertion likewise affirmed in the Samoan worldview. Culture is the arena of God's activity and therefore a source and resource for theology.[1]

At the same time, it is important to keep in mind that God's revelation cuts across all contexts. It is not restricted to any culture, ethnicity, or religious tradition, and all contexts are open to critique. Culture is God-given, but it is shaped and lived out by imperfect human beings. This means that the Samoan context, while exhibiting core values that offer profound riches that can be drawn upon to create a compelling public theology, is also a context that does not always live up to the core values it espouses.

CULTURE AND CHRISTIANITY IN SAMOA

Samoa is a small nation-state in the Polynesian subregion[2] of the South Pacific (Oceania), comprising two relatively large islands, Upolu and Savaii, two smaller inhabited islands, Manono and Apolima, and a number of smaller uninhabited islands. Samoa has an estimated population of 198,576, and the population of neighboring American Samoa is around 55,700.[3] Approximately 440,000 Samoans live outside Samoa,[4] and they make their own distinctive contributions to Samoan culture, but these are beyond the scope of this study.

Samoa regards itself as a Christian nation, and Samoans almost universally consider themselves Christians. As Manfred Ernst writes, "It would be hard to find any other nation in the world where society and the churches are so closely interwoven, and where the historic mainline churches have had and still have such a great impact on nearly every aspect of life, as Samoa."[5] In the most recent survey, 99.9 percent of the population reported belonging to a Christian denomination.[6]

Responding to the question, "Is Samoa a Christian nation?" Rex Ahdar draws this conclusion: "We can say that, yes, Samoa is a Christian nation in a demographic sense (most people identify themselves as Christians). And in the following ways: the Christian faith is a major source of moral guidance for ordinary citizens, Christian doctrines are still widely believed, and the ethos that governs political life is Christian."[7] However, despite Ahdar's claim, the overwhelming confession of Christian allegiance among the population of Samoa does not automatically make Samoa a Christian nation. This would not be the case unless core Christian values were manifestly lived out in the public sphere in which people exist and interact with one another.

Toleafoa Afamasaga, a Samoan social critic, has noted the contradiction entailed in the assertion that Samoa is a Christian nation: "If Samoa is indeed such a violent place, how might this be explained in the light of our preoccupation with religion and anything remotely connected to religion?"[8] Afamasaga's comment questions the authenticity of the claim enshrined in Samoa's national motto, *Fa'avaei le Atua Samoa* ("Samoa is founded in God"). This claim is reiterated in Article 1 of Samoa's Constitution, which states: "Samoa is a Christian nation founded on God the Father, the Son and the Holy Spirit,"[9] a specifically Christian conception of God. This statement promotes the message that Samoa as a Christian nation follows Christian values. This claim is also assumed in the common practice of including Christian prayers and devotions performed by clergy on all public occasions.

The Constitution of Samoa still allows for the freedom of religion. Samoan government does not require religious groups to register. This has left an opening for a variety of religious groups to enter Samoa in recent decades, regardless of their beliefs or practices. Nonetheless, despite the competition between these newer religious groups and the established mainline churches, and the competitiveness among the established churches, Samoa still sees itself as united in its Christian identity. Almost all Samoans, regardless of denominational affiliation, view Christianity as an inherent part of what it means to be Samoan. This syncretistic blend of Samoanness and Christianity has occurred largely at the level of complementary underlying moral values, but it has not resulted in any understanding that Samoan Christians have a calling to "speak truth to power" in the public sphere.

The Samoanized traditions and practices of church life, the patriarchal hierarchy that controls both church structures and governance (in which pastors have become as powerful as *matai* [chiefs], and in certain respects more powerful), and the sacrificial commitments made by church members to support the church and clergy—these are among the most striking examples of how neatly Christianity and culture co-exist in Samoa. What is missing is an appeal to shared Christian and Samoan ethical values to confront social issues that may challenge the status quo or cause public discomfort. This is why a contextual public theology is so necessary in order to create a framework that can empower those who feel called to address these issues in the name of both the Christian gospel and the values affirmed by the *fa'asamoa*.

CULTURE AND GOVERNANCE IN SAMOA

Samoa is a fiercely traditional nation with continuing strong ties to its indigenous culture and customs, its *fa'asamoa*. Traditional social structures and institutions are very resilient in Samoan society and are cemented by the *aiga* (extended family) and the *fa'amatai* (chiefly system). Today Samoa is governed according to both the *fa'amatai* and the imported Westminster parliamentary system. The *fa'amatai* governs mostly at the village level, but is given recognition at the national level by virtue of the fact that, except for some representatives of individual voters, only *matai* (chiefs) can become members of Samoa's national parliament. The chiefly system operates in tandem with the Westminster parliamentary form of government, which functions according to principles of representative democracy, premised on the notion of a secular government appointed not by God but by "the people."

The *fa'amatai* presumes a divine warrant for its authority but, unlike monarchical rule, it has no notion of absolute and inalienable power. The two governing systems run parallel with each other, with the secular state garnering, more often than not, greater political power. This means that despite deference paid in Samoa's 1960 constitution to the *fa'asamoa* (as well as Christian principles), Samoa's secular state privileges the power of parliamentary politicians. The parallel tracks of the government and the *fa'amatai* are often a contested space.

The *fa'amatai* and the parliamentary system are said to operate symbiotically in order to protect the harmony and welfare of Samoan society. Political leaders are expected to demonstrate the values implicitly upheld by both systems. However, a close study of religious[10] and secular[11] governance in Samoa suggests that adherence to these moral virtues is more often than not found wanting. The old adage that "power corrupts" is evident in Samoan political life, as in other countries, whether in parliament or in village councils.

The current social reality of Samoa also evinces a false demarcation of sacred and secular spheres, encouraged by the presumption that church ministers should concern themselves only with spiritual matters, not secular matters. Indeed, clergy are condemned by the state, as well as by church authorities, if they publicly preach or take a stand against the social injustices affecting Samoa.

For example, before the passage of the Casino Bill in 2010 (since amended in 2018), which legalized casino gambling in Samoa, many of the sermons aired on television and radio targeted the personal, familial, and societal damage associated with gambling. The chairman of the Samoa National Council of Churches, Kasiano Le'aupepe, stated that he "feared the perils of gambling will shake Samoa's Christian foundation."[12] In response, Prime Minister Tuilaepa sternly reminded the clergy that it was not their role to interfere in public matters.

Such reminders serve to promote and perpetuate a naïve consciousness which endorses the false view that the church is a completely autonomous domain that has nothing to do with the state. This false consciousness creates a culture of silence and passivity in the churches, similar to that addressed by Paulo Freire's liberationist pedagogy, with its critique that those who wield unquestioned power overwhelm the populace with their normative worldview, resulting in mindsets which Freire refers to as *semi-intransivity* and *naïve transivity*.

Semi-intransivity refers to a

> consciousness that is typical of closed structures. . . . This consciousness fails to perceive many of reality's challenges, or perceives them in a distorted way. . . . This mode of consciousness cannot objectify the facts and problematic situations of daily life.[13]

In naïve transivity, one "engages with the world, but in simplistic ways, without argument and discussion, following established patterns unquestioningly."[14] As a result, citizens are passive and do not even see their situation as oppressive. They assume that their personal problems have no relationship to larger social structures, and that they have no constructive role to play in reshaping those social structures so as to alleviate the injustices they face.

In order to develop a public theology for Samoa, this widespread social reality of false consciousness, complicity, and passivity must be addressed. Public theology in this context can only be developed through the cultivation of what Freire calls *critical consciousness*,[15] in which the Samoan people are able to objectively analyze their lived experience as a society and become active participants in changing situations and structures of injustice through action for social transformation.

Before introducing the core values that undergird the Samoan context, it is important to touch briefly upon three interrelated foundational concepts that provide the framework within which Samoan values are manifested. These are the concept of *va* (relational space); the Samoan understanding of the self within the *va* framework; and *aiga* as the primary location for the inculcation of values.

UNDERLYING CONCEPTS

Va

The concept of *va* lies at the heart of the *fa'asamoa*. *Va* refers to the space (literal, figurative, emotional, or symbolic) between people, places, things, and the supernatural. The most common expressions used to illustrate the imperative of respecting the *va* are *ia teu le va* ("let us cherish/care for *va* relationships"); *vafeiloai* (referring to the rules of relational behavior); and *vatapuia* (referring to the boundaries within relationships). A regulating social construct like *va* is crucial in communal cultures that value group unity more than individualism. In the *fa'asamoa*, all relationships are held in balance by *va*. According to Aiono-Le Tagaloa, "*Va* is first of all the relationships between the Creator and the created.... *Va* is relationship, connection, affiliation, boundaries, difference, separation, space, distance, responsibility, obligation, state of being, position, standing, and so much more."[16]

Jeannette Mageo summarizes the significance of this relational orientation by highlighting the expression *teu le va* (nurture *va* relationships). As a Samoan, "one does not act on one's own behalf but as an ambassador of one's group; therefore, one gives respect in a representative capacity to the ambassadors of other groups. It [*teu le va*] also can be seen as symbolizing the relationships among and within communities."[17]

The Samoan novelist Albert Wendt argues for the importance of respectful relational space because it reflects and protects Samoans' unique collective identity.[18] This is encompassed in the concepts of *fa'asinomaga* (communal character and places of belonging), *tupuaga* (genealogical lineage), and *tofiga* (roles and responsibilities to protect our heritage). *Va* "relationships of respect" are lived out in spiritual, interpersonal, social, economic, and political contexts.

The Samoan Self

Within the *va* framework, the self is a relational being rather than an autonomous individual. For Samoans, any dissociation between the individual and the community, or any separation of the physical and spiritual aspects of the self is anathema to one's well-being.[19] The Samoan self cannot exist in isolation from others or from an integrated physical-spiritual reality. This understanding of personhood is consistent with descriptions of Samoa as a socio-centric or collectivist society. The well-being of the group is perceived to be of greater importance than the individuals who make up the group.[20]

There are both gifts and risks entailed in this construction of the self. While this relational selfhood has advantages that are lost at times in the Eurocentric focus on the individual as an autonomous being, there is a risk of a lack of balance in either worldview. As Upolu Vaai points out, "Western cultures often run the risk of putting too much emphasis on the autonomy of the self at the expense of social relations. Samoa and many Pacific island cultures, in contrast, run the risk of putting emphasis on relationships at the expense of individual uniqueness and distinctiveness."[21] It could be argued that the core Samoan-Christian values revealed in this study are ideally a moral fulcrum that seeks to find a balance between the extremes of individualism and collectivism.

Aiga: Locus for Inculcation of Values

Another important consideration in any attempt to understand Samoan core values is an appreciation of their rootedness in the web of familial relatedness that is the *aiga*. This is evident in the comments of Research Participant CVG021. As a housewife, she spends most of her time caring for her children and attending to family, village, and church commitments. In her comments, she highlights her *aiga* as the primary setting for imparting the values she has internalized and embraces today: "Good manners, respect, love, justice and humility . . . these are Godly values. These are also the values that I was socialized into as I grew up in my family. I remember my parents teaching us every day about these values; I saw them within my own family and they became part of who I am."

SAMOA'S CORE VALUES

This study centers its framing of a public theology for Samoa in the core values of the *fa'asamoa* and the *fa'akerisiano* (Christian faith). These are the values of respect (*fa'aaloalo*), selfless service (*tautua*), justice (*amiotonu*), consensual dialogue (*soalaupule*), and love (*alofa*). In constructing a Samoan public theology based on these values, this study incorporates a synthetic approach to contextual public theology, following Bevans', also drawing on insights from his translation model, anthropological model, and praxis model. These core values are briefly introduced below, along with their Christian parallels, and will be fleshed out in greater depth in succeeding chapters.

Fa'aaloalo (Respect)

Fa'aaloalo is most commonly translated as "respect" but also encompasses the attributes of courtesy, politeness, and pleasantness.[22] Tui Atua Tupua Tamasese Taisi Efi (hereafter referred to by his more common designation, Tui Atua) suggests a deeper meaning in his claim that "*fa'aaloalo* is *alo mai* and *alo atu*."²³ The expressions *alo mai* and *alo atu* are akin to the biblical injunction to "do unto others as you would have them do unto you." This understanding reinforces the importance of nurturing reciprocity in relationships.

In such relationships there is a focus not only on respecting the space between people but on reciprocity. *Alo mai* and *alo atu* may be translated as "face meeting face" or "I face you and you face me." Once there is loss of face through disrespect, there cannot be a meeting of faces, and therefore the foundation upon which *fa'aaloalo* is premised disappears. In this sense, *fa'aaloalo* can be understood as the honoring of the other's value and dignity.

Fa'aaloalo is sometimes practiced in Samoa in a manner that validates unequal power relations. For example, *fa'aaloalo* can be misused in the context of the relationship between a *matai* and his/her extended family (*aiga*), a church minister and his parish, or in relations between men and women. There are chiefs who expect respect from members of their *aiga* but do not respect them in return. There are pastors who expect deference from their parishioners simply because they are *faifeau* (pastors). There are husbands who expect obedience and submission from their wives only because they are men. Still, *fa'aaloalo* in its ideal form must be reciprocated. It is not meant to be a one-way street.

In both Samoan and Christian values, respect is based on the sacredness of relationality. *Fa'aaloalo* resonates with the covenantal relationship between God and God's people described in the Hebrew scriptures. God showed enduring respect for the people of Israel, even though they continued to break their covenant with God and follow other gods. The Hebrew scriptures are a story of the Israelites' struggle to live out their commitments in their covenantal relationship with God.

A metaphor for God's *fa'aaloalo* is found in Hosea's relationship with his wife Gomer, in the third chapter of Hosea. Although she was a "promiscuous woman" (NIV), a "harlot" (NASB), and a "whore" (KJV), Hosea married her and, like God, he showed respect and love for her. *Fa'aaloalo* is a value that is associated with this relational attribute of God. It is meant to be enacted in relationships among people in all spheres of life, including the public sphere. *Fa'aaloalo* toward the other entails respect in relationships with God, society, and creation.

Tautua (Selfless Service)

A related core value in the *fa'asamoa* is selfless service, or *tautua*—service for the *matai* (the titled head of one's extended family), one's parents, one's grandparents, and one's community and church. Both Samoan proverbs and the Bible are often cited to support this value.²⁴ Gataivai Nepo has written that *tautua* is "concretely founded upon complete obedience, mutual loyalty and mutual respect."[25]

Linguistically, *tau* carries the meaning of struggling, while *tua* means "back." In this sense, *tautua* entails serving "from the back," as in service from the kitchen, which is at the back of the *fale* (Samoan house), in terms of the service rendered by the family, and especially the untitled men, to the *matai*. At the heart of the concept of *tautua* is humble and sacrificial service for others. The *tautua* (both the act of service and the person who performs the service) struggles without complaint to provide whatever is needed for the benefit of others.

Authentic *tautua* in the *fa'asamoa* entails the engagement of one's whole self, relying on one's strength and the motivation of one's mind to provide exemplary service. Typically this is seen in acts of providing food or whatever is needed for the survival of the family and community. These acts of service are formulated in the inner being of a *tautua* as he or she strives wholeheartedly to satisfy the needs of the *matai*, family, and community. Devotion and honesty are essential for these tasks, and in performing acts of *tautua* one must at all times demonstrate genuine love.

Jesus in his own ministry became the role model for such servanthood. He described himself in this way: "I am among you as one who serves" (Lk 22:27). Jesus demonstrated this when he undertook the most humble service imaginable, washing the dirty, dusty feet of his disciples on the night of his Last Supper with them before his crucifixion (Mt 26:14–39; Lk 22:24–27; Jn 13:1–17). Jesus used this act of *tautua* to call his followers to offer the same kind of service to others. In Jn 13:14–15, he says to his disciples, "So if I, your Lord and Teacher, have washed your feet, you also ought to wash one another's feet. For I have set you an example, that you also should do as I have done to you."

Amiotonu (Justice)

Amiotonu is derived from two words, *amio* (behavior) and *tonu* (right or just). The literal translation of *amiotonu* is "correct or just behavior." Milner's *Samoan Dictionary* translates *amiotonu* as "justice and righteousness."[26] In the Samoan context, justice is seen in actions of integrity in day-to-day life and the manner in which people conduct their daily affairs. In this sense, *amiotonu* is intimately linked with *fa'aaloalo* (respect). Any deviation from the norms regarding "right relationships" is an undermining of the principle of *amiotonu*. Without *amiotonu* there can be no peace or harmony in Samoan life, whether in families, villages, or the nation.

Justice in the Hebrew scriptures is likewise associated with the living out of "right relationships." This is reflected in the way God related to the people of Israel: "The Lord works vindication and justice for all who are oppressed" (Ps 103:6). The Book of Exodus tells the story of the Israelites being rescued from oppression in Egypt so that their relationship with God could be restored.

Biblical justice is also about creating a world that is fair, generous, and merciful, especially for those who are poor or outsiders. This kind of justice includes providing "hospitality to the stranger." Lv 19:33–34 is among the passages that mandate this kind of justice: "When an alien resides with you in your land, you shall not oppress the alien; . . . you shall love the alien as yourself, for you were aliens in the land of Egypt."

The appeal to this understanding of justice is a common theme of the Old Testament prophets. They often describe justice using metaphorical language. Am 5:24 says, "Let justice roll down like waters, and righteousness like an ever-flowing stream." Is 40:4 speaks of justice in this way: "Every valley shall be lifted up, and every mountain be made low; the uneven ground shall become level and the rough places a plain." This imagery suggests that, when justice prevails, everyone shares equally in a good life. As Mi 4:4 puts it, in a just society everyone "shall sit under their own vines and under their own fig trees, and no one shall make them afraid."

In the New Testament, Jesus calls people to seek first God's kingdom and God's justice (Mt 6:33). As noted earlier, Jesus began his public ministry by announcing it as a ministry of justice and liberation (Lk 4:18). The justice that is the centerpiece of Jesus's New Covenant is also inclusive. It aims to renew all broken relationships, as epitomized in parables such as the story of the Prodigal Son in Lk 15:11–32.

This vision of justice is especially for those who are marginalized in society. Indeed, the Old Testament theme of justice as "hospitality to the stranger" is given a new twist by Jesus in his singling out of society's most despised for extravagant hospitality. In Lk 14:12–13, Jesus says, "When you give a luncheon or a dinner, do not invite your friends or your brothers or your relatives or rich neighbors, in case they may invite you in return, and you would be repaid. But when you give a banquet, invite the poor, the crippled, the lame, and the blind." This suggests that justice is a turning-upside-down of society's status quo, without any expectation of being repaid, and this is a principle that resonates with the ideal of *amiotonu*, although it is not always fulfilled in practice.

Soalaupule (Consensual Dialogue)

Soalaupule refers to the process of decision-making in the *fa'amatai*. It is a process in which all participants voice their opinions until consensus is reached. It consists of three root words: *soa, lau,* and *pule*. Fanaafi Aiono-Le

Tagaloa translates *soalaupule* as follows: "*Soa* means two or a pair; *lau* means to recite or declare; *pule* means to distribute or portion out, and conveys authority."[27] The meanings of these three elements of *soalaupule* should make evident the inclusive approach to decision-making in the *fa'amatai*, where decisions are made on a consultative basis. At least two people must be involved in the making of a decision, but the ideal is to involve all relevant people.[28] A final decision is reached when all members of the *aiga potopoto* (network of extended families) or *fono* (village council) come to a mutual agreement, rather than a decision being made by any one individual, or even by a majority. Elise Huffer and Asofou So'o explicate this clearly:

> *Soalaupule* suggests being part of a decision-making process where everyone freely discusses the issues involved, puts forward their views and weighs all views against each other for their merits and practicality. This eventually results in a decision that everyone is happy and comfortable with. It explicitly establishes the fact that the decision has been made by more than one person. The more people involved in the decision the better, as dictated by the Samoan proverb, *O le tele o sulu e maua ai figota* ("The more lit fire we have, the more fish we are likely to catch").[29]

The principle of *soalaupule* as a consensual style of decision-making is a concept widely used not only in Samoa but throughout Oceania. It is a fundamental feature of group deliberation and an important characteristic of the *fa'asamoa* and other Oceanian ways of being and doing. It is a term with which people identify and which they use with pride.[30]

Jesus also used a dialogical approach in his interactions with others. For example, in Jesus's encounter with the Samaritan woman at the well (Jn 4:5–29), he engaged in dialogue with her not only to encourage her liberation from her current situation (in which she was socially ostracized) but also so that she could authenticate God's purpose in her life. She was an active participant in that dialogue.

Jesus often posed searching questions in his conversations with others, which was a way of inviting them into deeper conversation. He also engaged people by telling parables, which resonates with Samoans' way of teaching through retelling myths and legends. Jesus's main purpose in his open dialogues with others was for their lives to be transformed so that they could experience God's love. In *soalaupule*, the goal is to reach a decision that will ensure peace and harmony.

Alofa (Love)

Alofa is literally translated as "love" but also refers to compassion or charity.[31] *Alofa* is encapsulated in the act of giving from the heart. It encompasses not only ideals of love, charity, and compassion but acts of caring, sacrifice, service, and consideration, all of which are closely associated with *tautua* and *fa'aaloalo*.[32] *Alofa* is such a central value of Samoan society that former Head of State Tui Atua, considered the paramount living custodian of Samoan indigenous knowledge, has asserted, "*fa'asamoa* is founded on *alofa*."[33] *Alofa* is so much associated with heartfelt giving that it is used, for example, to describe financial contributions in the Congregational Christian Church in Samoa. The act of donating money to support the minister and his family is considered an act of *alofa*. This action epitomizes the Samoan understanding of *alofa* as *gift*.[34]

The New Testament also speaks of love as being at the heart of all that is good: "And now faith, hope and love abide, these three; but the greatest of these is love" (1 Cor 13:13). This love is from God and is a reflection of God's Spirit. It came to its fullest expression in God's gift of Jesus Christ to the world, a love best captured by the New Testament Greek word *agape*. *Agape* is selfless, Christ-like love that alone can bring about genuine transformation in individuals and societies. Augustine described *agape* as "the soul's movement," the deepest force that drives persons toward the good.[35]

FINAL THOUGHTS

This chapter's brief introduction to the contextual background of Samoa has highlighted the Samoan context in terms of the inextricable linkage between the Samoan culture and Christianity, and the significance of the core values that characterize both the *fa'asamoa* and the Christian faith. It is contended that these values, embedded in both the *fa'asamoa* and the Christian faith, can complement one another in forming the foundation of a public theology that has relevance and efficacy in the Samoan context. In order to do public theology in Samoa, the relationship between Christianity and culture in Samoa must be understood, critically analyzed, and acted upon. Public theology must make sense in the context wherein it is situated, in terms of its rationality and applicability. The Samoan context will thus be further unpacked and analyzed in succeeding chapters.

NOTES

1. Bevans, *Models of Contextual Theology*, 16–17.
2. Polynesia is one of the three sub-regions of Oceania, along with Melanesia and Micronesia. Polynesia comprises more than 1,000 islands spread over the southern and central Pacific Ocean. Its indigenous peoples share many ethnic similarities, cultural values, customs, and a similar language family, although each island group has its own distinct language and traditions. Polynesia's island nations or territories

include Samoa, American Samoa, Tonga, French Polynesia (Maohi Nui), Niue, Cook Islands, Easter Island (Rapa Nui), Hawaii, Tokelau, Tuvalu, Wallis & Futuna, and the indigenous Maori of New Zealand.

3. "Samoa Population 2019," *World Population Review*, accessed March 11, 2019, http://worldpopulationreview.com/countries/samoa-population/. American Samoa is a U.S. territory consisting of the main island of Tutuila and the smaller islands of Tau, Olosega, Ofu, and Aunuu. Its estimated population is 55,700. See "American Samoa Population," *Worldometers*, accessed November 21, 2019, https://www.worldometers.info/world-population/american-samoa-population/.

4. Ibid. In addition to the 55,700 Samoans in American Samoa, there are 380,000 Samoans living in the diaspora (New Zealand, Australia and the United States), and several thousand Samoans living in other Pacific Islands nations.

5. Manfred Ernst, ed., *Globalization and the Re-shaping of Christianity in the Pacific Islands* (Suva, FJ: Pacific Theological College, 2006), 695.

6. The most recent official data on religious affiliation in Samoa is found in the 2011 census. See Samoa Bureau of Statistics, *Samoa: Populations and Housing Census 2011 Analytical Report* (Apia, WS: Census-Surveys Division, Samoa Bureau of Statistics, 2012).

7. Rex Tauati Ahdar, "Is Samoa a Christian State?," *Public Lecture*, National University of Samoa, Le Papaigalagala, Samoa, October 6, 2011.

8. Toleafoa Afamasaga, "Of Sacred Cows and Cash Cows and Violence in God's Own," *Samoa Observer*, October 7, 2007, 2.

9. Grant Wyeth, "Samoa Officially Becomes a Christian State," *The Diplomat*, June 16, 2017.

10. Rex Tauati Ahdar, "Samoa and the Christian State Ideal," *International Journal for the Study of the Christian Church* 13, no. 1 (2013): 59–72.

11. See Iati Iati, "The Good Governance Agenda for Civil Society: Implications for the Fa'asamoa," in *Governance in Samoa: Pulega i Samoa*, ed. Elise Huffer and Asofou So'o (Suva, FJ and Canberra: Institute of Pacific Studies, University of the South Pacific and Asia Pacific Press, 2000), 67–78; and Elise Huffer and Asafou So'o, "Consensus Versus Dissent: Democracy, Pluralism and Governance in Sāmoa," *Asia Pacific Viewpoint* 44, no. 3 (2003): 281–304.

12. Nicola Marie Hazelman, "PM: Church Warning on Casinos a Joke," *Samoa News*, July 16, 2012, 3.

13. Paulo Freire, *The Politics of Education: Culture, Power and Liberation*, trans. Donaldo Macedo (Westport, CT: Bergin & Garvey Publishers, 1985), 75. See also Paulo Freire, *Cultural Action for Freedom* (Cambridge, MA: Harvard University Press, 1972), 17.

14. Paulo Freire, *Education for Critical Consciousness* (New York, NY: Continuum, 2005), 14.

15. Ibid.

16. Aiono-Le Tagaloa, *Tapuai: Samoan Worship*, 5.

17. Mageo, *Theorizing Self in Samoa*, 81.

18. See Vilsoni Hereniko and David Hanlon, "An Interview with Albert Wendt," in *Inside Out: Literature, Cultural Politics, and Identity in the New Pacific*, ed.

Vilsoni Hereniko and Rob Wilson (Lanham, MD: Rowman and Littlefield Publishers, 1999), 85–94.

19. Kiwi Tamasese, Carmel Peteru, Charles Waldegrave, and Allister Bush, "O Le Taeao Afua, the New Morning: A Qualitative Investigation into Samoan Perspectives on Mental Health and Culturally Appropriate Services," *Australian and New Zealand Journal of Psychiatry* 39, no. 4 (1997): 300–9.

20. Ibid.

21. Ibid.

22. See Pa'u T. Mulitalo-Lauta, *Fa'asamoa and Social Work within the New Zealand Context* (Palmerston North, NZ: Dunmore Press, 2000).

23. Tui Atua Tupua Tamasese Taisi Efi, "More on Meaning, Nuance and Metaphor," in *Su'esu'e Manogi: In Search of Fragrance*, ed. I'uogafa Tuagalu, Tamasa'ilau Sualii-Sauni, Tofilau Nina Kirifi-Alai, and Naomi Fuamatu (Le Papaigalagala, WS: Centre for Samoan Studies, National University of Samoa, 2008), 71.

24. Cluny Macpherson and Laavasa Macpherson, "When Theory Meets Practice: The Limits of the Good Governance Program," in *Governance in Samoa: Pulega i Samoa*, ed. Elise Huffer and Asofou So'o (Suva, FJ and Canberra: Institute of Pacific Studies, University of the South Pacific and Asia Pacific Press, 2000), 30.

25. Nepo, "A Theological Study of 'Tautua'," xi.

26. G. B. Milner, *Samoan Dictionary* (London: Oxford University Press, 1966), 18.

27. Fanaafi Aiono-Le Tagaloa, "The Samoan Culture and Government," in *Culture and Democracy in the South Pacific*, ed. Ron Crocombe et al. (Suva, FJ: University of the South Pacific, 1992), 122–23.

28. Ibid., 123.

29. Huffer and So'o, "Consensus Versus Dissent," 282.

30. Ibid.

31. See Mulitalo-Lauta, *Fa'asamoa and Social Work*.

32. Tamasailau M. Suaali'i-Sauni, "*E Faigata le Alofa*: The Samoan *Fa'amatai*: Reflections from Afar," in *Changes in the Matai System: O Suigai le Fa'amatai* (Le Papaigalagala, WS: Centre for Samoan Studies, National University of Samoa, 2007), 52.

33. Efi, "More on Meaning, Nuance and Metaphor," 52.

34. Jeannette M. Mageo, *Theorizing Self in Samoa: Emotions, Genders, and Sexualities* (Ann Arbor, MI: University of Michigan Press, 1998), 12–24.

35. For Augustine's depiction of *agape* and its association with the love of God, see St. Augustine, *The Trinity (De Trinitate)*, 2nd ed., trans. Edmund Hill, ed. John E. Rotelle, Works of Saint Augustine Book 5 (Hyde Park, NY: New City Press, 2012). Paul Tillich reminded us that *agape* does not exist apart from justice. See Paul Tillich, *Love, Power and Justice: Ontological Analysis and Ethical Applications* (Oxford: Oxford University Press, 1954).

Chapter 3

Interwoven Strands of *Fa'asamoa*

Chapter 2 offered an introductory description of the Samoan context and its core values, highlighting the congruence between Samoan and Christian values. In this chapter, I examine the *fa'asamoa* (Samoan way) in greater depth, as it is manifested in its three underlying frameworks: *aganu'u* (culture), *agaifanua* (customs), and *fa'akerisiano* (Christian life). This necessarily includes a summary of the historical foundations out of which contemporary manifestations of the *fa'asamoa* have emerged and evolved. This discussion also notes the importance of language, signs, and institutions in the *fa'asamoa*. It is important to understand how the interrelated strands of *fa'asamoa* function if one is to construct a meaningful public theology in the Samoan context.

THE COMPLEXITY OF *FA'ASAMOA*

A Multiplicity of Definitions

The literature on *fa'asamoa* elicits many interpretations from Samoan scholars[1] and non-Samoan scholars.[2] Interpretations from the Samoan public[3] are also considered a collective treasure, embodying the wisdom and knowledge often associated with age and experience. In the writings of both Samoan and non-Samoan scholars, *fa'asamoa* is explained as an established yet ever-evolving concept, continually taking on new interpretations over time.

While early scholarship on Samoa, chiefly that of anthropologists Felix Keesing and F. J. H. Grattan, focused on the effects of Western influences on Samoan socioeconomic and political structures, since the 1960s research on Samoa has broadened to more critically examine the interface between Western ideals and the social ideals imbedded in the *fa'asamoa*.

To confine *fa'asamoa* to one definition is impossible. Tui Atua asserts that *fa'asamoa* "is a body of customs and usage. It is a mental attitude to God, to fellow man [*sic*] and to his surroundings. It is a distinctive lifestyle. . . . It is a collection of spiritual and cultural values that motivate people. . . . It is the heritage of [the] people."[4] Tui Atua's description implies that *fa'asamoa* is not an easy concept to define because it entails such a multiplicity of elements of the Samoan worldview, customs, and values.

Commenting on cultural studies of Samoa by Shore, Freeman, Mageo, and Schoeffel,[5] the American anthropologist Douglas Drozdow-St. Christian concludes that "what each of these studies stress is that life in Samoa is never static."[6] He goes on to say that "while Fa'a Samoa is spoken of as a totalizing code, . . . it is a Samoan's dream of what Samoa should be, a process of desire rather than a fixed standard of regulation."[7]

Fa'asamoa, in other words, represents the ideals of Samoan culture and identity. Samoans believe that they have a unique understanding of who they are, which is best described as *fa'asamoa*. This self-awareness is described by Melanie Anae as "the art of remembering who our mothers and grandmothers told us we were, and how these memories have impacted on our life experiences, and vice versa. Our ethnic identity is situated historically, socially, politically, culturally, but, more importantly, emotionally."[8]

Fa'asamoa can thus be envisaged as an umbrella term for a worldview that inculcates distinctive ethical principles, traditions, and collective identity, actualized by means of adherence to customs and shared values. This is captured in Drozdow-St. Christian's statement that *fa'asamoa* "is a kind of shorthand Samoans use to indicate a wide range of things. These include their perception of how their ancestors lived, to their persistent concern with propriety and a truly Samoan way of living, to the tension between what many see as conflicting interests of tradition and the need for . . . development."[9]

A Holistic Existence

Tui Atua describes *fa'asamoa* as the essence of Samoans' holistic sociocentric existence, writing,

> I am not an individual; I am an integral part of the cosmos. I share divinity with my ancestors, the land, the seas and the skies. I am not an individual, because I share a "*tofi*" (an inheritance) with my family, my village and my nation. I belong to my family and my family belongs to me. I belong to my village and my village belongs to me. I belong to my nation and my nation belongs to me. This is the essence of my sense of belonging.[10]

The Samoan theologian who has perhaps contributed the most in recent years to an elaboration of this interconnectedness that defines the *fa'asamoa* is Upolu Lumā Vaai. In *The Relational Self*, he develops the image of *tino* (body) as a "cosmic-inclusive" way of speaking of the embodied relatedness of humans, communities, and creation.[11] Vaai reflects on the essence of Samoanness as an "inescapable connection to the whole":

> The living faces of my parents, family, ancestors, village, land and ocean are active in my way of being. "I am because of them!" Because of the interconnectedness of *tino*, one living face cannot rule over others. . . . Recognising people, land, ocean, tree and sky as "our" *tino* raises a deep awareness for securing and protecting all those faces.[12]

Imbedded in this statement is an ethical foundation underlying the relational core of *fa'asamoa*. If "one living face cannot rule over others," this has profound implications for how a Samoan public theology should be constructed. Pa'u Mulitalo-Lauta has likewise referred to *fa'asamoa* as forming the ethical basis for "the principles, values and beliefs that influence and control the behavior and attitudes of Samoans."[13] He uses the metaphor of the umbilical cord to capture this life-giving and life-sustaining underlying ethic. Here *fa'asamoa* is an agent of life in its personal, social, political, economic, and religious manifestations.

We can summarize this discussion by asserting that *fa'asamoa* must be viewed in a holistic way as embodying Samoans' interconnectedness with their ancestors, the created world, the Creator, their understanding of how Samoans should live in terms of their values, and even their conflictedness encountered in attempting to embody *fa'asamoa* in the contemporary era.

Since this study aims to develop a Samoan public theology, it is crucial to understand the interplay between Samoan culture, its customs, and Christianity, as these are the three settings within which *fa'asamoa* is enacted. Samoan culture (*aganu'u*) and customs (*agaifanua*) have always been the concrete representations of *fa'asamoa*. With the arrival of Christianity (*fa'akerisiano*), new ethical principles and religious institutions, in the form of the church, were incorporated as a fresh expression of *fa'asamoa*. Consequently, *fa'asamoa* now represents an integration of culture (worldview and values), customs (group rituals and behaviors), and Christianity (the church).

AGANU'U (CULTURE)

In the traditional Samoan understanding, culture was recognized as *aganu'u*, where *aga* is the essence of the nature of things, while *nu'u* represents the sum total of humans' learned experience, as well as the social organization of the *fa'amatai* (chiefly system).[14] Le Tagaloa-Aiono describes *aganu'u* as defining the unity "between man [sic] and God, the unity between the material and the spiritual, the unity between the physical and the psychic, the unity between the sociopolitical and the economic, the unity between the practical and the aesthetic, the unity between male and female, [which] is of absolute importance."[15]

Unity in Le Tagaloa-Aiono's depiction describes the search for harmony that characterized the pre-Christian Samoan culture, where it was believed that persons, communities and everything in nature and the universe must exist in harmonious relationship. This harmony was achieved through the balance and equilibrium required to maintain relationships among individuals and groups, humans and nature, and humans and the divine. A similar explanation of *aganu'u* is given by the Samoan theologian Amaamalele Tofaeono:

> The word *aga* refers to the moral and social or behavioral character of a *nu'u* (village or a community). *Aga* bespeaks the spiritual (from *agaga*—spirits) character of the community, including the thinking process or the philosophy and psychology of a certain community. It includes their visions, dreams, anticipations, fears and hopes, or the way they conceive and face the ups and downs of life. This means that the spiritual and social behaviors of the community are intimately interwoven to foster a specific ethos and way of life.[16]

The Samoan understanding of culture, then, is much more than a description of the Samoan people's distinctive customs—how they choose to organize themselves as a society. Culture for Samoans is their understanding of interrelatedness, held in balance by values that are designed to create and sustain harmony. A Samoan public theology must exhibit this same quest for relational harmony in the public sphere. Feleterika Nokise describes this quest in the following way:

> Samoan culture epitomises the centrality of relationships. . . . The "self" only makes sense within this communal framework. A person is part of the whole, and is made up of many parts. . . . The ordering of space between people—*teu le va*—in all relationships, safeguarded by the demands and expectations of the *fa'asamoa*, is for Samoans the path that brings meaning, balance and harmony in life.[17]

AGAIFANUA (CUSTOMS)

Agaifanua refers to customs that, while sharing similarities throughout Samoa, are manifested in distinctive ways in particular villages and extended families. Samoans at times use the terms *aganu'u* and *agaifanua* interchangeably, depending on the context. These customs were not only manifestations of the *fa'asamoa* in old Samoa but also are still very much part of Samoan life today.

For example, in a Samoan wedding *fa'asamoa* is expressed through the exchange of gifts between the families of the bride and groom. Samoans refer to this custom as *fesagaiga o paolo*, the "facing of connections by marriage."[18] This involves not only the exchange of gifts between the two families but also gifts for invited guests, especially those of higher status such as church pastors.

The same practice of gift-exchange is evident in Samoan funeral customs. The act of *si'ialofa* ("gifts presented out of love") is presented to the bereaved family, who in turn provide hospitality for visitors. *Si'ialofa* is enacted through the gifts of "fine mats"[19] and monetary donations. This custom is a way of sharing responsibilities in the face of the experience of grief.

Regrettably, the practice of *si'ialofa* is now at times tainted by excess or insensitivity, stemming from a mindset premised on the belief that cultural customs are above scrutiny. This corrupted view negates the real essence of the *fa'asamoa* as honoring all communal relationships. A current initiative of the government is designed to lessen the burdens which customs such as this have placed on the poor in recent history.[20] An example of how this initiative is being taken on board can be seen in the villages of Sala'ilua and Sili on the island of Savai'i, which have now banned the use of imported canned fish, various red meats, and chicken parts in village funeral exchanges, after some families were left financially ruined attempting to meet their material obligations.

Yet despite such initiatives, challenges remain regarding the tendency for funeral customs to leave some families impoverished. To illustrate this point, I offer an anecdotal account of the expensive protocols surrounding my mother's funeral. My mother passed away in 2002. Since she was a *matai*, we honored her with a proper chiefly send-off. However, what became apparent in the process of organizing her funeral was that the *matai* who was in charge of these protocols was most concerned with proving that he was an important *matai*, with the result that he sidelined my sisters and me in his decision-making.

As a result, we were left with heavy debts to pay, while the *matai* whom we looked upon as *matai ai* ("eyes toward" or "all attention on to acquire guidance") was oblivious to the hardships his decisions had placed on our family. In this and other similar incidents, many Samoan families have gone beyond their limited resources to fulfill the expectations of *si'ialofa*. As a result, families are burdened with debts that take years to repay, which is not in the true spirit of the *fa'asamoa*. Such generosity is certainly an expression of the core values of love, service, respect, and justice that must undergird any Samoan public theology, but it should not be enacted in a way that creates suffering and deprivation for some.

In Samoa there are also ritual customs that are specific to certain villages. These practices are often seen on occasions such as weddings, funerals, or the installation of a *matai* title. I will describe one of these customs, the *afitunu*. The ritual of the *afitunu* epitomizes the identity of the village of Salelesi. It harks back to the legendary service performed by two sisters, Sa and Lesi, to So'oamalelagi, the daughter of their chief. Sa and Lesi are considered the ancestors of the village of Salelesi, on the eastern side of Upolu.

In performing their service, Sa and Lesi would go fishing and, upon their return, broil fish in a fire for So'oamalelagi's meal. In time, Tuiatua Matautia Fa'atulou, the high chief in Atua, married So'oamalelagi, who was the daughter of the high chief of Leulumoega. So'oamalelagi brought her servants Sa and Lesi with her to Chief Tuiatua's village after her marriage, and Sa and Lesi continued their service to So'oamalelagi and Tuiatua. When Tuiatua died, So'oamalelagi was fetched to return to Leulumoega to her family. As she departed, she made a parting request to her husband's family to show compassion to Sa and Lesi regarding anything they needed, because of their exemplary service.

The *afitunu* ritual extols the virtue of this genuine service shown by Sa and Lesi, and is enacted through a ritual offering, given out of respect and love. Traditionally, the *afitunu* consisted of fish broiled in fire, wrapped in a breadfruit leaf. It was delivered to its recipient by boat, which was associated with the boat in which Sa and Lesi traveled from the village of Neiafu on the island of Savaii. The boat signifies the solemnity of the presentation of the *afitunu*, and the *afitunu* came to symbolize the highest form of respect and honor given to a paramount chief or relatives of a paramount chief.

A fairly recent enactment of the *afitunu* ritual took place during the ceremonial events surrounding the installation of the Head of State of Samoa, Tui Atua, at the end of 2008. All *matai* and untitled men participated in the presentation of the *afitunu*. Instead of fish, a cow was used as the *afitunu*. This ritual is still reserved for gifts of respect to the highest chiefly titles, such as the Head of State. A question arising from this kind of ritual in relation to public theology concerns how such rituals of respect might be enacted more broadly in the public sphere.

LOTU (RELIGION) / *FA'AKERISIANO* (CHRISTIANITY)

The word "*lotu*" is Tongan in origin, its primary meaning being "system of worship." The term "*tamalotu*" was initially used to distinguish between those who had accepted Christianity, at least nominally, and those who had not.[21] In Samoa, the word was applied only to the Christian religion. Subsequently, it also came to have the connotation of "denomination." A distinction was made early on between the *lotu Toga* and the *lotu Taiti*. The *lotu Toga*, which was associated with the Wesleyan Methodist Missionary Society, had its origins in the fact that a Samoan returning from a visit to Tonga first introduced Tonga's Methodist form of Christianity to Samoa. Likewise, it was a Samoan returning from Tahiti who introduced a form of Christianity that had been influenced by the London Missionary Society (Congregationalists), who were active in Tahiti.[22]

Early Contact with Foreign Missionaries

Lalomilu Kamu identifies three groups of people who independently introduced Christianity to Samoa: random Europeans (sailors,[23] traders, whalers, escaped convicts, and beachcombers[24]); islanders from other island groups, such as Tonga, Fiji, and Tahiti; and European missionaries.[25] This has been confirmed by other research as well.[26] Each of these groups contributed something to the proclamation of the gospel in Samoa, and a vital role was played by the initial Tongan and Tahitian missionaries referred to earlier, but the greatest impact was made by the European missionaries.

Gratton's research on the history of religion in Samoa concluded that "there are few [mission] fields in which Christianity has been more readily embraced and where missionaries have had to face less widespread . . . resistance than in Samoa."[27] In the period leading up to the introduction of Christianity, the Samoan religious scene was in fact ripe for change. In the midst of widespread unrest and war just prior to the arrival of the first European missionaries, the goddess Nafanua[28] revealed a prophecy to the high chief Malietoa which was interpreted as signifying that a new religion was coming to replace the old gods. A common perception among Samoans is that this prophecy predisposed war-weary Samoans to be open to a new solution to the brutal warfare ravaging the land.

Indeed, some historians maintain that "the assassination of the notorious tyrant Tamafaiga . . . ushered in a period that was opportune for [religious] innovation."[29] It is part of a widely embraced Samoan mythic narrative that the defeat of Tamafaiga by the high chief Malietoa paved the way for the mass conversion of Samoans to Christianity, since Malietoa became a pivotal early convert of the pioneering missionary John Williams.[30]

However, it would be simplistic to assume that Samoans accepted Christianity because of Nafanua's prophecy, or as a way of seeking relief from social stress, or in blind submission to the dictates of their chiefs. There were other factors at work as well. First, from a theological perspective,

Samoans could easily have seen parallels between their understanding that all of life was infused with divinity and the new notion of a powerful intervention by the Christian God in the world through the incarnation of Jesus. This was a familiar relational concept.

Moreover, Samoans accepted Christianity for pragmatic reasons. They were impressed by the possibilities for material gain associated with aligning themselves with the missionaries. Malama Meleisea argues that "Samoans ... embraced Christianity ... with deliberation, for the most materialistic of reasons."[31] John Williams gives examples in his journals of chiefs arguing for Christianity in their villages on the basis of the wealth this would bring.

> One pointed to the ships, clothes, scissors, beads, and other material goods of the *papalagi* (Europeans) and stated that he thought "the God who gave them all these things must be good and that his religion must be superior to ours. If we receive and worship him, he will in time give us all these things as well."[32]

Perhaps the most accurate conclusion is that Samoans' motives for accepting Christianity were multifaceted. Historian Richard Gilson argues that Samoans at the time of first contact with foreign missionaries were "a polytheistic and practical people, tolerant of the gods of others, and inclined to judge a deity at least partly in terms of the favors he lavished upon the living."[33] Given the material goods which the missionaries introduced into Samoan society, their invitation to Samoans to worship the new God may even have been perceived, "in Samoan eyes, as a gesture of good will and generosity."[34] The chiefs who cooperated with the missionaries and led their *aiga* to mass conversions may have been both sincere in accepting the new *lotu* and, at the same time, also strategic in hoping to manipulate the missionaries in order to make the most of their material largesse.

Finally, it is not possible to describe this early phase of the missionary period without acknowledging the contested spheres of religious influence it created within Samoan society. Controversy surrounding the question of whether Congregationalists or Methodists were the first Samoan Christians, and conflicts between these two dominant mission organizations over "turf" and supremacy,[35] led to an extremely competitive form of denominationalism in Samoa. One can still discern the legacy of these competing missionary movements in the contemporary Samoan church scene. Some villages with a long-standing historical connection to a particular denomination do not accept other churches in their village, leading to conflicts that can turn violent and even lead to banishment. Selota Maliko examines this phenomenon in his study of banishment in Samoa:

> Despite the pre-Christian religious pluralism, once the mainline churches became fused with the *fa'asamoa* and the ruling authorities, they came to

dominate religious life in Samoa. The introduction of new churches or religious groups has thus often created hostility and rejection in Samoan villages. . . . Some villages have banned the introduction of any new religious groups, allowing only the very first Christian churches accepted by their ancestors.[36]

On the one hand, the apparent ease with which Samoans accepted Christianity, despite the complex motives associated with this acceptance, has meant that most Samoans, even today, take the Christian faith for granted as an inherent part of the *fa'asamoa*. This should theoretically ease the path toward developing a public theology grounded in shared Samoan-Christian values. On the other hand, the very taken-for-grantedness of Christianity in Samoa has contributed to a lack of reflection and analysis about how Samoans should live out the Christian faith in the present. Further, the hotly contested space of denominationalism has created disunity and competition, which mitigate against the ecumenical spirit needed to articulate and live out a shared public theology.

Missionaries and *Matai*

Beyond the early cooperation between the missionaries and *matai*, which certainly facilitated the successful evangelization of the Samoan people, some historians contend that the missionaries actually enhanced the authority of the *matai*. Prior to first contact with foreign missionaries, the *matai's* authority was centered in familial and village leadership, rather than being overtly priestly.[37] Suddenly, as collaborators with the missionaries, "they had only to embrace the new faith to become elders in the church,"[38] and in this way they expanded their sphere of influence. This was a shrewd strategic move by the missionaries—transferring the *matai's* respected status from the village into the church so as to facilitate a smoother acceptance of Christianity by the people.

Selota Maliko's research reveals how the missionaries also, perhaps inadvertently, expanded the political power of the *matai* in their villages. Writing about the social changes ushered in by the missionaries, he notes:

> A number of new village restrictions emerged due to the missionaries' influence. For example, in order to ban the practice of night dancing, which was considered evil in the eyes of the missionaries, night-time curfews were introduced in the villages as a means of restricting "salacious" dances and sexual practices. At 10:00 p.m. a bugle was sounded, after which people had to remain in their houses. Because only *matai* were allowed on the road to police the curfew, the sound of the bugle became an affirmation of their power. . . . As a result, the freedom of people to move around in their villages was taken away for the first time. This freedom was replaced by the newly enhanced control of the *matai*.[39]

This finding indicates that the authority of the missionaries and the authority of the *matai* were mutually reinforcing, and that the *matai*'s status actually increased due to the influence of the missionaries. The respect accorded to *matai* made the missionaries determined to focus their mission strategy on persuading the chiefs to embrace the faith. The missionaries' acceptance of most of the cultural norms of the *fa'asamoa* (other than what they deemed blatantly "heathen" practices) also enabled Samoans to identify the missionaries with preexisting cultural roles, thus further easing the path toward acceptance of the new religion.

In turn, the missionaries themselves were placed on a pedestal by the Samoan people and accorded what amounted to a kind of chiefly status of their own. Aiono-Le Tagaloa describes the social reception of the early missionaries in Samoa in the following way:

> The Teachers of the Faith [missionaries] were given a highly respected place within the social organization of the Samoans. They were given a status similar to that of the *tama'ita'i*—the female heirs of the *matai*. They were placed in these groups because it was observed that the Christian teachers carried out the responsibilities or *nafa* normally carried out by the *tama'ita'i* or the *feagaiga*—the covenant. . . . It was from this privileged position that I believe the faith took root and became firmly established in Samoa.[40]

This elevation of the missionaries in turn influenced the social structure of Samoan society. Missionaries were directly involved in the shaping of what would become the modern Samoan nation-state. This involvement in public life facilitated the move toward the establishment of formal institutions of national government in Samoa. It should be noted, however, that this involvement of the missionaries in the public sphere was not continued by Samoan clergy after the end of the missionary period. The public sphere became the domain of the *matai*, while ministers were elevated in status but relegated to the spiritual domain.

Missionary Influence on Samoans' Belief System

Once Samoans accepted Christianity, the Christian belief system quickly became part of the *fa'asamoa*, which legitimated Christian beliefs, practices, and institutions. Yet the *fa'asamoa* itself did not change fundamentally after the acceptance of Christianity; the authority of the *matai* and the *fono*, and most customary practices, remained intact. Indeed, the established moral framework of the *fa'asamoa*, grounded in the core values identified in this study, melded well with Christian teachings. Moreover, cultural traditions such as hierarchical status in the family, village, and chiefly system were supported by the church.

Despite this largely harmonious amalgamation of Christianity and *fa'asamoa*, it must be acknowledged that the form of Christianity that was transplanted to Samoa by foreign missionaries also reflected the foreign value system of the West. This Eurocentric worldview had a significant impact on the structures, theology, practices, and polity of the Samoan churches. It included approaches to biblical interpretation and theology that were typical of nineteenth-century English Protestantism and its missionary movement, with its evangelical orientation and focus on the judgment and wrath of God. The missionaries also brought with them a Pietist[41] streak that did not predispose Samoan Christians to embrace a social gospel or a prophetic role of "speaking truth to power" in society.

The Victorian Era's (1830s–1900) deeply entrenched patriarchy also held sway in the missionaries' understanding of church leadership, which persists even today in the continuing restriction of the clergy to males only, despite women having been accepted into ordained ministry in most churches around the world for some time, and despite the fact that women are allowed to be *matai*. One visual reminder of this Victorian worldview that accompanied the missionaries is the legacy of its insistence on feminine modesty. This can still be seen today in the prescribed dress code in Samoan churches, with women continuing to wear hats and long dresses covering the whole body that are more reminiscent of nineteenth-century England than reflective of Samoa's hot tropical climate. Although European in origin, this custom has been thoroughly internalized as Samoan.

Nonetheless, despite the influence of European notions of church, theology, and social conventions, this did not completely eradicate the indigenous Samoan religious orientation. In formal Samoan gatherings even today, the orator (*tulafale*) always employs, during speech-making, traditional sayings which refer to the old religion.[42] From such religious survivals we can see that Samoa's traditional religiosity is still alive. Events in Samoans' lives are interpreted within a diffuse religious framework.

It might even be said that this traditional religiosity was strengthened by the introduction of Christianity. As Aiono-Le Tagaloa points out, "When Christianity arrived in Samoa it was embraced wholeheartedly. I believe this is because so many facets of the new faith found parallels within the Samoans' own beliefs. They believed in one great God. He was unseen and yet was in all places, for the name Le Tagaloa [the ancient creator God] means Boundless Freedom."[43]

Role of the *Faifeau* (Pastor)

Anthropologist Lowell Howell made the observation that village pastors are the most highly respected people in all of Samoa: "No religious leader under the ancient Samoan religion ever equalled the paramount position of the village pastor."[44] In contemporary Samoa, this high status and esteem is still evident in the prominent status given to the *faifeau* (pastor). As Emma Kruse Vaai asserts, "In Samoa, being a *faifeau* is strongly associated not only with spirituality and pastoral care but with wealth and wellbeing."[45]

While the implied critique in the latter part of this statement has merit, it may also be regarded as something of a generalization, as not all *faifeau* are wealthy. I have come across *faifeau* who rely on the support of their extended families in order to meet their needs. One example is a Methodist parish in a village where I conducted some of my field research for this study. The minister and his wife only receive the equivalent of NZ$300 fortnightly. From this income they donate a portion back to the church, including donations to the women's fellowship, development needs of the parish, and Church synod activities. Some of the poorer parish members also come to this *faifeau* for financial help. Thus, based on what I have observed and experienced, I would qualify Vaai's critique of the wealth of *faifeau* as an apt generalization but not true of all *faifeau*.

At the same time, it is true that the *faifeau* is a person of great status and authority in Samoan society. During the missionary period, the *faifeau* was given the title *fa'afeagaiga*, with the prefix *fa'a* meaning "to cause to become" and *feagaiga* meaning "covenant." This means that the relationship between the congregation and the pastor is a sacred covenant. *Feagaiga* is a term that was traditionally ascribed to the sister, signifying the sacred covenant between sister and brother. With the establishment of Christianity, this notion of covenant was extended to the relationship between the pastor, who holds a sacred status (like the sister), and his congregation. Here the status of the pastor complements that of the chief.

The legacy of the missionaries concerning the role of the clergy is that Samoan pastors are expected to proclaim the gospel through preaching and leading worship, and to provide spiritual counsel to their church members, and to the village council when requested. Such counsel may occasionally influence political matters in the village (as in the few reported cases of pastors who have intervened to save those who are under an edict of banishment from their village council), but by and large pastors accept the rulings of the village *fono* and the national government without question.

The roles of the pastor also vary somewhat depending on the historic traditions of particular denominations. Some churches are slightly more flexible regarding the expectations placed on their pastors, while others have more formalized and rigid policies to which pastors and their wives must adhere. The consequence of not abiding by these rules may be banishment and being stripped of ministerial standing. The drawback of this understanding of the role of the minister for the task of developing a public theology is that, despite the esteemed status of the *faifeau*, there is very little leeway built into this role for confronting social problems, especially if this entails challenging the status quo.

Lotu and *Fa'akerisiano*: A Summary

What is most important to keep in mind, for the purposes of this study, is that there was historically a symbiotic relationship between the missionaries, *matai*, clergy, and *fa'asamoa* that has had a lasting impact on both church and society in Samoa. While the missionaries wielded considerable influence and were elevated to positions of great respect, the *matai* also made use of their close ties to the missionaries for their own benefit. They seized on the advantages for their people of the formal education introduced by the missionaries, and the prospects for material benefit associated with European wealth.

Samoans accepted wholesale the brand of Christianity brought by the missionaries, while at the same time never completely abandoning their innate Samoan religiosity. The missionaries, by largely accepting the precepts and practices of the *fa'asamoa*, ensured a smooth pathway toward the embrace of Christianity by all Samoans. However, although this made Samoa one of the most thoroughly Christianized countries in the world, it left unanswered the question of how Samoan Christians, including pastors, could live out their calling to witness in the public sphere—how they could speak truth to power when they were and are so intimately intertwined with and answerable to those with power.

SAMOAN TRADITIONAL RELIGION

Tala o le Vavau (Traditional Myths)

Referring to the Samoan cosmology that supported the religious worldview in pre-contact Samoa, Lalomilu Kamu writes, "Their understanding of God, Creation, the culture and their worldview were drawn from the myths of creation."[46] The ancient gods of Samoa played a significant role in religious life. The supreme god was Tagaloa, the god of creation. As Penelope Schoeffel explains,

> Both Tongan and Samoan myths of origin explain the creation of the universe through the potent procreative forces of the *atua* Tagaloa who introduced matter

and form into the void, whereupon the marriage of like and like gave rise to new forms, until the geological formation of the physical environment, and the geographical form of the islands and the surrounding oceans was complete. Above and below this physical world lay the non-physical sky and underworlds, the realms of the spiritual. Then Tagaloa created human beings and through his impregnation of a mortal female, in some versions his daughter, he transferred divine essence or *mana* to the human race.[47]

At the same time, many other deities existed as manifestations of the supreme god Tagaloa. Families, villages, and districts all had their own gods, who were petitioned to secure safety, well-being, and blessings. There were also more important gods who linked the Samoan people together, such as Nafanua, the goddess of war.[48]

The traditional myths (*tala o le vavau*) that explain this cosmological panoply of gods are closely associated with the concept of *fa'avavau*, meaning "forever into the future." Samoan mythology has a sense of timelessness, regardless of changing times or the historical past. It is believed that Samoan myths can never disappear, as they are more than just stories: they are living connections to a spiritual essence that has no end. Although Christianity has altered some aspects of the mythological culture of old Samoa, ancient Samoan myths are still very much alive in Samoan oratory. The use of myths in formal oratory reinforces the enduring truth that *fa'asamoa* is deeply rooted in its rich religious heritage, and that this heritage will continue to have resonance for Samoans for the rest of time.

Before the arrival of the missionaries, Samoans depended on these myths to explain their existential realities and the mysteries of life—the interwoven strands of the natural and the supernatural. The wisdom associated with these myths is still felt to be evident in the core values that hold Samoan society together. They cement the enduring yet evolutionary nature of Samoan identity. These myths are interpreted somewhat differently within each Samoan district, a fact affirmed in the common saying, *E tala lasi Samoa* ("Samoa has many stories"). But although these stories may be told somewhat differently from place to place, their significance remains the same. The never-ending search for harmony resides in these myths. As has always been the case, they direct the collective search for wisdom.

Tapuaiga (Religious Experience)

Before the arrival of Christianity, Samoans were rooted in a pervasive experience of the divine. In old Samoa, almost every domain of life was infused with the sacred, and a *tapuaiga* or religious ceremony always took place before, during and after a communal activity. For example,

When a group of villagers prepared to go hunting, a *tapuaiga* would take place before they left, and while they were engaged in this activity the *tapuaiga* was held by other members, led especially by the elders, including chiefs and others present. The villagers would remain silent, patiently awaiting the return of the group. During this . . . silence no one was allowed to walk in front of the chiefs or the place where the worship was held, unless urgently needed.[49]

In addition, many religious rituals in old Samoa took place within the *aiga*. Family gods were "invoked for the purpose of enhancing the welfare of the *aiga*. The hopes and expectations of families for a successful outcome of expeditions and projects involved . . . an offering to the gods, in the form of a chant or prayer-like incantation . . . accompanied by a display of appropriate movements and actions. The aim was to please the gods and win their favor."[50]

Religious experience in this context can be explained not only in terms of an intense awareness of divine presence but in terms of a universally accepted value system that related spirituality to morality. In Samoan society, past and present, religious experience has provided a rationale for one's behavior—for ethics. In old Samoa, people petitioned gods for protection or success, but this devotion also carried with it assumptions about the kinds of behaviors that were expected of one in order to maintain "right relationships"—with others, with nature, and with the gods.

Tapuaiga is the noun form of the verb *tapua'i*, which means "to make a spiritual connection with God for another person or for a situation. . . . The assumption is that as I *tapuai* for another person and their situation, someone else carries out the same act for me and my situation. In simplest terms, *tapuai* is the worship of God for the good of someone else."[51] It is the making of a spiritual connection between the inner person (the *mauli*) and God, in situations concerning *tagataola* (living persons).[52]

Aiono-Le Tagaloa's research confirms that there were traditionally two forms of Samoan *tapuaiga*: private and public. Public worship began with *alofisa* (the *ava* sacrifice), and ended with *anapogi* (fasting).[53] In the missionary James Newell's *Papers and Diaries on Samoan Tapuaiga*,[54] discovered by Aiono-Le Tagaloa during archival research in London, he recorded his observations of public worship rituals such as the following:

> The lighting of the fire until the flames shot up and lit up the whole house . . . was referred to as *fanaafi o fa'amalama*. The setting of the worship was inside the *fale tele* or roundhouse. The *fale tele* had one, two or three center pillars. In front of the pillars was the *magalafu*, a stone lined (with a) shallow hollow where the fire was placed and was never allowed to go out completely. . . . The *fanaafi o fa'amalama* was observed twice a day; in the early morning, at

approximately five o'clock, . . . and in the evening when the fires are blown—*ula afi*. This is when the ashes are blown and allow the embers/coals to come alive. When the dry tinders are thrown on them, flames would flare, illuminating the house and the worshippers—this was the sacrifice or fire votive to God.[55]

Four of the prayers typically recited during the *fanaafi o fa'amalama* were recorded by Newell. Note the confession of wrongdoing in the prayer cited below, and also the practical plea to the fire god to send the foreigners ("gods" of the sea) away to uninhabited islands, as they were bringing in disease. This was a practical concern at the time this prayer was recorded, as the diseases brought by Europeans who landed on Samoa's shores were in fact decimating the local population by the time the missionaries arrived. In the following prayer, when the fire would burst into flames, the priest or priestess says:

This is a fire votive for you, our God.
May you wrap us, cloak us in your goodness and kindness.
(Again the fire flares)
This is a fire votive to you, our God.
Our erring, wrongful, defiant ways are blatant before you.
(Again the fire flares)
This is a fire votive to you, our God.
Direct those "gods" of the seas—seafarers—to uninhabited lands,
for they bear sickness and curses.
This is the fire votive to you, our God.
Cover us, hide us in the broad mantle of your love.[56]

The words of this prayer make a spiritual connection between humans and God in the hope of securing the people's survival and well-being.[57]

One of the participants in my field research, Participant GM005, described traditional Samoan religion the following way:

> Before the establishment of the God of theology, the God of history was already prevailing in Samoa. This means that, in this view, theology is a new thing. It is important for all these countries to remember [that] before the arrival of these men to record their theology, it [Samoa] had long been guided by rules of culture and custom and the indigenous reference in the administering of government and [care for] each family.

The essence of this participant's comment is that, before the arrival of Christianity, Samoans were already rooted in religious awareness and experience, which guided all aspects of life. Evidence of this can be found in the ancient Samoan story of creation which, according to Tui Atua, "outlines a theory of creation and a theology of life."⁵⁸ Samoans in the past may have expressed their religious beliefs differently than they do today, but their awareness of the sacred was an essential cornerstone of their lived experience.

Religion in old Samoa was also intertwined with the highly developed social and political organization with which it was closely identified. Even though respect for the priestly class (the *taula-aitu*) was based on fear of their sacred power, they were also seen as part of the web of authority that controlled life in community.⁵⁹ Today, although there is a strong prohibition against Christian pastors "meddling" in secular affairs, we can still see vestiges of this web of authority, in that *matai* hold important religious positions in the church, and the clergy are "as powerful as chiefs."

Aiono-Le Tagaloa concludes that it was difficult if not impossible to separate the secular from the sacred in pre-Christian Samoa. It was only when Christianity took over the *tapuaiga* that the church introduced, knowingly or unknowingly, the notion of a split between the sacred and the secular, a split that was a by-product of the eighteenth-century European Age of Enlightenment⁶⁰ which separated the world of reason and science from that of spiritual experience.

In old Samoa, the art of passing on religious knowledge fell to a select few. Such knowledge gave power and status to its custodians, especially those respected as custodians of district or national histories. The knowledge of this inner circle of custodians was generally uncontested.⁶¹ In contemporary Samoa, in contrast, the practice of passing on indigenous knowledge is now formally associated with the Lands and Titles Court, because custodians often cannot come to any consensus. The influences of materialism and Western education have manipulated the authentication of the knowledge of custodians. There is no longer the implicit belief that their knowledge is God-given—that the origin of all knowledge and wisdom is from God.⁶²

The interrelatedness of all things that was implicit in pre-Christian Samoan religious experience holds great promise as a resource for constructing a Samoan public theology. The understanding that all of life is infused with divinity means that the public sphere today can be viewed as a sacred sphere. As God's agents, we are called to speak and act in this sacred public space. The core values which give substance to our moral behavior in the public sphere all flow from and are interconnected in this ancient and eternal Samoan quest for the harmony and well-being of all of creation.

LANGUAGE AND *FA'ASAMOA*

In addition to the three settings of the *fa'asamoa* elaborated in the preceding sections, a related category which infuses all of these settings is the care with which *fa'asamoa* is communicated through language. There are two aspects of the Samoan language: the chiefly and the common, sometimes referred to as the chiefly and the ordinary; or, to use Milner's distinctions, the polite and the ordinary.[63] Ordinary language is used in informal conversations, among friends or peers.

Linguistic anthropologist Alessandro Duranti argues for an interpretive theory of meaning to understand the relationship between the Samoan language and culture. As Duranti explains,

> For Samoans, meaning is seen as the product of an interaction (words included) and not necessarily as something that is contained in someone's mind. In engaging in interpretation, Samoans are not so much concerned with knowing someone else's intentions as with the implications of the speaker's actions/words for the web of relationships in which his life is woven.[64]

In other words, for Samoans, language is the very bedrock of their interwoven relational identity. Indeed, Aiono-Tagaloa goes so far as to assert, *A nimo pe solo la ta gagana, onaleai lea o le Atunuu o Samoa; a leai la ta gagana, onaleai lea o sa ta aganuu.*[65] ("If the Samoan language disappears or fades, then there will be no Samoan country; if we don't have a language, then we don't have a culture.") Without the Samoan language, there is no Samoan identity sufficient to constitute a nation. Aiono-Tagaloa speaks of language as being the core of a Samoan person's point of reference or *fa'asinomaga*, together with *igoamatai* (*matai* title) and *eleele ma fanua* (land). The difference between these aspects of *fa'asinomaga* is that, while there can be more than one *matai* title or physical location to which a Samoan is connected, there is only one Samoan language.

It is in this light that the way Jürgen Habermas speaks of language is relevant for Samoa. Habermas identifies the following core functions served by language: "(1) that of reproducing culture and keeping tradition alive; (2) that of social integration or the coordination of the plans of different actors in social interaction; and (3) that of socialization or the cultural interpretation of needs."[66]

These functions of language are very much evident in contemporary Samoan society, where the *fa'asamoa* is articulated and strengthened both in ordinary conversations and formal oratory. The Samoan language in all its complexity is taught in the curriculum of all schools and tertiary institutions. This helps not only to maintain the language but to keep Samoan traditions and culture alive. The Samoan language functions as the "cement" or "glue" of social integration, and as a primary agent of socialization and cultural interpretation. This means that any authentically Samoan public theology must be communicated with linguistic sophistication and integrity, an issue raised explicitly by some research participants in this study (see especially the section in chapter 6, "Communicating Values Effectively").

Signs

Signs imbedded in the *fa'asamoa* convey significant meanings. These meanings are associated with the core values guiding Samoans' existence. For example, the practice of *tulou* is a sign of respect. When one walks past a person, one lowers oneself physically as a sign of respect. At the same time one utters the word *tulou* (excuse me). Both the vocal utterance and the physical movement convey an awareness of respect toward the other. They are a sign that one is observing the *va* or sacred space in relationships.

Another sign is discovered in both ordinary and formal speech through the use of the phrase *vaeatu*. As explained by Emma Kruse Vaai, *vaeatu* means "setting myself apart," being "conscious of the distance between us," or "maintaining the balance in our relationship."[67] Using this phrase is a sign that one is about to utter a form of apology for what one is about to say, in case what one says is wrong or causes offence.

Meaning is also conveyed through signs in the *fa'asamoa* based on the way one speaks—not only one's words but one's tone and demeanor. This is highlighted in the saying *E iloa le tamali'i i lanatu ma lana tautala* ("A noble is determined by the way (s)he stands and talks"). This refers both to ordinary speech and formal speech. A chief or orator who is well versed in the culture reflects this knowledge in the way he or she speaks in Samoan oratory. If this is done well, people repeat the wisdom saying, *O le fa'ailoga o le tagata sa tautua fa'amaoni i ona matua ma lona aiga* ("A sign of a person who has served his/her parents and family honestly"). But if a person does not exemplify this value through adhering to proper protocols and demeanor during formal speech, the reaction is *O le fa'ailoga o le tagata e le'i tautua fa'amaoni i ona matua ma lona aiga* ("A sign of a person who did not serve his/her parents and family honestly"). As with the use of language, the significance of signs in the *fa'asamoa* must be understood and respected in the enactment of an authentic Samoan public theology.

Oratory

Samoan oratory or *lauga fa'asamoa* takes as its point of departure traditional Samoan beliefs, practices, and repositories of history and wisdom. Ceremonial *lauga* celebrates an ancient world, replete with mythical-historical characters and places, eternal values, and absolute hierarchies. It is a formal type of speech which can be delivered in a village council meeting, in a gathering on the *malae* (open field, or "village green"), or during special occasions and rituals.

Lauga fa'asamoa is typically performed by the *tulafale*, or talking chiefs, on behalf of their extended family, village, church, or district. In a public *lauga*, a *tulafale* always begins with the *fa'atau*, or debate among orators for the purpose of finding a representative to speak. Each *tulafale* engaged in the *fa'atau* recalls connections to myths and legends, as well as hierarchical statuses, to support his claim to speak. As Mageo notes,

> Some of the recurrent properties of traditional oratory found in ceremonial performances of *lauga* are the frequent use of proverbial expressions [derived from mythology, history and everyday life] to indicate the high status of the people present; the celebrative tone of voice; reference to people in terms of their position; the identification of the speaker with the voice of tradition; the pre-allocation of turns [to speak]; and the unavoidable presentation of past, present and future events.[68]

Whether Samoan oratory is used in secular or sacred spheres, it must always include ceremonial addresses (*fa'alupega*) by and to those present. *Fa'alupega* refers to a set of honorific addresses for the titles of a particular locality. It is an acknowledgment of one's identity in terms of *aiga* (extended family) and *nu'u* (village). The importance of using this honorific language correctly can be seen in an incident that happened in a theological college during a time of fellowship with a neighboring theological college. While introducing the keynote speaker, the lecturer who was giving the introduction forgot to include the *fa'alupega* of the speaker, in terms of the location of the parish he was serving, his place of origin, his village, and his family.

Before the speaker started his speech, he made the following comment: *kaukuaga ma oukou . . . e a'o fa'alelei fa'alupega o gu'u*. What is significant here is not the translation, but the fact that the speaker's use of *k* and *g* instead of the normative *t* and *n* was seen as a way of countering the disrespect associated with the introducer's ignorance of his *fa'alupega*, by using coarse speech. The response to this lapse reinforced the significance of *fa'alupega* as a marker of identity and an understanding of *fa'asamoa* protocols, highlighting the importance of one's awareness of the need to show respect for the other. Such linguistic rubrics and meaning-laden signs cannot be ignored in the project of developing a public theology that speaks to Samoans in a way they understand.

Preaching

Church ministers perform *lauga* in the church setting in the form of sermons. An interesting aspect of contemporary sermons is their continual reference to Samoan cultural and proverbial expressions. Each sermonic *lauga* represents the preacher's awareness of the audience to whom he is speaking. Church sermons have in this way taken on board the importance of contextualization.

In the introductory portion of a sermon, the preacher refers to Samoan events and expressions to find a point of entry into the actual biblical text on which his sermon is based. A church sermon could thus potentially be a valuable form of public theology, to the extent that it engages with issues affecting the well-being of the general public. In this sense, it could be argued that public theology already has an entry point in the Samoan church context. Church ministers only need to be reminded that part of their calling is to speak through their ministry of proclamation about issues that affect the well-being of their people.

INSTITUTIONS OF *FA'ASAMOA*

Institutional *fa'asamoa* refers to all of the structures and polities which are intended to ensure cohesiveness and provide for the needs of those within its social structure. As a highly stratified society with complex roles and responsibilities, Samoa is structured in such a way as to ensure social stability. The basic political unit in Samoa is the *nu'u*, which has been translated as "village" or "polity." The *nu'u* is made up of a number of extended families and is governed by a council (*fono*) of chiefs (*matai*) elected as representatives of each extended family. The *nu'u* can therefore be seen as collectively representing each *aiga* in a locality. *Aiga* and *nu'u* are thus inseparable, and both may be referred to as the central organizational units of Samoan life.

Aiga (Family)

Aiga is often translated "extended family" but it also means family in the sense of immediate relations. The *aiga* is the most basic social unit of Samoan life, comprising grandparents, parents, children, and other relatives. Sometimes a Samoan *aiga* even includes strangers who are taken in when they have no other place to live. Indeed, in Samoa no one can truly be a stranger because everyone has a place of origin, a sense of direction, and a space in a particular social location.

Samoans find their most basic sense of identity in their kin-group. The basis of this identification is knowledge of one's *faia* (how one is related to other people in the *aiga*). Sa'iliemanu Lilomaiava-Doktor writes,

> *Fa'asamoa* conceives of individuals foremost as integral members of *aiga*, irrespective of where they currently reside. The developmental cycle of the *aiga* refers to its social, spiritual, physical and economic improvement in parallel with the life cycles of the individuals within an *aiga*. Individuals are constantly reminded of their important contributions to the collective welfare. One

develops one's *aiga* relationships through responsibilities that are maintained over time.[69]

Within the *aiga*, one is part of both the *aiga potopoto* (relatives living in the same village and different villages) and the *puiaiga* (relatives living in the same village). Each member of the *aiga* has a particular role to play, depending on his or her age and status. The *aiga* signifies relationships of people headed by a titled person, the *matai*, who is selected by the *aiga* to hold their title.

The *matai* directs economic and political activities for the *aiga* and is the custodian of *aiga* assets, including customary land and titles. Each *aiga*, as a social unit, may also be seen as a self-sustaining economic entity. Amaamalele Tofaeono describes the relationship between the *matai* and the *aiga* using the image of concentric rings of relations, at the center of which is the *matai* as the leader, custodian, and power broker. Where one is located on these concentric rings signifies how close or distant one is to the *matai*.[70]

However, all members of the *aiga* are tied together through a reciprocal relationship wherein the *matai* serves as the guardian of family assets, while the family retains the right to remove the title if they are unhappy with the *matai*'s service. As a self-sustaining group, all members of the *aiga*, including the head, cooperatively contribute the products of their labor for the common good of the whole *aiga*.[71] Individuals are highly motivated to act in the best interests of the *aiga*. As Ronald Crawford puts it, "A Samoan's conception of himself is closely tied to his identity as a member of a family—from it he receives security and the necessities of life; to it he offers his service."[72] The centrality of the *aiga* will be confirmed in research participants' location of public theology in the concerns of families in their communal settings.

Nu'u (Village)

As noted above, the *nu'u* comprises groups of *aiga*. *Nu'u* encompasses everything with which the community identifies, in terms of its geographic and social location, ceremonial grounds, people, social hierarchy, governance, and history. Meleisea confirms that "the basic political unit of Samoa is termed *o le nu'u* [the village]."[73] Before annexation by Germany in 1900 (with the eastern island group now known as American Samoa becoming a U.S. territory), Samoa was divided into geographical districts, each comprising a number of villages, which acknowledged one or more leading or paramount chiefs. However, every village was politically autonomous.

The word "village" does not accurately capture the meaning of the word *nu'u*. "Village" suggests a contained settlement, but the *nu'u* was traditionally much more than that. It was a slice of territory from the top of the highest central range of mountains in the interior of the island to the outermost reef. Every *nu'u* included between twenty and forty extended families (*aiga*) who collectively owned the territory. Some of the land formed the shared estate of each extended family, while some of it—the forest and lagoon—belonged to everyone in common. The social groupings within Samoan society are thus based on the Samoan saying, *O Samoa ua uma ona tofi*, meaning "Samoa is already defined."

The social organization of the *nu'u* originally consisted of three groups: the *tama'ita'i* (ladies), the *aumaga* (untitled men), and the *matai* (chiefs). Two more groups were added over time: wives of *matai* and children of *matai*, reflecting changes since the introduction of Christianity in 1830.[74] Members of the *nu'u* are today arranged into six groups: *tama'ita'i* (ladies), *aumaga* (untitled men), *faletua ma tausi* (wives of chiefs), *tamaiti* (children), *matai* (titled men or women), and *aualuma* (daughters of the village). Each of these groups has its own responsibilities. The guiding principle behind all of these divisions is *o leva fealoa'i*, or "relationship of respect." These relationships function to maintain peace and cooperation. It is out of respect that each individual is oriented to her or his place in the *nu'u*. The six groups are discussed more fully below.

Tama'ita'i (ladies): The *tama'ita'i* are the healers, the teachers, the priestesses, and the makers of wealth (*faioa*). They are also the *pae ma le auli* (peacemakers), and the unit in the social structure that mirrors, among females, the authoritative level of the *matai* group itself. The *tama'ita'i* group was traditionally considered the *feagaiga* (covenant between sister and brother) of the village. As sisters, women occupy an honorary status compared to that of their brothers. Brothers are obligated to serve and protect their sisters, and in old Samoa it was believed that a sister had the power to place a curse on her brother if he did not live up to his covenantal role. This covenant guarantees sisters equal rights with their brothers. Basic to the organization of the family is the respect which males must pay to their sisters, their father's sisters, and the children of these female relatives.

Aumaga (untitled men): This group is referred to as *o le malosi o le nu'u* (the strength of the village). Village work, beyond work obligations to each young man's *aiga*, is done by the *aumaga*. In old Samoa, the *aumaga* were quite literally the *malosi o le nu'u*, in that they functioned as the army, fishermen, horticulturalists, cooks, and sportsmen. For an untitled man to be granted a *matai* title, he must have demonstrated exemplary service to the *aiga* and *nu'u* during his time as part of the *aumaga*. He is called *taule'ale'a* (one who is youthful and untitled). However, even if an untitled man is of advanced age, he still retains his *taule'ale'a* status if he does not hold a *matai* title.

Faletua ma Tausi (wives of chiefs): This group represents the foreign element in the social organization of Samoan society. The *faletua* is the wife of the *alii* (chief), and the *tausi* is the wife of the *tulafale* (talking chief). They are the "non-heirs" of the *matai* title, although they possess their own kind of authority. *Faletua* means "house at the back," while *tausi* means "to nurture." Their roles and status are defined by the customary duties and traditional service they offer to their husbands.

These roles are important in maintaining the stability, unity, and welfare of the *aiga*. *Faletua* provide significant support for the *matai*, while at the same time undertaking most of the work in raising the family. They are considered to be the backbone of the *aiga*, although they are *fafine nofotane* ("in-marrying wives") in the context of their husbands' *aiga*. However, they are accorded dignity and respect as *feagaiga* when they return to their place of birth.

Tamaiti (children): Traditionally, *tamaiti* referred to children of the *matai*, although today this is a more general designation for children. The children of *matai* have the right to be included in the selection of *matai* titles, but like other Samoan children they are generally to be "seen but not heard." Samoan children are socialized in a manner that fosters respect and obedience. Grattan notes that "it is one of the duties of children who are older to keep the young quiet by any reasonable means, especially within the hearing of gatherings of adult people."[75]

Children's responsibility to keep quiet is a cultural characteristic because it reflects the nurturing of the *va* or respectful space. The rationale behind this custom is not to oppress children but to nurture them in the ways of respect and obedience. Their silence will be rewarded as they become adult members within their *aiga, nu'u,* and church. They will then become active in decision-making as responsible adults, for they will have been learning through observation throughout their childhood.

Matai (chiefs): In the governance of the *nu'u*, as noted earlier, each extended family is represented by a leader chosen by the family. Traditionally these heads of families were given ancestral names as titles. Today the titled heads of families are simply called *matai*. We have seen that each *matai* belongs to the council (*fono*) which governs the village. Although the *matai* are not equal in rank, all have an equal voice in the government of the *nu'u*.

There are two types of *matai*. One is referred to as *ali'i* (chief) and the other as *tulafale* (talking chief). The chief is the exalted ritual authority; the talking chief is the custodian of Samoan customary law and the spokesman for the chief in the *fono*. Together these *matai* constitute a ruling class or nobility. Serge Tcherkezoff's research shows that the word *matai*, universally translated into English as "chief," did not originally mean "chief" in old Samoa. It referred to someone who was the best in his specialized activity. The meaning evolved over time into a new connotation—"head of the family"—before it took on the broader political meaning it has today and incorporated a hierarchical ranking system of lesser and more important chiefs.[76]

The word *matai* is derived from *mata i ai*. This term has the nuance of being set apart or consecrated. The literal meaning of *mata i ai* is "someone to whom all eyes are turned for guidance, direction and leadership," and who is therefore a role model for the family. *Matai* are seen to hold *pule* (authority) over the village, land, and people. This *pule* is given to them through their chiefly titles. In theory, both men and women can hold *matai* titles, but it is far more common to have a titled male than a titled female.

At the highest levels, *matai* titles were traditionally, at least in theory, hereditary. A family may have more than one *matai* title, but only one title has senior rank and high respect. For example, in my father's family he is one of several *matai*. His role is to support the senior *matai*, who is responsible for the welfare of the whole *aiga*. It was traditionally believed that *matai* titles were divinely bestowed, endowing them with the divine right to represent the *aiga* in the *nu'u*.[77]

The leadership role of the *matai* in old Samoa continued and, as noted previously, even expanded with the introduction of Christianity. Bevans' translation model is relevant here because of its concern with the preservation of tradition, while adapting faith expressions to a particular context. In this case, the missionaries utilized the *matai* system to acquire access to the Samoan social structure, resulting in mass conversions. Once the *matai* accepted the new faith, their extended families all became Christians. After the introduction of Christianity, the *matai*'s influence extended beyond the village *fono* into the church.

Aualuma (unmarried daughters): This is the female counterpart of the *aumaga* (untitled men). The *aualuma* consists of the unmarried women of each family, who perform ceremonial and labor functions for the village. The traditional practice was that when young girls reached the stage of womanhood, they were made aware, mostly by their mothers, that it was their time to join the *aualuma*, where they would learn the skills of providing correct hospitality and serving their families and village. This group prepared young girls for their future roles as wives and mothers, and played a very important role in the education of females.

The wives of the *matai* and untitled men of the village are not members of the *aualuma* and have no public role in their husbands' village. This is reserved for the *aualuma*. With the arrival of Christianity, the young unmarried girls in the *aualuma* were sent to the pastor's wife to learn new skills, such as cooking, sewing, and other domestic skills. In her field research in Samoa, cultural anthropologist Margaret Mead observed that all of these village subgroupings of males and females upheld the central political structure of the *nu'u*.[78]

What is crucial in terms of developing a Samoan public theology is that all of the underlying structures that define the *fa'asamoa*, including the social groupings designed to insure harmony in families and communities, are grounded in the concept of *va*—the sacred space that is essential for right relationships. Although some of the inherent inequalities in status in the *fa'asamoa* may be challenged from a Christian perspective (given the oneness of all in Christ), the sacred *va* undergirding all relationships must also lie at the heart of a Samoan public theology of values, as it is premised on relationships of respect. This concept is upheld in the contributions of many research participants in this study in chapters 5 and 6.

FA'ASAMOA TODAY

The Fusion of *Fa'asamoa* and Christianity

The formal marriage between *fa'asamoa* and Christianity is now firmly enshrined in the principles of the *fa'amatai* (chiefly system), but in both theory and practice this is a complicated partnership that has necessarily entailed changes and compromises in both the *fa'asamoa* and Christianity, as is the case in any marriage. The *fa'asamoa* is expected to work together with Christianity to provide the governing framework for the Samoan nation, its families, and villages.

Since Samoans' religious awareness is expressed through the *fa'asamoa*, any deliberations in the Samoan public square must reflect the values of both Christianity and *fa'asamoa*. My contention is that these values are based on shared principles of love, justice, dialogue, service, and respect; these values are both sacred to the *fa'asamoa* and exemplified by Jesus in his public ministry. Consequently, any Samoan public theology must incorporate the language, culture, and religious beliefs of Samoa while it engages with the theological foundations of the Christian faith.

Fa'asamoa and Governing Principles

As noted earlier, Samoa's form of government combines both traditional Samoan and Western democratic practices. Although Western democracy has at its core the principles of universal rights, good governance, accountability, and transparency, these principles in the Samoan context are worked out in a way that reflects Samoan culture and Christian influences. The government ostensibly makes laws and provides public services for the common good of Samoans within this framework.[79]

The present-day form of government recognizes the importance of the *fa'asamoa* through the institution of *fa'amatai*. This institution is respected because it is the "matrix within which power and responsibility are exercised for the general good of the community rather than solely for the individual."[80] Emma Kruse Vaai adds, "At the village level, all are accounted for, are under the power of, and are cared for by the *matai* system, which is adhered to and believed to be sanctioned by God."[81]

Samoa has also adopted a constitution that embodies elements of both *fa'asamoa* (which incorporates *fa'akerisiano*) and Western democracy. As Meleisea explains,

> When Samoa became independent in 1962, it adopted a constitution which, it hoped, would combine the best elements of Samoan and Western political institutions. . . . One was the system of chiefly authority, which was based on the idea that titleholders would represent the interests of the extended families who gave them their titles. The other was more vaguely defined—a set of Western liberal principles, such as individual rights, religious freedom, equality under law, and so on.[82]

The effectiveness of this attempted marriage between parliamentary democracy and the *fa'amatai* remains an open question. At times there are conflicts between the two partners. For example, there have been instances when the Lands and Titles Court has adjudicated in favor of a family under an edict of banishment by a village council, only to have the council ignore the government's ruling and proceed with the banishment.[83] The question of "who has the final say?" is not always clear.

Moreover, problems associated with the abuse of power plague both systems of governance at times. Corruption can occur in any system when individuals become greedy or power-hungry and ignore the needs of those whom they are called to serve. The uneasy marriage between Western democracy and the *fa'amatai* is still a work in progress. Meanwhile, the church has tended to steer clear of taking a firm stand in relation to justice issues that emerge in both spheres of power, preferring the safety of the status quo in which its prestige is ensured. It is in this contested space that public theology must speak prophetically into the Samoan public sphere.

FINAL THOUGHTS

This chapter has explored the complexities of the *fa'asamoa* by examining its manifestations in the *aganu'u*, *agaifanua*, and *fa'akerisiano*. At the core of *fa'asamoa* are the fundamental principles that define Samoans' self-understanding. *Fa'asamoa* reflects the unity of all Samoans, including those living in the diaspora, under a homogenous cultural umbrella. It incorporates several related aspects—"traditions," "way of life," and "distinctive identity." *Fa'asamoa* is at its core a way of defining and circumscribing relationships and interconnections. This chapter has shown how the *fa'asamoa* has adapted to, incorporated, and made most of the Christian religion that arrived from foreign shores but was seamlessly folded into the *fa'asamoa*.

Understanding this relational core of the *fa'asamoa* is essential for the task of constructing a Samoan public theology, for it is out of this framework that the core values which must undergird any authentic Samoan public theology emerge. Since this study's examination of those values relies on how they are appropriated by a cross-section of the Samoan public, it is necessary in chapter 4 to explain the research methodology that led to these research participants' elaboration of their understanding of Samoa's core values, and how they might be utilized in a Samoan public theology.

NOTES

1. Relevant works include Saleimoa Vaai, *Samoa: Fa'afetai and the Rule of Law* (Le Papaigalagala, WS: Centre for Samoan Studies, National University of Samoa, 1999); Ioana Chan Mow, *The Effectiveness of Cognitive Apprenticeship Based Learning Environment (CABLE) in Teaching Computer Programming* (PhD Thesis, University of South Australia, 2006); Fanaafi Aiono-Le Tagaloa, *Culture and Democracy in the South Pacific* (Suva, FJ: Institute of Pacific Studies, University of the South Pacific, 1992); Tui Atua T. T. T. Efi, "Tupualegase: The Eternal Riddle," in *Su'esu'e Manogi: In Search of Fragrance*, ed. I'uogafa Tuagalu, Tamasa'ilau Sualii-Sauni, Tofilau Nina Kirifi-Alai, and Naomi Fuamatu (Le Papaigalagala, WS: Centre for Samoan Studies, National University of Samoa, 2009), 207–13; and Malama Meleisea, *The Making of Modern Samoa: Traditional Authority and Colonial Administration in the History of Western Samoa* (Suva, FJ: University of the South Pacific, 1987).

2. See, for example, works such as: Derek Freeman, *Margaret Mead and Samoa: The Making and Unmaking of an Anthropological Myth* (Cambridge, MA: Harvard University Press, 1983); Brad Shore, *Sala'ilua: A Samoan Mystery* (New York, NY: Columbia University Press, 1982); Jeannette M. Mageo, "Aga/Amio and the Lotu: Perspectives on the Structure of the Self in Samoa," *Oceania* 59 (1989): 181–99; and *Theorizing Self in Samoa: Emotions, Genders, and Sexualities* (Ann Arbor, MI: University of Michigan Press, 1998); Penelope Schoeffel, "The Ladies' Row of Thatch: Women and Rural Development in Western Samoa," *Pacific Perspective* 8, no. 2 (1979): 1–11; and "Rank, Gender and Politics in Ancient Samoa: The Genealogy of Salamāsina O Le Tafaifā," *The Journal of Pacific History* 22, no. 4 (1987): 174–93.

3. The Samoan public here refers to the selected groups used in this study.

4. Cited in Michael Field, *Black Saturday: New Zealand's Tragic Blunders in Samoa* (Auckland: Reed Books, 2006), 15–16.

5. See Shore, *Sala'ilua: A Samoan Mystery*; Freeman, *Margaret Mead and Samoa*; Mageo, *Theorizing Self in Samoa*; and Schoeffel, "The Ladies' Row of Thatch."

6. Douglas Drozdow-St.Christian, *Elusive Fragments: Making Power, Propriety and Health in Samoa* (Durham, NC: Carolina Academic Press, 2002), 40.

7. Ibid., 41.

8. Melanie Anae, *Fofoai-vao-ese: The Identity Journeys of New Zealand Born Samoans* (PhD Thesis, University of Auckland, 1998), 44.

9. Drozdow-St. Christian, *Elusive Fragments*, 40–41.

10. Tui Atua Tupua Tamasese Efi, "Fa'asamoa Speaks to My Heart and My Soul," in *Su'esu'e Manogi: In Search of Fragrance*, ed. I'uogafa Tuagalu, Tamasa'ilau Sualii-Sauni, Tofilau Nina Kirifi-Alai, and Naomi Fuamatu (Le Papaigalagala, WS: Centre for Samoan Studies, National University of Samoa, 2008), 80.

11. Upolu Lumā Vaai, "Tino Theology," in *The Relational Self*, ed. *Upolu Lumā Vaai and Unaisi Nabobo-Baba* (Suva, FJ: University of the South Pacific and Pacific Theological College, 2017), 227.

12. Ibid.

13. Pa'u Mulitalo-Lauta, *Fa'asamoa and Social Work within the New Zealand Context* (Palmerston North, NZ: Dunmore Press, 2000), 15.

14. Fanaafi Aiono-Le Tagaloa, "The Samoan Culture and Government," in *Culture and Democracy in the South Pacific*, ed. Ron Crocombe, Uentabo Neemia, Asesela Ravuvu, and Werner Von Busch (Suva, FJ: University of the South Pacific, 1992), 121.

15. Ibid.

16. Tofaeono, *Eco-Theology: Aiga—the Household of Life*, 28.

17. Feleterika Nokise, "Ecumenism in the Navigators' Archipelago—An Elusive Reality: Samoa and American Samoa," in *Navigating Troubled Waters: The Ecumenical Movement in the Pacific Islands Since the 1980s*, ed. Manfred Ernst and Lydia Johnson (Suva, FJ: Pacific Theological College, 2017), 264.

18. See George Pratt, *Pratt's Grammar and Dictionary of the Samoan Language* (Apia, WS: Malua Printing Press, 1977).

19. A "fine mat" (*'ie tōga*) is a delicately woven mat that has great cultural value. Fine mats are not used to sit on, like ordinary mats, but are highly treasured items used in cultural exchanges.

20. "Samoans Urged to Return to Origins of Fa'asamoa," news release, Radio New Zealand, January 19, 2009.

21. Crawford, The Lotu and the Fa'asamoa, 1.

22. Ibid.

23. "Sailor cults" were religious cults that evolved during the early contact period in Samoa and several other Pacific Islands settings, in which it was believed that certain sailors who arrived with material goods were semi-divine figures who would bring material wealth to those who accepted the new Christian religion. See Elia Ta'ase, *A Study of the Siovili Cult and the Problems Facing the Church in Samoa Today* (BD Thesis, Pacific Theological College, 1971).

24. "Beachcomber" was a term applied to Europeans who arrived in the early stages of contact in Samoa and other Pacific islands, who "combed the beaches" scavenging for items they could use for barter. Since they at times engaged in immoral behavior, the term acquired a negative connotation. See Harry E. Maude, "Beachcombers and Castaways," *Journal of the Polynesian Society* 73, no. 3 (1964): 254–93.

25. Kamu, *The Samoan Culture and the Christian Gospel*, 24.

26. See, for example, Sharon W. Tiffany, "The Politics of Denominational Organization in Samoa," in *Mission, Church and Sect in Oceania*, ed. James A. Boutilier, Daniel T. Hughes, and Sharon W. Tiffany (Lanham, MD: University Press of America, 1978), 427.

27. F. J. H. Gratton, "Religion in Samoa," in *An Introduction to Samoan Custom* (Apia, WS: Samoa Printing and Publishing Company, 1948), 126.

28. Nafanua is considered by Samoans to be both a historical and a mythical figure. Historically, she is seen as a "fierce warrior and the paramount political strategist of Samoa," who solidified Samoa by appropriating the four paramount chiefly titles in the fifteenth century. Melanie Anae, "Nafanua and Reflections on Samoan Female Sexual Personhood," in *The Relational Self: Decolonising Personhood in the Pacific*, ed. Upolu L. Vaai and Unaisi Nabobo-Baba (Suva, FJ: Pacific Theological College and University of the South Pacific, 2017), 206. As a legendary figure, Nafanua is believed to have been a goddess who "reigned on earth, carried off victories, established a measure of order, and then, just before she disappeared, announced to . . . Malietoa Vainu'upo that he would soon be a great chief and that his 'kingdom would come from the sky'" (Ibid., 207).

29. Ibid., 206.

30. This Malietoa–Tamafaiga–Williams connection may be somewhat overblown, as there is evidence that Malietoa in fact "ignored pleas from Williams and his fellow missionary Charles Barff to stop fighting [with Tamafaiga's forces]. Furthermore, the much-repeated idea that Malietoa's victory removed an anti-Christian tyrant, Tamafaiga, thus opening the path for conversion, is complicated by the fact that Christianity pre-dated Williams in Samoa, and there is no evidence that these earlier Christians were suppressed by Tamafaiga." Andrew Robson, "Factors in the Conversion of Samoa, Then and Now," *Pacific-Credo Publications*, (September 2018), 51. See also Andrew Robson, "Malietoa, Williams and Samoa's Embrace of Christianity," *The Journal of Pacific History* 44, no. 1 (June 2009): 21–39.

31. Meleisea, *Lagaga: A Short History of Western Samoa*, 17.

32. Cited in Richard M. Moyle, ed., *The Samoan Journals of John Williams 1830 and 1832* (Canberra: Australian National University Press, 1984), 237.

33. Richard P. Gilson, *Samoa 1830–1900: The Politics of a Multi-Cultural Community* (Melbourne: Oxford University Press, 1970), 72.

34. Ibid.

35. Due to an agreement made in London between the Wesleyan Methodist Missionary Society (WMMS) and the London Missionary Society (LMS), the pioneering Methodist missionary Peter Turner was ordered to leave Samoa. The LMS missionary John Williams was very influential in the decision to remove Turner. He

urged the mission agencies in London to leave Samoa to the LMS while the Methodist mission concentrated on other island groups, such as Fiji and Tonga. Nokise, "Ecumenism in the Navigators' Archipelago," 258.

36. Selota Maliko, *Restorative Justice: A Pastoral Care Response to the Issue of Fa'ate'a Ma Le Nu'u (Banishment) in Samoan Society* (PhD Thesis, University of Otago, 2016), 120.

37. Nokise argues that old Samoa "did not have a distinct priestly class. . . . It would be misleading, therefore, to regard the *matai* as priests. They had multi-dimensional roles that were tied up in the complex web of the peoples' social and political life." Nokise, "Ecumenism in the Navigators' Archipelago," 257. However, there was a group who might be considered religious experts, known as *taula-aitu*, who "received and made offerings at small temples, ascertained the causes of illness and misfortune, and when possessed by the gods could speak their will." Raeburn Lange, *The Origins of the Christian Ministry in the Cook Islands and Samoa* (Christchurch: Macmillan Brown Centre for Pacific Studies, University of Canterbury, 2006), 115.

38. Gratton, "Religion in Samoa," 127.

39. Maliko, "Restorative Justice," 10–11.

40. Ibid.

41. Pietism was a movement, first espoused by the German Lutheran theologian Philipp Spener in the seventeenth century, which came to influence Protestantism across Europe. It emphasized personal piety and spiritual renewal, and influenced the growth of evangelicalism in the eighteenth century and John Wesley, the founder of Methodism, in the nineteenth century. See Christian T. Winn et al., eds., *The Pietist Impulse in Christianity* (Eugene, OR: Wipf & Stock Publishers, 2012).

42. An example is the common saying, "*Se'i muamua se fa'asao a manu vao,*" literally translated "before bird-catching an offering should be made." This saying is still included in the introductory ceremonies for many functions. It originates from a traditional Samoan hunting practice. When men prepared for the hunt of the *manuali'i* (swamp hen), they first made an offering to the gods, such as a bunch of bananas. The offering was called *fa'asao a manu vao*. See Erich Schultz, *Proverbial Expressions of the Samoans* (Wellington: The Polynesian Society, 1965), 37.

43. Aiono-Le Tagaloa, *Tapuai: Samoan Worship*, 37.

44. Lowell D. Holmes, "Samoan Oratory," *The Journal of American Folklore* (1969): 342.

45. Emma Kruse Vaai, "Religion," in *Samoa's Journey 1962–2012: Aspects of History*, ed. Leasiolagi Malama Meleisea, Penelope Schoeffel, and Ellie Meleisea (Wellington: Victoria University Press, 2012), 92.

46. Kamu, *The Samoan Culture and the Christian Gospel*, 87.

47. Penelope Schoeffel, "Rank, Gender and Politics in Ancient Samoa: The Genealogy of Salamāsina O Le Tafaifā," *The Journal of Pacific History* 22, no. 4 (1987): 175.

48. See Kaydee Schmidt, *The Aitu Nafanua and the History of Samoa: A Study in the Relationship between Spiritual and Temporal Power* (PhD Thesis, Australian National University, 2011).

49. Meleisea, *Lagaga: A Short History of Western Samoa*.

50. Nokise, "Ecumenism in the Navigators' Archipelago," 256–257.
51. Aiono-Le Tagaloa, *Tapuai: Samoan Worship*, 31.
52. Ibid.
53. Ibid., 46.
54. James Newell was a London Missionary Society missionary who began his service in Samoa in 1881. His *Papers and Diaries on Samoan Tapuaiga* are held in the archives of the School of Oriental and African Studies Library in London.
55. Ibid., 39–41.
56. Ibid.
57. Ibid., 60.
58. Tui Atua T. T. T. Efi, *Tau Mai Na O Le Pua Ula: Fragrancing Samoan Thought* (Dunedin, NZ: University of Otago Press, 2009), 21.
59. See John B. Stair, *Old Samoa: Or, Flotsam and Jetsam from the Pacific Ocean* (London: Religious Tract Society, 1956 [1897]).
60. The Enlightenment, also known as the Age of Reason, dominated European thought in the eighteenth century. It undermined the authority of the church in society by insisting on reason as the primary source of authority. This led to the separation of church and state and a split between the religious (which became privatized) and the secular. The Enlightenment promoted individual liberty, progress, and the scientific method, and had a profound influence on the development of modern Western democracies. See Milan Zafirovski, *The Enlightenment and its Effects on Modern Society* (New York, NY: Springer-Verlag, 2011).
61. Stair, *Old Samoa*, 3.
62. Ibid.
63. See G. B. Milner, *Samoan Dictionary* (London: Oxford University Press, 1966).
64. Alessandro Duranti, "Intentions, Language, and Social Action in a Samoan Context," *Journal of Pragmatics* 12 (1988): 13–33.
65. Fanaafi Aiono-Le Tagaloa, *O La Ta Gagana* (Alafua, WS: Lamepa Press, 1996), 1.
66. Cited in Omer Turan, *The Triangle of Publicness, Communication and Democracy* (MSc Thesis, Middle East Technical University, 2004), 36.
67. Emma Kruse Vaai, *Producing the Text of Culture: The Appropriation of English in Contemporary Samoa* (Le Papaigalagala, WS: Centre for Samoan Studies, National University of Samoa, 2011).
68. Mageo, *Theorizing Self in Samoa*, 81.
69. Sa'iliemanu Lilomaiava-Doktor, "Beyond Migration: Samoan Population Movement (Malaga) and the Geography of Social Space (Va)," *The Contemporary Pacific* 21, no. 1 (2009): 8.
70. Tofaeono, *Eco-Theology: Aiga—The Household of Life*, 31.
71. Ibid.
72. Ronald James Crawford, *The Lotu and the Fa'asamoa: Church and Society in Samoa, 1830–1880* (PhD Thesis, University of Otago, 1977).
73. Meleisea, *Lagaga: A Short History of Western Samoa*, 28.

74. The inclusion of these two groups reflects the ability of the *fa'amatai* system to adapt to the social changes associated with the impact of Christianity.

75. F. J. H. Grattan, *An Introduction to Samoan Custom* (Apia, WS: Samoa Printing and Publishing Company, 1948), 166.

76. See Serge Tcherkezoff, "Are the Matai out of Time? Tradition and Democracy: Contemporary Ambiguities and Historical Transformations of the Concept of Chief," in *Governance in Samoa*, ed. Elise Huffer and Asofou So'o, 113–132 (Suva, FJ and Canberra: Institute of Pacific Studies, University of the South Pacific and Asia Pacific Press, 2000).

77. Ibid.

78. Margaret Mead, *Coming of Age in Samoa: A Psychological Study of Primitive Youth for Western Civilization* (New York: Harper Perennial Modern Classics, 2001), 15.

79. Le'apai Lau, Asofou So'o, and Rob Laking, "Samoan Public Sector Reform: Views from Apia and the Villages," *Policy Quarterly* 4, no. 3 (September 2008): 59.

80. Vaai, *Producing the Text of Culture*, 25.

81. Ibid.

82. Evotia Tamua, Graeme Lay, Tony Murrow, and Malama Meleisea, *Samoa: Pacific Pride (Peoples of the Pacific)* (Auckland: Polynesian Press, 2000), 191.

83. Several instances of this are described by Selota Maliko in his study of banishment in Samoa. Describing one such case, he writes, "When the [Lands and Titles] Court dismissed the decision of the village *fono* and ordered Afu and her family to return to the village, the youths of the village [*aumaga* acting on behalf of the *fono*] attacked Afu's family, threw stones at the family's houses, smashed the interiors of the houses, and burnt their cars." Maliko, Restorative Justice, 23.

Chapter 4

Listening to "the Public"
A Talanoa *Approach to Field Research*

An indispensable partner in any public theology is "the public" who are the subjects of public theology. The objective of this chapter is to bring the Samoan public to the forefront by outlining the contextual methodology used in the field research portion of this study, noting how it guided the collection and analysis of information. The chapter first locates the researcher as a partner within this research process. It then discusses the methodologies that guided data collection, collation, and analysis.

LOCATING THE RESEARCHER

A Samoan and *Faletua* (Pastor's Wife)

I was born and raised in Samoa within my Samoan *aiga*, their culture, and the Christian faith. I was nurtured from infancy to believe in and engage with Samoan cultural values and Christian principles. Both have informed my sense of self and my relationships. I am also the wife of an ordained minister, and the *faifeau* (pastor) and his wife (*faletua*) have a highly respected status in Samoa, especially in their own denomination but also more broadly.

Being a *faletua* meant that I have had relatively easy access to a network of people who could assist as participants in my study or help me to recruit participants. Because of this, I had to be careful to ensure that my participants genuinely wanted to participate in the study. I had to be aware of how my role as a *faletua* might predispose participants to restrict or temper their communications with me, as a person with perceived status. This required adopting an approach that can free participants to express themselves in a dialogue without reservation.

A Student and Teacher of Theology

My time living in Fiji and New Zealand as a student has also had a significant influence on my perception of Samoan values (by drawing comparisons) and the place of the Christian faith within this value system. In those broader contexts, I was introduced to the skills of critical analysis regarding both the *fa'asamoa* and the Christian faith.

After graduating from theological schools in New Zealand and Fiji, I returned to Samoa with my husband and children. I discovered when I sought to teach at the Methodist Church's Piula Theological College, where my husband had joined the faculty, that it was not possible for a woman to be employed in this role. There were no female students, since the Methodist Church in Samoa does not ordain women. Those who taught at Piula were all men and *faifeau* of the Methodist Church. However, when the College experienced a teacher shortage, as a *faletua* I was finally able to take up a non-theology teaching position.

Before I was given this position at Piula, I found employment at the National University of Samoa (NUS). My time at NUS stimulated an interest in the relationship between the religious and public spheres in Samoa. It was an interest that was inspired by a quote from John Wesley, the founder of the Methodist movement, who made the powerful declaration that "all the world is my parish."[1] This resonates with my understanding of the Christian faith as necessarily welcoming to all, regardless of gender or any other factor, which has ramifications for the role of the church in the Samoan public sphere.

An Insider Researcher

The main challenge of being an insider researcher has been discerning how to utilize my insiderness in such a way as not to bias my study but, instead, to maximize opportunities to communicate well with my research participants and to faithfully represent their views, while at the same time engaging critically with literature on matters relevant to my study.

A particular challenge for this study is that one can never simply ask a Samoan individual about his or her values, as they are the collective values of family, village, and ancestors. One scholar has even stated, off the record, that whenever one asks a Samoan about her or his values, (s)he will respond with a story designed to avoid what is being pursued. This is because discussing values involves a questioning of one's communal self. A question such as "what are your core values?" could imply that the researcher is questioning the values of the interviewee's parents, *aiga*, and village.[2] As an insider researcher, I had to be constantly mindful of this complex "selfhood."

AN INDIGENOUS RESEARCH PARADIGM

In the primary research portion of this study, I adopted both constructivist grounded theory and *talanoa* methodologies in my collection, collation, theorizing, and analysis of primary data. My approach to qualitative research utilizes the constructivist grounded theory advocated by Kathy Charmaz.[3] My appropriation of a *talanoa* framework for interviewing is located within Timote Vaioleti's *talanoa* research methodology for Pacific Islands indigenous research.[4]

The "Pacific" in Indigenous Research Methodology

Pacific Islander academics have in recent years increasingly developed indigenous research approaches and employed Oceanian concepts and metaphors as aids to research. Indigenous Pacific Research (IPR) subscribes to the presupposition that research strategies must be designed so as to focus on obtaining contextual insights, insider perspectives and particularities, as these unfold during investigation.

A helpful summary of indigenous approaches to Pacific Islands research is provided by Cresantia Koya-Vaka'uta.[5] In "Rethinking Research as Relational Space in the Pacific," she begins by revisiting the Maori researcher Linda Tuhiwai Smith, whose frank critique of the imposition of Eurocentric research paradigms onto indigenous peoples in *Decolonizing Methodologies* asserts that even "the term 'research' is inextricably linked to European imperialism and colonialism. The word itself, 'research,' is probably one of the dirtiest words in the indigenous world's vocabulary."[6] This is because the imposed Western research models have come with their own assumed values that have not taken into account indigenous people's self-understanding and ways of viewing and being in the world.

Koya-Vaka'uta argues that "a first step toward much needed research reform must begin with the recognition of an Indigenous Research Paradigm as valid and critical to Pacific understandings of contextual places, spaces and knowledges."[7] She sees this as a decolonizing project that relies on Pacific Islanders' common core value of the sacredness of relational space. Here research becomes "an act of negotiation, rendering the researcher and the researched tied in a relational space determined by the cultural understandings of reciprocity, and governed by the rules of engagement that this negotiation demands."[8]

Koya-Vaka'uta identifies a number of IPR approaches that have emerged in recent years, tied together by this central theme of relational space. In addition to *talanoa*, which I adopt in this study and which is perhaps the best known of these models, the following are just some of the other IPR paradigms summarized by Koya-Vaka'uta:

- *Fonofale*—Attributed to the initial work by Fuimaono Karl Pulotu-Endermann, . . . [and] built on the metaphor of the traditional [Samoan] house, it reinforces the dual philosophy of holism and continuity.
- *Kakala*—First articulated to Konai Helu Thaman . . . , it details processes involved in [Tongan] garland-making in alignment with research practice, and emphasizes the values, ethics and relationships within these processes.
- *Ta-Va*—Developed by "Okustino Mahina, it . . . is presented as a [Tongan] theory of time and space, providing a framework for intellectual critique and interpretation, taking into account cultural transformations over time that privilege a focus on relational spaces within this holistic construct.
- *Vanua*—First emerging in the work of [Fijian] Rev. Dr Ilaitia Sevati Tuwere . . . in contextual theology discourse, it is based on the metaphor of the land . . . including conceptions of place, and people as custodians of the land, in relationship with God and the wider cosmos.
- *Teu Le Va*—Developed by Melanie Anae, it is . . . a [Samoan] philosophical and methodological approach to informed research praxis . . . premised on relational spaces and ways of valuing, negotiating and acting within these spaces.
- *Iluvatu*—Developed by Sereima Naisilisili . . . around the metaphor of a particular kind of [Fijian] mat, . . . it highlights guiding principles of respect, inclusivity, cohesiveness, and the values and practices surrounding cultural notions of place and spiritual connectedness with family and community.[9]

I take seriously Anne-Marie Tupuola's reminder that any researcher who does research with Oceanian indigenous communities needs to have a "full understanding of Pacific knowledge and an awareness of Pacific cultures."[10] In support of this prerequisite, Sitiveni Halapua calls on all Pacific Islander researchers to honor the concept of *va* or relational space.[11] Regardless of which indigenous metaphor one employs, Pacific researchers must take seriously the relational underpinnings of all approaches to learning and sharing knowledge in the Pacific.

Kabini Sanga argues that, in undertaking IPR, there are two basic assumptions that are axiological in nature. These are stated as opposing perspectives: "(1) that the social world and research of that world are value-free; and (2) that the social world and research of that world are value-bound."[12] I contend that Pacific Islander researchers, consciously or unconsciously, take for granted that research is value-bound and is therefore influenced by the researcher, the researched, the conceptual framework used, the methodology, and the context. To the extent that this Pacific worldview is normative, no research is value-free.

Sanga further argues that the debate regarding IPR is based on two additional opposing assumptions: "(1) that the social world for people is tangible and external to their cognition, whether or not they perceive this; and (2) that the social world for people is intangible and internal to their cognition."[13] Both assumptions are valid. But whether reality is experienced as tangible/external or intangible/internal, IPR acknowledges a commonly shared assumption about Oceanian social reality: that all human interactions are infused with *mana* (sacred power).[14]

Talanoa Research Methodology

The *talanoa* research methodology, according to Timote Vaioleti, is "a personal encounter, where people story their issues, their realities and aspirations, [that] allows more *mo'oni* (pure, real, authentic) information to be available for Pacific research than data derived from other research methods."[15] Vaioleti links *talanoa*, "along with qualitative research, grounded theory, naturalistic inquiry and ethnography . . . to the phenomenological research family."[16] This is supported by Semisi Prescott's statement that "The epistemology of *talanoa* is . . . closely associated with that of the interpretive (constructivist) paradigm."[17] The researcher and the participant (research partner) are regarded as equal and inseparable in their search for revealed meanings. They both have a valid contribution to offer to each other, and together they co-construct their *talanoa*.

Talanoa as a means of communication is shared across the island nations of Oceania, particularly in Fiji, Samoa, the Solomon Islands, Hawaii, the Cook Islands, and Tonga.[18] It is rooted in the oral traditions of island societies. Prescott writes that while it is wrong for any one island nation to claim *talanoa* as uniquely its own, "nevertheless, each nation appears to apply it in their own unique way across a variety of contexts, which may be the reason behind such a claim."[19]

In Vaioleti's framework, *talanoa* can be referred to as a conversation, a discussion, an exchange of ideas, or thinking together, whether formal or informal. It is almost always carried out face-to-face.[20] Linguistically, *talanoa* is made up of two words, *tala* and *noa*. In Tongan, *tala* means "to inform, tell, relate and command, as well as to ask or apply," while *noa* means "of any kind, ordinary, nothing in particular."[21] Hence *talanoa* on one level means "talking about nothing in particular," without a rigidly prescribed framework for the discussion.[22] It is, most importantly, a personal encounter where people freely story their realities and their aspirations.[23]

The development of *talanoa* as a formal research methodology can be traced to two Tongan scholars, Timote Vaioleti and Sitiveni Halapua.[24] Vaioleti transformed the concept of *talanoa* such that it is not just about the "talk" of participants but about the way that talk is set up and analyzed for academic research purposes—in other words, how interview data is framed.[25] Halapua emphasizes that "*Talanoa* does not have a rigidly preconceived agenda. It is very open, you can tell your story. Prior to the advent of Western civilization and the coming of missionaries, *talanoa* was how our history was created. Nothing was written. Anybody could tell his or her story about what was important to him or her."[26]

Talanoa has parallels with the concept of dialogue advocated by Paulo Freire, who used open dialogue to reveal and enhance participants' common humanity of love, humility, and faith. Both *talanoa* and Freirean dialogue are processes that "require intense faith in human beings, in their power to make and remake, to create and recreate, to include and exclude."[27]

The *talanoa* methodology has been used in a number of recent research studies, in areas such as education,[28] housing,[29] and gambling.[30] *Talanoa* has also been employed in theological and hermeneutical discourse, in particular by Jione Havea[31] and Nasili Vaka'uta.[32] Sitiveni Halapua proposed *talanoa* as a potential means of conflict resolution following the 2000 coup in Fiji.

The *talanoa* process can be used in one-to-one interviews or focus group discussions, and has proven to be a useful approach in cross-disciplinary research.[33] *Talanoa* is advantageous because of its flexibility, which, according to Prescott, reflects "the need to accommodate the multitude of situations in which it is used and the personalities of those who participate."[34]

As with any valid approach to research, *talanoa* may at times not achieve the results anticipated by the researcher. This may be frustrating for the researcher at times, but is not a bad thing. This will be discussed further in the section on data collection. This is to be expected in any qualitative research, where the researcher is dealing with people's experiences and emotions. Qualitative research, according to Marilyn Lichtman, is always fluid and ever-evolving, having a dynamic nature because it uses complex ways of thinking and describing.[35]

I understand *talanoa* as "holistically intermingling the researcher's and participants' emotions, knowledge, experiences and spirits."[36] *Talanoa* in this sense necessitates a face-to-face conversation, whether formal or informal. The use of *talanoa* in this study takes into account contextual nuances of meaning, cooperation, and flexibility, and the concept of *va* which is at the core of *fa'asamoa*.

I have also viewed the *talanoa* approach to research through a critical lens. It is true that the way in which this research methodology has been presented has at times idealized the *talanoa* process, which could lead to a "warm and fuzzy" notion of empathic dialogue that runs the risk of the researcher being unable to interpret data with sufficient objectivity and critical analysis. Trisia Farrelly and Unaisi Nabobo-Baba have concurred with Suaalii-Sauni's concern that "*talanoa* research has been veiled in metaphors and rhetoric, rendering it politically and academically powerful, albeit somewhat mystical."[37]

A related risk is that *talanoa* research may be viewed simplistically as mere open-ended conversation, rather than the complex process of engaged listening, attending, checking for clarification of meaning, and probing for interpretation which is actually entailed in *talanoa* research. I have countered this danger by paying careful attention to both questions and responses, accurate note-taking and coding, and clarificatory follow-up.

While acknowledging the potential pitfalls of the *talanoa* research methodology, I nonetheless argue for its relevance in undertaking insider research as a Samoan, as it honors Samoan collectivist conceptions of self and ways of communicating, and thereby facilitates the uncovering of honest, insightful views about Samoan values and their role in constructing a Samoan public theology.

CONSTRUCTIVIST GROUNDED THEORY (CGT)

CGT was developed by Kathy Charmaz as an alternative to classic and Straussian grounded theory (GT) (grounded theory being defined as the systematic generating of theory from data).[38] The appeal of CGT is its flexibility and its appreciation of the theoretical orientation and social location of the researcher. CGT enables a richly nuanced interpretive understanding of the social realities and perspectives of participants.

CGT differs from GT because of its emphasis on how data, analysis, and methodological strategies become constructed, and because of the way it takes into account the research context and the researcher's perspectives and priorities. The goal of CGT is to give unfettered voice to participants. Charmaz encourages grounded theorists to incorporate the multiple voices, views, and visions of participants in rendering their lived experiences, in order to accurately interpret participants' meanings.

CGT assumes that there are multiple social realities, rather than any one and only "real reality."[39] As Charmaz writes, CGT "assumes the relativism of multiple social realities, recognizes the mutual creation of knowledge by the viewer and the viewed, and aims toward interpretive understanding of subjects' meanings."[40] Merilyn Annells highlights the way in which CGT "reshapes the interaction between researcher and participants in the research process, and in doing so brings to the fore the notion of the researcher as author."[41]

Charmaz has asserted since the mid-1990s that a constructivist approach to GT is needed because "data do not provide a window on reality. Rather, the "discovered" reality arises from the interactive process and its temporal, cultural, and structural contexts."[42] Data is constructed through an ongoing interaction between researcher and participant. This is also what happens in *talanoa*.

A SYNTHESIS OF *TALANOA* AND CGT

Data Collection

The aim of the primary data collection in this study was to gather information on adult Samoans' views about core Samoan values. This process also enabled the researcher and participants to identify corollary Christian values, with the aim of articulating a public theology for Samoa. The aim of the secondary data collection was to review the relevant scholarly literature and situate those findings alongside that of the primary data.

A decision was made to protect the anonymity of participants by using coded identifiers rather than identifying them by name. Although there would have been merit in elevating the "voice" of participants by naming them, in the Samoan context anonymity opened up a pathway for participants to participate much more freely than would have been the case had they been named. Indeed, most participants would likely not have taken part in the *talanoa* had they been identified. In a society like Samoa, where preference is given to a select few to speak (chiefs, orators, church ministers, politicians), the anonymity guaranteed by using codes rather than proper names was a liberating device, especially for those whose voices are otherwise muted in the public sphere.

Selection of Participants: The main criteria for involvement in the study were being a Samoan adult, residing in Samoa, and belonging to a village, church, nongovernmental organization, parliament, or government department. It is worth acknowledging again that Samoans living in the diaspora have much to offer to the construction of a Samoan public theology, but because their diasporic experience is not identical to that of Samoans living in Samoa they deserve their own investigation, beyond the capacity of this study. It was also not feasible to include American Samoans in the field research. Although their collective life is grounded in the *faa'samoa*, the fact that they are, in effect, an American colony means that their social realities are unique to that context and merit their own public theology approach.

Twenty participants were selected from the Village group; twenty from the Church group; fifteen from the NGO group; and twenty from the Politicians and Government Workers group. These four groups cover the four main sociopolitical groupings in Samoa. Seventy-five *talanoa* interviews were conducted, with forty-three males and thirty-two females. All participants were over twenty-one years of age. Their participation was determined by availability and interest.

Participant Groups: The Village group consisted of members of the *aualuma, faletua ma tausi, aumaga,* and *matai* sub-groups. Their responses were shaped by their specific roles within the village system, as explained in chapter 3. The NGO group ranged from those who addressed particular social issues to those who dealt with environmental or religious issues and some who worked in private businesses. All participants in this group were helpful and eager to participate in this research.

The Church group included both representatives of mainline denominations, including some theologians, and religious groups or churches that are not members of the Samoa National Council of Churches. Those from the non-mainline groups had as much to contribute to this research as those from churches under the umbrella of the National Council of Churches. The last group consisted of Government Workers and Politicians, whose work and public behaviors are guided by the government code of ethics.

Talanoa Interviews: These were carried out with selected participants over a period of six months. Each of the seventy-five participants had one interview with the researcher. These interviews had no set time limit, although in formal work settings participants' time tended to be less flexible than that of the villagers. The *talanoa* interviews were guided by a topic directory that listed seven thematic areas for discussion. Participants were encouraged to share on these themes, in whatever way they felt comfortable. Initially most participants stated that they had no or little knowledge of public theology. They engaged more willingly and openly in the *talanoa* when it was explained that I was interested in their personal understanding and experiences.[43]

The following themes were selected by the researcher, based on literature findings:

1. Core values (in relation to participants' social location/s)
2. Understanding of public theology (personal understanding)
3. Relationship between core values and public theology
4. Avenues for Samoan theologians to enter public debates
5. Training received by public theologians
6. Role of public theology in society
7. Enactment of theology in public life

Talanoa Format: I began each *talanoa* with a brief word of welcome and an expression of appreciation to the participant for accepting the invitation to *talanoa*. The interviews were conducted on a one-to-one basis, fleshing out the identified themes through focused questions that opened up *talanoa* sharing. It was felt that conducting group *talanoa* about core values and understandings of public theology might hinder the more reserved participants from sharing their genuine views.

The social position of each participant affected the structure of the *talanoa*, in the sense that this could cause the *talanoa* to shift from a free-flowing dialogue to a more structured conversation influenced by external factors such as time constraints and other obligations. With some of the more "professional" participants, the process ended up being more formal than I had anticipated. In some instances, instead of being informal dialogue, these became quite formal conversations that entailed the use of Samoan protocols. This could have been because their professional positions had made them more accustomed to formal communication, or because Samoan conversations involving serious issues tend to become more formal.

It is important to note that cultural protocols in Samoan society reflect power relations that can hinder the acquisition of information sought by the researcher. It would have been disrespectful, for example, for me to ask questions while the participant was speaking. This was especially the case with politicians and church ministers. The status these participants held in Samoan society obligated me to abide by the protocols of Samoan culture, language, and social mores.

A gift of the equivalent of NZ$20 in money and food was given to each participant. However, there were cases when participants did not accept this gift out of respect and a sign of *alofa* toward the researcher, who was at that time a graduate student, a common response being *tu'u lau tupe e fesoasoani i lau aoga* ("keep your money to help with your studies"). This interaction indicates that both parties in the *talanoa* were being guided by cultural protocols regarding generosity, respect, and hospitality.

All *talanoa* interviews were conducted in the Samoan language, and later translated by the researcher into English. Given the largely English-speaking readership of this work, only the English translations are included here; the original Samoan transcripts remain in the author's possession. All sessions were held at the participants' designated group location, or at a place selected by the participant. A number of participants initially expressed some concern about the topic under discussion. Two reasons were given: first, they were afraid they might not give useful responses; second, they had never heard of public theology.

Those who did not have confidence about their participation were mostly those from the Village group. They were mainly wives of chiefs or daughters of the villagers who were unemployed. Their lack of confidence in their ability to articulate their ideas in appropriate ways may be due to a common myth in Samoan thinking that it is only those with a good education who have anything worth saying on serious topics. Giving the "wrong" answer poses a threat to their communal self, as this might bring shame to their *aiga*.

Listening to "the Public" 105

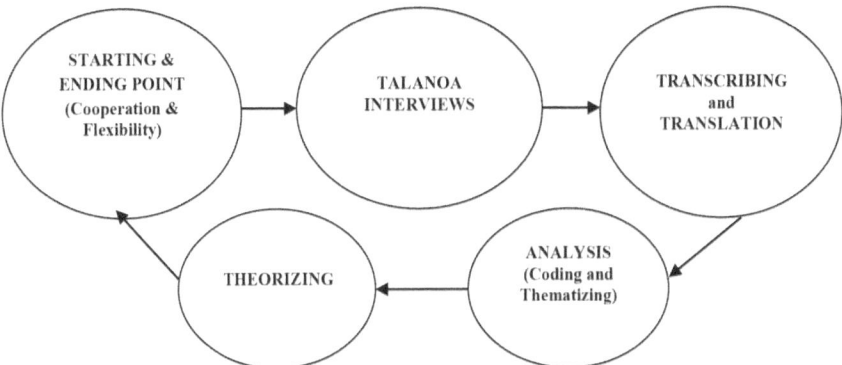

Figure 4.1   Steps in the *Talanoa* Process.

However, this was generally resolved with an explanation of the research topic and the methodology used. Trust and confidentiality were openly reinforced. The *talanoa* process is traced in figure 4.1.

Data Analysis

Within the analytical framework of CGT, *talanoa* interview data was subjected to a multilevel analysis through a successive coding process. Charmaz employs a two-step CGT coding procedure—Initial Coding and Focused Coding—both of which I used.

Initial Coding: I began the initial process of coding after reading through the transcripts. This entailed a close examination of each line, allocating codes to prominent words or groups of words. This took more time than the actual fieldwork and required a great deal of patience, especially when reading through lengthy transcripts. The initial code areas derived were:

1. Samoan custom and traditions
2. Core values of respect and service
3. Choice of values
4. Blessings from family, church, and village
5. Service to church
6. Becoming a *matai*
7. Influence of family, church, and village
8. Group identity
9. Suitability for a task

Focused Coding: The nine initial codes were then refined to three: (1) Core Values; (2) Public Theology; and (3) Theology and Public Life. Under *core values*, sub-codes emerged such as "family" and "identity." Under *public theology*, the sub-codes that surfaced were "understanding of public theology," "relationship between core values and public theology," "avenues for theologians to participate in public life," "the training of theologians," and "the role of public theology." In *theology and public life*, the sub-codes were "power and leadership," "indigenous reference and spirituality," "village and church ministers," and "faith marginalization."

Coding rigor is critical to the trustworthiness of the information gathered in field research. Guba and Lincoln find that sound qualitative research requires credibility, transferability, dependability, and confirmability in order to show rigor.[44] In my study, a transcribed copy of the interview was posted or e-mailed to each participant before translation started. Once the interviews were translated, a copy was sent to each participant for transparency purposes and to check that the translation was a true record of what he or she said during the *talanoa*.

Memo Notes to Self: Assessing primary data included writing memo notes to myself about key points arising from the *talanoa* interviews. This is in line with the role of reflection in CGT, which records the researcher's thinking about what is revealed in the interview process while the interview experience is still close at hand. In my memos, I noted my thinking about what had been revealed and how it might influence the analysis of data. This gave me an opportunity to remember, question, analyze, and make meaning of the time spent with participants and the insights generated during the *talanoa*. Charmaz does this by consistently including the participants' voices throughout the process of analysis.[45] I have likewise inserted participants' words into the text throughout the interpretive chapters. The process of CGT analysis is mapped in figure 4.2 below.

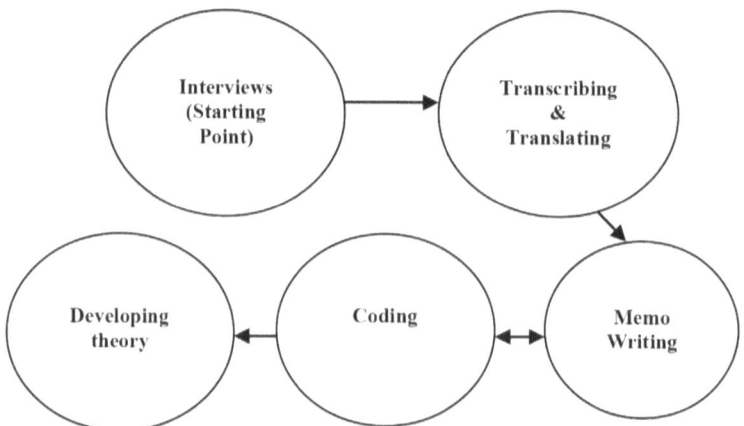

Figure 4.2   Steps in Developing a Grounded Theory.

Evaluation of CGT

The preceding sections have indicated the ways I have incorporated CGT into the process of conducting *talanoa* interviews and interpreting the findings. The techniques of coding (initial and focused) were particularly helpful in identifying core themes and sub-themes. The ways in which these emerged through the *talanoa* interviews will become clear as the core Samoan values, and their relevance for a Samoan public theology, are unpacked in the ensuing chapters.

CGT has also been helpful for my research in its insistence that the researcher's own perspectives must undergo critical interpretation alongside those of the participants. This enabled me to adhere rigorously to the principle of autocriticality—the capacity to be self-critical. This is highlighted by Jenna Breckenridge, who notes that CGT "does not assume the naive objectivity of the researcher, but rather, through the rigorous application of the methodology, researcher biases are revealed and accounted for."[46] By, in effect, consistently "interviewing myself," I have utilized CGT to avoid the pitfalls of researcher bias. The entire process of eliciting the views of participants, by means of the CGT/*talanoa* framework, has enabled the insights of Samoan participants about their core values to be uncovered, interpreted, and applied in the construction of a public theology.

Ethical Considerations

I engaged in this research making every effort to conform to the highest ethical standards expected in serious qualitative research. Contact persons were utilized in organizing interviews with selected participants, although occasionally I had to approach the participants directly in order to set the date, time, and place of interviews. In situations where the participants requested to meet straightaway, an explanation of the objectives of the field research was given by telephone in order to acquire their permission and consent.

A written explanation of the research was prepared to inform the participants about the purpose of the study. A consent form was made available for each participant to sign before the interview. Information regarding the research purpose, consent, and themes of *talanoa* interviews were all provided in the Samoan language. Participants were informed that they could withdraw from the *talanoa* at any time if they wished to do so, and that confidentiality was protected at all times, particularly through the use of identifying codes rather than names.

FINAL THOUGHTS

This chapter has introduced and explained the research methodology and methods used in this study, indicating how CGT and *talanoa* were employed to collect, organize and analyze data pertinent to the research topic. The chapter has made a case for the importance of Pacific Indigenous Research and the use of *talanoa* as an indigenous research method. Data collection procedures, including a profile of participants, and ethical considerations have also been explained.

At the same time, I have applied a critical eye to both *talanoa* and CGT, noting the possible risks inherent in this more subjectivist approach to qualitative research, and indicating how I have attempted to mitigate those risks. A strong argument has been made that, despite these risks, these research approaches are the most relevant for this particular kind of research, especially given the fact that *talanoa* is an authentically Samoan way of communicating, and that I am undertaking this research as an insider researcher who understands how to navigate the intricacies of such communication.

NOTES

1. John Wesley, personal journal, June 11, 1739, last modified June 1, 2005, http://www.ccel.org/ccel/wesley/journal.vi.iii.v.html.

2. Tui Atua had just such a conversation with a fellow Samoan, who "took exception to the question, 'what do you think?' He argued that it is offensive and intrusive because he would have to ask: What does my mother think? What does my father think? What does my family think? What does my village think? . . . before he can respond to the question, what do I think? Because he is accountable to his family, his village and himself when he answers." Efi, "More on Meaning, Nuance and Metaphor," 71.

3. Kathy Charmaz, *Constructing Grounded Theory: A Practical Guide through Qualitative Analysis* (London: Sage Publications, 2006), 23.

4. Tamasa'ilau M. Sualii-Sauni and Sauni Maa Fulu-Aiolupotea, "Decolonising Pacific Research, Building Pacific Research Communities and Developing Pacific Research Tools: The Case of the 'Talanoa' and the 'Faafaletui' in Samoa," *Asia Pacific Viewpoint* (May 16, 2013): 4. Timote Vaioleti is a Tongan academic and education researcher at the University of Waikato in New Zealand, and is most often cited as the founder of the *talanoa* research methodology.

5. See Cresantia Frances Koya-Vaka'uta, "Rethinking Research as Relational Space in the Pacific: Pedagogy and Praxis," in *Relational Hermeneutics: Decolonising the Mindset and the Pacific Itulagi*, ed. Upolu L. Vaai and Aisake Casimira (Suva, FJ: Pacific Theological College and University of the South Pacific, 2017), 65–84.

6. Linda Tuhiwai Smith, *Decolonizing Methodologies: Research and Indigenous People* (London and New York, NY: Zed Books, 1999), 1.

7. Koya-Vaka'uta, "Rethinking Research as Relational Space," 69.

8. Ibid., 71.

9. Ibid., 75–77.

10. Anne-Marie Tupuola, "Raising Consciousness: The Fa'a Samoa Way," *New Zealand Annual Review of Education* 3 (2007): 54.

11. See Sitiveni Halapua, *"Talanoa*—Talking from the Heart," Interview, *SGI Quarterly* (January 2007): 9–10.

12. Kabini F. Sanga, "Making Philosophical Sense of Indigenous Pacific Research," in *Researching the Pacific and Indigenous Peoples*, ed. Tupeni M. Baba, Nuhisifa Williams, and Unaisi Nabobo-Baba (Auckland: University of Auckland Press, 2004), 57.

13. Ibid., 46.

14. *Mana* is a shared concept in many Oceanian cultures, especially throughout Polynesia. Although English translations are insufficient, it is most commonly translated as "power" or "prestige," and it is associated with sacred and at times even supernatural power. For a discussion of how the concept of *mana* has evolved historically and in the contemporary era in Oceanian cultures, see Matt Tomlinson and Ty P. Kāwika Tengan, eds., *New Mana: Transformations of a Classic Concept in Pacific Languages and Cultures* (Canberra: ANU Press, 2016).

15. Cited in Timote Masima Vaioleti, "Talanoa Research Methodology: A Developing Position on Pacific Research," *Waikato Journal of Education* 12 (2006): 21.

16. Ibid., 25.

17. Semisi Prescott, "Using Talanoa in Pacific Business Research in New Zealand: Experiences with Tongan Entrepreneurs," *Alternative, Special Edition* 1 (2008): 131.

18. Ibid., 133.

19. Ibid.

20. Vaioleti, "Talanoa Research Methodology," 23.

21. Ibid.

22. Ibid.

23. Ibid., 21.

24. Sualii-Sauni and Fulu-Aiolupotea, "Decolonising Pacific Research," 5.

25. Vaioleti, "Talanoa Research Methodology," 23.

26. Halapua, *"Talanoa*—Talking from the Heart," 9.

27. Paulo Freire, *Pedagogy of the Oppressed*, 30th anniversary ed. (New York, NY: Continuum, 2000), 21.

28. Timote Masima Vaioleti, "Talanoa Research Methodology: A Perspective on Pacific Research," Paper Presented, *Pasifika Nations Educators Association Conference*, Wellington, NZ, April 15–17, 2003.

29. Moses N. Alatini, *Housing and Related Social Conditions of the Tongan Community Living in Otara (Ko E Fale Nofo'anga Pea Mo 'Ene Fekau'aki Mo E Mo'ui 'a E Kainga Tonga Nofo 'i Otara)* (MA Thesis, University of Auckland, 2002).

30. Sione Tui'hai, Yvette Guttenbeil-Po'uhila, Jennifer Hand, and Tim Htay, "Gambling Issues for Tongan People in Auckland, Aotearoa-New Zealand," *Journal of Gambling Issues* 12 (December 2004): 43–49.

31. See, for example, Jione Havea, ed., *Talanoa Ripples: Across Borders, Cultures, Disciplines* (Auckland and Albany, NZ: Masilamea Press and Office of the Directorate Pasifika, Massey University, 2010).

32. See, for example, Nasili Vaka'uta, *Talanoa Rhythms: Voices from Oceania* (Albany, NZ: Office of the Directorate Pasifika, Massey University, 2013).

33. Judy T. McFall-McCaffery, "Getting Started with Pacific Research: Finding Resources and Information on Pacific Research Models and Methodologies," *MAI Review* 1, no. 8 (2010): 1–5.

34. Prescott, "Using Talanoa in Pacific Business Research," 134.

35. Marilyn Lichtman, *Qualitative Research in Education* (London: Sage Publications, 2006), 9.

36. Vaioleti, "Talanoa Research Methodology," 24.

37. Trisia Farrelly and Unaisi Nabobo-Baba, "*Talanoa* as Empathic Research," Paper Presented, *International Development Conference*, Auckland, NZ, December 3–5, 2012, 3–4. They cite Tamasailau Suaalii-Sauni, "To *Talanoa, Fa'afaletui*, or Not? Reflections on the Development of Pacific Research Methods," Paper Presented, *Vaaomanu Pasifika Units VASA Seminar Series*, Victoria University, Wellington, NZ, June 20, 2012.

38. Barney G. Glaser, *Theoretical Sensitivity: Advances in the Methodology of Grounded Theory*, Vol. 2 (Mill Valley, CA: Sociology Press, 1978), 2. Glaser was critical of constructivist grounded theory because of his insistence on the construction of empirical data as the basis of theory.

39. Jane Mills, Ann Bonner, and Karen Francis, "Adopting a Constructivist Approach to Grounded Theory: Implications for Research Design," *International Journal of Nursing Practice* 12, no. 1 (2006): 8–13.

40. Kathy Charmaz, "Grounded Theory: Objectivist and Constructivist Methods," in *Strategies of Qualitative Inquiry*, ed. Norman K. Denzin and Yvonna S. Lincoln (London: SAGE Publications, 2003), 250.

41. Jane Mills, Ann Bonner, and Karen Francis, "The Development of Constructivist Grounded Theory," *International Journal of Qualitative Methods* 5, no. 1 (2008): 7.

42. Charmaz, "Grounded Theory," 524.

43. Prescott notes a similar movement from non-engagement to engagement, based on a number of *talanoa* sessions carried out in Tonga in 2006. See Prescott, "Using Talanoa in Pacific Business Research."

44. Egon G. Guba and Yvonna S. Lincoln, "Competing Paradigms in Qualitative Research," in *Handbook of Qualitative Research*, ed. Norman K. Denzin and Yvonna S. Lincoln (Thousand Oaks, CA: SAGE Publications, 1994).

45. Kathy Charmaz, "Between Positivism and Postmodernism: Implications for Methods," *Studies in Symbolic Interaction* 17 (1995): 43–72.

46. Jenna P. Breckenridge, "Choosing a Methodological Path: Reflections on the Constructivist Turn," *Grounded Theory Review: An International Journal* 1, no. 11 (2012): 1.

Chapter 5

Talanoa about *Aga Tausili* (Core Values)

Scholarship on Samoan cultural values draws on insights from diverse academic domains such as philosophy, political history, theology, education, sociology, anthropology, and cultural studies. Prominent in the literature on Samoan values is Tui Atua,[1] who has written extensively about values from an indigenous perspective. Tui Atua accentuates the core values of *alofa* (love), *amiotonu* (justice), and *fa'aaloalo* (respect), and elaborates on nuances and metaphors within *fa'asamoa*. Elise Huffer and Asofou So'o discuss the values of *alofa* and *fa'aaloalo* in relation to their work on consensus in Samoan social relations.[2] Frank Smith, a Samoan biblical theologian, has interpreted the values of *tautua, alofa, fa'aaloalo*, and *tautua* in relation to the Gospel of John.[3]

Chapter 2 introduced the Samoan context and identified five Samoan core values, with Christian parallels, that are foundational for this study, providing a brief overview from both cultural and theological perspectives. Chapter 3 situated these values within the broader historical and contemporary framework of the *fa'asamoa*, noting points of contact with the concerns of public theology. This chapter turns to a more in-depth examination of Samoa's core values, taking into account how they are frequently interwoven. These core values are fleshed out by highlighting key themes emanating from each of the four participant groups (Village, Church, NGOs, and Government Workers/Politicians).

FA'AALOALO (RESPECT)

Osiaiga (Care for the Family)

Fa'aaloalo is expressed in varied but interrelated ways. A key example is seen in the practice of *osiaiga*. *Osi* means "to embrace" and *aiga* means "family," such that *osiaiga* literally means "to embrace the family." *Osiaiga* as a sign of respect is a way of supporting and maintaining the unity of the *aiga*. Participant CVG075 explains this concept in terms of her role as a chief, in her relationship with her extended family:

> When I became a chief I listened and learned . . . . It was the request of my parents that I become a chief. Then, as years went by, I was accustomed to caring for the extended family, my mother's family and my father's family—those who are close and those included in the extended family. When I thought about it, the important value that became the direction for me was *osiaiga* [embracing or caring for families]. That value can be placed alongside love and reciprocity.

Here *fa'aaloalo* is implied in the statement "I was accustomed to caring for the extended family, my mother's family and my father's family." This tangible demonstration of respect is coupled with the values of *alofa* and *tautua*, as illustrated in Participant CVG075's commitment to love and serve her *aiga*. This is an essential part of a Samoan person's socialization in the *aiga*.

This respectful caring is often concretely demonstrated in the context of families' *fa'alavelave* or "giving" at weddings, funerals, and other special occasions. These outworkings of *fa'aaloalo* derive from traditional links through the extended family that encourage and strengthen *aiga* connections.[4] At the same time, they strengthen communal relationships in villages and wider contexts. *Fa'aaloalo* encourages one to participate in public acts of generosity and support pertaining to the *aiga, nu'u,* and *lotu*. In these social locations, each person contributes whatever support he or she is able to provide, even if one has nothing material to give. One's presence in these gatherings is both a sign of *fa'aaloalo* and a concrete expression of solidarity in one's *va* relationships.

These practical displays of *fa'aaloalo* are at times criticized, because they can be viewed as being based on vertical and unequal social relations—"lower" people showing respect to "higher" people. However, ideally *fa'aaloalo* is meant to be practiced by all to all; everyone should both give and receive *fa'aaloalo*. At the same time, it is important to acknowledge that any ideal has the potential for abuse, and if those who have the least to give show their respect by making sacrifices that are to their own detriment, this is an abuse of the true intention of *fa'aaloalo*. Its effectiveness depends very much on the corollary practices of love and justice among those who practice it.

Alo mai, Alo atu (Face-to-Face Engagement)

According to Fofo Iosefa Sunia, *fa'aaloalo* is the motivating factor that guides moral action in Samoan life.[5] The essence of *fa'aaloalo* is signified in the etymology of the root word *alo*, which can be translated as "stomach or belly."[6] We might say that *alo* relationships necessitate respect "at the gut level." Pratt translates *alo* as "the seat also of affections or feelings."[7]

Showing respect for the other requires meeting the other face-to-face or "belly to belly"—or, among females, "womb to womb." In other words, *fa'aaloalo* emanates from the very center of the person. In this face-to-face way of relating, *fa'aaloalo* becomes associated with *tautua* (selfless service), *alofa* (love, compassion), and *mamalu* (dignity).[8] It requires humility and an awareness that all relationships are meant to be respectful.

One should not underestimate the balance required in the enactment of *fa'aaloalo* understood as *alo mai, alo atu* ("you face me and I face you"). Without this balance, one is no longer practicing *fa'aaloalo* but has become *tufanua* (literally, "rude person"). *Tufanua* refers to any kind of interaction that is regarded as disrespectful.

Feiloaiga Taulealeausumai's discussion of *fa'aaloalo* features terms such as authority, boundaries, and obedience. She states that every Samoan—child, parent, *matai*, or minister—relates to others within a clear sense of boundaries, which must not be overstepped in order to maintain peace and social equilibrium.[9] Laufai Sauoaiga similarly argues that the *fa'asamoa* has established rules for persons to follow in order to achieve the essence of *fa'aaloalo*, which is the honoring of the other.[10] Upolu Vaai echoes this point when he writes, "Clustering around the concept of *fa'aaloalo* is the depth of honouring one another."[11]

This essence of *fa'aaloalo* is seen in the practical application of hospitality in Samoa. When a Samoan family hosts visitors, they serve them generously without expecting any reward. They offer hospitality in the form of food, drink, or accommodation to anyone who needs it.[12] In practical terms, this hospitality aspect of *fa'aaloalo* incorporates the ideal of reciprocity, even if the hospitality is "given" by one party and "received" by another in a specific instance. Although the hosts expect nothing in return for their hospitality, they know that they can count on others offering hospitality to them when needed in the future.[13] The element of surprise in *fa'aaloalo* is experienced in the blessings one receives for such actions at some point in the future, despite not expecting any reward.

TAUTUA (SELFLESS SERVICE)

The motivation behind the concept of *tautua* is found in the Samoan saying, *O le ala i le pule o le tautua* ("The path to power is through service"). Participant CRG045, a member of the Church group, explains this selfless service as follows:

> You serve from the back until you can come to the front. Jesus said, if you don't humble yourself . . . if you don't come from the back, you don't get to go to the front. Service is a task done freely without wanting a reward. It is a

responsibility or an obligation. If there is a Samoan untitled man who serves but thinks of becoming a *matai*, then Samoans would name him as an anticipated *matai*, or wanting to be a *matai*. This means that you should never serve with ambitions. You should serve with a righteous heart without expecting a reward for your service.

O le ala i le pule o le tautua (The path to power is through service) is a common Samoan saying often applied to a person who may be under consideration to obtain a *matai* title. Felise Va'a characterizes *tautua* as serving a *matai* through work, time, and money.[14] This service raises the status of the chief in the eyes of the community because it increases his ability to meet his chiefly obligations. The servant remains in the background but is eventually rewarded, most importantly through succession to the family *matai* title.

Tautua Matavela

There are various forms of *tautua*. The first is *tautua matavela*, or service which refers metaphorically to the experience of the face becoming heated through exposure to the sun during work in the plantation (garden), or to fire during the preparation of food in the traditional earth oven. This imagery accentuates the fact that discomfort and sacrifice are to be expected in the act of providing service. This service is not done on sporadic occasions, or for short bursts of effort; it is service that is continuous. The longer one serves, the more knowledge and experience one gains of the values that uphold Samoan culture. The rationale behind this sacrificial service is that one will grow in maturity by serving well.

Tautua Tuavae

The second type of good service is *tautua tuavae*. In a literal sense, this refers to the type of service which involves following behind in the footsteps of the *matai* wherever he goes. If a *matai* travels from his village to Apia, the untitled men will travel as well, so that they can continue their service. While the *matai* has his meal, the untitled men sit at the back, waiting with a bowl of water. When the *matai* finishes eating, the untitled men present the basin of water for hand washing. When the *matai* is satisfied with the service provided by the untitled men, he will utter words such as *fa'amalo le gasese, ia e manuia* ("a service well done, be blessed").

Tautua and Blessing

The story of the origin of the *ava* plant conveys the consequence of blessing associated with *tautua tuavai*. In this legend, it was the *tautua* of two sisters that resulted in the gift of Samoa's treasured *ava* plant. Tui Atua relates this story as follows:

> There were once two sisters, Ualā and Malomamae. They were responsible for the care of their grandfather, Tuisuga of Fagalii. One day Tuisuga craved *tuitui* (sea urchins) and so sent the girls to the sea to collect some for him. Along the way, the girls got bored and decided to do something else. When their grandfather found them idling and the basket not yet full, he got angry. He scolded and banished them. The girls left their grandfather and walked towards Mulifanua. They came across a boat sent by the Tui Fiti (the King of Fiji). The Tui Fiti's daughter had taken ill and he had sent emissaries to Samoa to find a *fofo* (traditional healer). The two girls, who held the gift of *fofo*, decided to help the Tui Fiti's daughter and boarded the boat. . . . When they arrived, the Tui Fiti was waiting anxiously. He asked the captain whether they had found a *fofo*. The captain pointed to the two girls, who were coming towards them with their basket of traditional remedies, including *vaisamipala*, a fermented coconut concoction. When the two sisters reached the Tui Fiti's daughter, one began to massage the daughter's stomach area; the other helped her to imbibe some of the *vaisamipala*. In what seemed only a few moments, the Tui Fiti witnessed with joy the sudden recovery of his daughter. . . . Seeing that their work was done, the two girls said to the Tui Fiti that they were now ready to return to Samoa. The Tui Fiti, indebted to the two sisters, asked them to stay a while. During their stay, both of them became his wives. With Ualā he had three children and with Malomamae he had one. Ualā's children, in order of birth, were Suasamiaava (male), Aanoatamalii (male), and Muliovailele (female). Malomamae's child was Saolateteleupegaofiti (male). When orators who subscribe to this version recite the genealogy of the *ava* in the *ava* ceremony, they will recite one or more of these names. In particular, they make mention of Aanoatamalii, for it is believed that the *ava* plant grew from and is his flesh. In contemporary Samoan oratory, orators use this name as an honorific for the *ava* root. . . . The story ends with the last testament of Aanoatamalii. His dying wish was that he be buried in the area of his home where he spent most of his life serving, i.e. the *valusaga*. This is the place where his *tautua* or service, that of *gasese*, i.e., service associated with preparing food, was conducted. The *valusaga* was also the place where Samoan families would make their compost . . . to help fertilise our soil. This was where Aanoatamalii wanted to be buried. Aanoatamalii instructed his family that if a plant were to grow where he was buried, they were to look after it, because the plant was he. Once he was strong enough, they were to take him, i.e. the plant, to Samoa. . . . After some time, his sister Muliovailele saw a plant with some shoots or *tolo* growing where they had buried Aanoatamalii. She declared, *Ua toe ola mai Aanoatamalii!* ("Aanoatamalii has come back to life!"). As promised to her brother, she then dug him up and took him to Samoa, the original land or roots of their mother Ualā. They settled in Vailele, next to

Fagalii.... According to Vailele and Fagalii history, the name records the place where the *ava* first grew.[15]

Tui Atua concludes that the lesson to be learned from this story is that one's *tautua* accrues blessings (*fa'amanuiaga*) from God.[16] "Blessing" in this sense refers to a divinely given reward for service in the form of tangible signs of well-being or success for oneself and, by extension, one's *aiga*. This interpretation still exists today in many Samoans' belief that in the long-term blessings will come from faithful service to parents, family, community, and church.

It is even believed that the people of Samoa, especially the descendants of Ualā and Aanoatamalii, continue to receive blessings from the *tautua* of Ualā and Aanoatamalii, and Ualā's sister Malomamae, to the Tui Fiti. The *ava* plant, as the reincarnation of Aanoatamalii, continues this *tautua* to the people of Samoa as a whole.[17] In addition, this story highlights the virtue of humility. As the son of the Tui Fiti, Aanoatamalii had rights to the grandest burial site Fiji could offer. Instead, he asked to be buried at the humble site of his service, the *valusaga*—the compost heap.[18]

Tautua i le Lotu (Service to the Church)

An important influence of Christianity in Samoa is seen in the practice of *tautua i le lotu* (service to the church). This is demonstrated by Samoans' sacrificial commitments to church obligations as a sign of their faith. The churches depend on the financial support of their members for maintaining the church and supporting pastors. Money donated by church members also goes into the building of new church structures. For the church members involved, this is an important part of their spirituality. Cluny Macpherson and La'avasa Macpherson offer the following observation:

> It is readily apparent in Samoa that the social and spiritual security that donors derive from their support for the church is more important to them than the returns that might be derived from the investment of the same amount of money in, say, a financial institution. The religious and socio-political "dividends" derived from contributions to churches are considered more significant and more certain, and they are valued more highly than those derived from financial investments calculated on such narrowly conceived indices as rates of return on capital.[19]

I often hear complaints from Samoans, both in Samoa and in the diaspora, who experience financial difficulties because of *tautua i le lotu*.

Sociologists and other researchers have conducted studies on this particular aspect of *tautua*, largely critical of the financial burdens this practice places on parishioners.[20] At the same time, there are many Samoans who sincerely embrace this practice and explain it as part of the value system that has shaped their cultural and religious identity, a common saying being *O le mea a lea na a'oa'oina ai i matou e o matou matua, ina ia toaaga e tautua le lotu* ("This is something our parents taught us, to serve the church devoutly").

Like other Samoan values, *tautua i le lotu* is, in the best sense, about maintaining right relationships. Participant CVG075 speaks of how Samoan people view their relationship to the church: "You know that the culture of Samoa and the mentality of the people is that priority is given to the church . . . we see that people are poor and yet they live to serve the Lord through the church."

SOALAUPULE (CONSENSUAL DIALOGUE)

A Collective Exercise of *Pule* (Authority)

In George Pratt's Samoan-English dictionary, *soalaupule* means "to consult together, and not to confine the instructions to the authority of one person."[21] Even the *sa'o*, the leader of the *aiga potopoto* (network of extended families), has no leeway to dominate the process of decision-making in the *aiga potopoto*. The emphasis in *soalaupule* is on deliberating together, rather than operating individually. *Soalaupule* thus refers to a collective sharing of *pule*. *Pule* refers both to those with authority, such as the *matai*, and to the wealth of knowledge which each participant contributes to the dialogue. This *pule* is offered to assist the *aiga* or the village council in reaching a mutual understanding. In the process of *soalaupule* there is no room for individualism, and a decision cannot be reached until there is consensus.

Huffer and So'o have described how some of the respondents in their study interpreted consensus: "One respondent commented that consensus was the way Samoans live and make decisions, particularly at the village level, summing up the general understanding of consensus as a decision-making process. . . . Some respondents highlighted the "goodness" of consensus . . . , while others focused on its negative aspects."[22] Consensus is viewed negatively in situations where it is manipulated to maintain power and status. But in its positive manifestation, it is a process of decision-making that achieves the common good "by allowing people to attain it together."[23]

A Search for *Tofa* (Wisdom)

Group deliberations are entered into in order to engage in *tofa saili*, the search for wisdom. According to Alexander and Katie Fala, "If Samoan knowledge is to be shared, it must have . . . those with the *tofa saili* (search for wisdom) to reflect on it and enhance it with new insights."[24] *Soalaupule* is also involved in the search for *tofa liuliu* (turning wisdom), as explained by Fa'alepo Tuisuga:

> The concept of *tofa liuliu* is mainly found within "*gagana fa'aaloalo*" [language of respect] usage. This "objective self-assessed, self-evaluated and self-reflective wisdom" . . . concerns the interpretation and understanding accomplished by and derived from rigorous deliberations between two or more people who are willingly and genuinely open to one another's advice and support. . . . The knowledge shared in this process from one person to another goes with a sense of responsibility, transcends human boundaries, and goes beyond the actual participants in a deliberation.[25]

Soalaupule in this sense is not merely a way of conversing with the other, but is intimately connected with the pursuit of wisdom. This quest is achieved through a mutual desire for justice, love, and observing the space of respect (*va*).

Among my research participants, the following is what Participant CRG045 had to say about *soalaupule*:

> Consensual dialogue refers to an issue that is going to be discussed with the same views, without any bias. We must be free to share views with others so that in the end there is consensus. This means that the opposite of dialogue is dictating. It [dictating] is the wish to rule by yourself, without considering the views of others. There is no room for dialogue. He or she wants to [be the one to] talk, wants to be the chief. But dialogue is about the equality of all people, and the equality of sharing in order to arrive at a good and happy ending. The root word of dialogue is to share, *fa'asoa*. Sharing between people shows the sharing of authority and power.

Participant CRG045 highlights key aspects of *soalaupule*, such as equality, but also notes that it is related to the exercise of power and authority. This is seen in the *soalaupule* by which *matai* arrive at consensual decisions in the *fono*. Even in a hierarchical society like Samoa, *soalaupule* must always be implemented out of love and respect for all, or else it defeats the whole purpose of Samoa as a nation founded in God—a motto which assumes that the love of God which holds the nation together extends to all Samoans.

AMIOTONU (JUSTICE)

Justice and Honesty

The Samoan understanding of justice is centered in the concept of "right relationships" among people, honoring people's social location in society, and embodying the core values that govern their interactions. *Amiotonu* is especially associated with *fa'amaoni* (honesty). Unless there is honesty, there can be no justice. In fact, *fa'amaoni* and *amiotonu* communicate the same meaning in the Samoan mentality, whether in social, political, or religious traditions.[26] According to Vaaimamao, these two terms encompass a plethora of good behaviors and attitudes, such as *amiolelei* (good conduct), *alofa* (love), *fa'aaloalo* (courtesy, respect), and *lotolelei* (kindness, mercy).[27]

Justice and Leadership

Amiotonu is often associated with the virtues expected of leaders, whether in the church or in secular spheres. In my field research, *amiotonu* was identified with the leadership roles of *matai*, politicians, and clergy. Participant CVG074, who is a *matai*, used the concept of *amiotonu* to refer to the role of the *matai* in general and, more specifically, within the village council:

> My priority goes to caring for my family. This is where the *matai's* sense of justice is reflected. It is how he arranges his family. Because before it gets to the village council, the *matai* should lead his family in order to be good and achieve unity. Within the village, the *matai* should rely on God's guidance. He should not rely on his knowledge. Because in most of the villages, there is a lot of injustice. So the *matai* has to rely on God for courage, so that he can speak out against the injustice he sees, because it is not God's will. He should speak the truth regardless of the consequences. The role of the *matai* in the village is to speak the truth and to do justice.

A key point being made here is that one cannot be a just leader without "relying on God's guidance." This entails seeking the truth (again, an appeal to honesty), and the paramount sign of a good leader is one who "speaks the truth and does justice."

Like Participant CVG074, Participant CVG031 described justice as a priority for *matai*, with the implication that this same virtue should be practiced by all who hold leadership positions in Samoan society. If justice does not prevail in Samoan society, whether in the church, village, or government, the consequence is the disintegration of the harmony and peace necessary for the flourishing of all.

ALOFA (LOVE)

Alofa as Unconditional Sacrifice

The story below illustrates the depth of the Samoan practice of *alofa*. This is the story of a woman who survived the 2009 tsunami in Samoa, as shared by Tui Atua in a public address:

> A few days after the tsunami, my wife and I went to visit the hospital where some of the survivors were, and I was told a profoundly moving story by a grandmother who was grieving for the loss of her grandson. Her family lived close to the sea in Saleapaga, one of the worst affected areas of the tsunami tragedy. In the early morning, as was usual for their family, she and her grandchildren would wake and then go about their morning rituals. This morning was no different. She recalled how she had given some coins to her grandchildren to get some goodies at the local store. She remembers them going to the store, playing on the way. The next thing she recalls was the emergency warning for all to go to higher ground. In the chaos of trying to locate her grandchildren she remembers the roaring sound of the wave, screeching towards them with driving rage, as if belching from the bowels of hell, whistling eerily, taunting death and destruction. This grandmother tells of how she yelled to her grandchildren who were nearby to run for their lives. Being a big lady, she knew she would slow them down if they were to run together. As she tried to move herself along as quickly as possible, she was horrified to see her seven year old grandson come back for her. He grabbed her hand tightly and pleaded, "*Sau, ta o*" ("come with me"). Realising that the young boy was not going to leave her, she stood up, held his hand tightly and tried to move quickly. When the wave reached them, the sheer force and magnitude of it caused their hands to be ripped apart. When she recovered from the force of the wave, she realised that she was no longer holding his hand and that the wave had taken him. Amidst tears she told me of how she still sees his face, feels his hand gripping hers, hears his voice firmly telling her to hurry along. And, despite her loss and grief, she decides that she owes it to him, to the strength of his love and his gesture, to keep living and to be thankful for the gift of her life.[28]

The actions of this child capture the Samoan perspective that the only way to know love is through manifest action. It is the practical manifestation of compassion that bespeaks the inner self. Love in Samoan culture is authenticated through interactions with others, including strangers. This is evident in Samoan practices of hospitality, and in the sacrificial caring demonstrated by the young boy in the story toward his grandmother.

Alofa as Gift

Internalizing *alofa* as gift does not refer to material gifts only. A person's presence at *aiga* gatherings is in itself a demonstration of *alofa* as gift. One's presence is seen as a gifting of oneself. One then naturally takes up particular roles, from performing chores to taking part in decision-making processes, or merely offering advice. This presence is both an expression of *alofa* and a crucial way of maintaining and strengthening ties with others.

This is often seen in Samoan *fa'alavelave*. *Fa'alavelave* has been described as a gifting responsibility observed during special occasions such as weddings, birthdays, church festivals, and funerals. Participants in these events offer gifts in the form of food, traditional crafts, time, and money as a demonstration of their love and respect for those for whom the event is directed. In the case of a wedding, family members rally together to help by providing food, equipment, and fine mats as a mark of respect and love for the newlyweds and their families.

Tui Atua captures the essence of this practice in his comments on Samoan funeral traditions, when he writes, "In traditional Samoan funeral culture, people present according to *si'ialofa* [literally, "presenting out of love," referenced earlier in terms of its potential for abuse]; the presentation is intended to share the burden of grief and expense."[29] This is an unconditional and sacrificial love which has affinities with New Testament depictions of *agape*, patterned after Christ's love for all of humanity, the highest of all moral norms.[30]

Summary of Samoan Core Values

Aga tausili is literally translated "best moral action." This translation alludes to the fact that there are distinctive characteristics that determine one's nobility in terms of behavior. These qualities are evident in the way individuals talk, walk, and behave—that is, how they observe the *va*. This moral nobility applies to any Samoan person, regardless of status. Participant CVG030 shared the importance of this value system in shaping her identity. This happened through the way she was socialized by her parents. Her response illustrates the core values which this socialization inculcated in her: "In my family, before I was married, my parents taught me to love, respect, be humble, serve others, and be honest. These are the same values that I use in my role as a chief's wife in my family and my relationships with people in my village and church. Because these values reflect my true self, as well as [being] a reflection of my family."

THE BLENDING OF CHRISTIAN AND SAMOAN CORE VALUES

Since the arrival of Christianity in the 1830s, the Samoan and Christian value systems have become intertwined. The Christian virtues of love, service, justice, respect, and sharing have reinforced the entrenched values that uphold the *fa'asamoa*. One example of this commonality of values can be seen in Samoans' common appeal to Jesus's dual commandment in Mt 22:37–39: "You shall love the Lord your God with all your heart, and with all your soul, and with all your mind... And a second [commandment] is like it: You shall love your neighbor as yourself." It is the fusion of the *fa'asamoa* and the gospel that collectively maintains and reinforces social capital in Samoan society. It is this interwoven fabric of gospel and culture that sustains and nurtures the Samoan people.

Through the processes of socialization, agents such as family, village, church, school, and peer groups have integrated Samoan and Christian values so that today they are inseparable. With the coming of Christianity, the Bible became a foundational guide for Samoan behavior, and the *fa'asamoa* incorporated biblical stories into its own myths and legends, enhancing proverbial wisdom sayings in a way that has strengthened both the cultural and Christian value systems.

Participant CVG029, who is the wife of a *matai* in her village, explains this synthesis of Samoan and Christian values from the perspective of the context in which she lives out her communal roles:

> As a member of the circle of *matai*'s wives, I am socialized into core values such as respect, love, sharing, helping out, and selfless service. These values are the same values I was taught by my parents and extended family, as well as the church. I use these values because they determine the kind of person I am. If I don't love, respect, help others, share and do unto others as I would like others to do unto me, I would not be satisfied with life; but, more importantly, I am not Christ-like.

Participant CVG029's comments highlight family and church as key settings for the learning and nurturing of values. If she does not practice them, not only is she denying her culture but, as she puts it, "more importantly, I am not Christ-like."

This same integration of Samoan and Christian values is reiterated by Participant GM012, a woman holding a leading position in a government department, who describes the core values on which she bases her decisions as a leader.

All the rules that guide my work are based on love. For example, if we have a case that we need to discuss in order to make a decision, we bring in the policies, but it is balanced by love. We look at the sort of implications the decisions we make have on the person discussed, on her children, on her husband, on her parents, and on her duties. So it is balanced by a decision based on love; however, sometimes we have to act out of justice. There is a lot of the Samoan culture used within our decision-making. There is a lot of respect that contributes to the flexibility in our decisions. For me, flexibility is often used. As a leader, if there is evidence that supports a decision you should make, then you don't have to [continue to] dialogue but go ahead and make the decision. Because sometimes dialogue can water down the appropriate decision. That is where you rely on God to carry out a just decision. All the values mentioned are ones on which the decisions and relationships in my kind of work are based. It's both cultural values and Christian values. That is why I believe at this time, in the lives of people in leadership, we need . . . Christian understanding to help with one's work.

Participant GM012's core values are influenced equally by her Samoan culture and her Christian faith. These two interwoven value systems inform her decision-making. The decisions she makes in her interactions with those in her government ministry uphold the importance of love and compassion in making just decisions, and while these are Samoan values, she explicitly states that "we need Christian understanding to help with one's work." Against this backdrop, we now turn to an analysis of Samoan core values from the perspectives of each of the four participant groups in this study.

VILLAGE GROUP CORE VALUES

The core values identified by each of the constituent groups in Samoan villages are summarized in table 5.1.

Values Flowing from *Alofa* (Love)

In the *aualuma* (daughters) subgroup, *alofa* was the value mentioned most often, along with words that have similar meanings, such as *fefa'asoaa'i* (sharing) and *fesoasoaniatu* (to offer help). *Fesoasoaniatu* is premised on the belief that an individual or group is moved by a sense of *alofa* to help others. These related concepts connect *alofa* to the value of *tautua* (service).

Participant CVG023, from the *aualuma* subgroup, highlighted values such as respect, honesty, and obedience as they relate to *alofa*, describing them as essential for moral action: "It is good manners—respect, honesty, obedience,

Table 5.1 Core Values of Village Group

Aualuma
tausa'afia (well-bred); *fa'aaloalo* (respect); *alofa (love)*; *amiotonu* (justice); *lotomaualalo* (humility); *fa'amaoni* (honesty); *usita'i* (obedience); *onosa'i* (patience); *fefa'asoaa'i (sharing)*; *mafuta fa'atasi* (fellowship); *tautala fa'aaloalo* (speaking politely); *fesoasoani atu* (helping out)

Faletua and Tausi
fa'amaoni (honesty); *fa'aaloalo* (respect); *alofa (love)*; *fa'amagalo (to forgive)*; *agalelei* (generosity); *lotomaualalo* (humility); *le fa'aituau* (impartiality); *mafai ona tali atu* (accountability); *tautua* (selfless service), *lelei fa'afoe* (efficiency); *fefa'asoaai* (sharing); *fesoasoani atu* (helping out)

Aumaga
fa'aaloalo (respect); *tautua* (selfless service); *fa'amaoni* (honesty); *alofa* (love); *tausi* (caring); *fefa'asoaa'i* (sharing); *fa'amagalo* (to forgive); *lotomaualalo* (humility); *fesoasoani atu* (helping out)

Matai
fa'aaloalo (respect); *tausi* (caring); *amiotonu* (justice); *tautua* (selfless service); *ola fa'aleagaga* (spirituality); *tautala i le moni* (speak the truth); *tulaga tutusa* (equality); *osiaiga* (maintaining families); *alofa (love)*; *fetufa'a'i* (sharing); *maopopo* (unity); *pulega lelei ma le manino* (transparency); *mafai ona tali atu* (accountability); *feso'otaiga lelei* (good communication), *laufofoga fiafia* (smiling face), *fefa'asoaa'i ma isi* (share with others), *fa'amaoni* (integrity)

---

especially love—that cause these [moral] actions. . . . Because these are life actions that distinguish a person from the rest of creation in terms of understanding, development and dominion over all of creation." The implication here is that one can only live a moral life by embodying these values associated with *alofa*, and that this is the way we as human beings demonstrate that we are suitable to be the guardians of the created world, as God intended.

For the *faletua ma tausi* (wives of chiefs) subgroup, *alofa* was likewise frequently mentioned, in connection with companion words such as *fefa'asoaa'i* (sharing), *fesoasoani atu* (helping), *tautua* (serving), *lefa'aituau* (impartiality), *lotomaualalo* (humility), and *agalelei* (showing kindness). Love was the unifying force for all of these participants.

Tausa'afia (Well-bred)

In Participant CVG022's narrative, she used the phrase *i luma o tagata* (literally, "in front of people") to indicate the importance of showing that one is *tausa'afia* (well-bred). The gist of her comment was that one must be acutely mindful of how one behaves in front of others, for it is in terms of one's public "face" that a Samoan is most judged. She states, "The values that I demonstrate in front of people are cheerfulness, humility, happiness and polite speaking. The reason why I use these values is to show that I am a trained person, because there is a belief that your actions determine your nobility."

The phrase *i luma o tagata* ("conscious of one's public face") is related to the practice of *fa'aaloalo* (respect). *Fa'aaloalo* takes shape in the context of face-to-face interactions. Tui Atua suggests that Samoans demonstrate a more transparent display of respect when they are face-to-face. Such communication serves the dual role of providing a medium through which *fa'aaloalo* can be shared and in which relationships are preserved.

Maintaining *va* relationships in this face-to-face manner is the prime indication that one is well-bred (*tausa'afia*). This understanding is clear in Participant CVG022's comments that it is her public display of her core values that shows that she is someone who is *tausa'afia*, who has been taught the significance of Samoan values and knows how to demonstrate them. Her use of the words *i luma*, meaning "in front," is reminiscent of Brad Shore's comment that the "front of the [Samoan] house" is associated with light and with the respectful path for acknowledging and affirming relations. The "front of the house" is a metaphor for transparency, for showing respect by meeting "in front" rather than "behind," especially when meeting with those of higher status. *Tua* or "back," in contrast, "is associated with the bush (*vao*), with a place which is away from public vision and where less dignified behavior may occur."[31]

Participant CVG026 listed a number of qualities that exemplify someone who is well-bred, and asserted that these are the foundation stones for all Samoan families who seek to have a cohesive family and to raise their children in the Christian life: "Honesty, respect, love, forgiveness, generosity, humility, and do not pay back the wrong others have done unto you. This is the true foundation for any family to grow and stay together in a Christian way of life."

In the previous quote, Participant CVG022 used the phrase *O a'u o se tagata a'oa'oina* ("I am a trained person"). She used this phrase not in the sense of being educated formally through Western-styled education, but in the sense of being well-informed and nurtured in core values. There is an inference here about the importance of such an "education" for instilling self-respect and thereby becoming well-bred. As Tui Atua writes, "It is this nurturing that provides them [children] with the moral compass to being, feeling, knowing and doing what is right."[32]

In contrast, when a Samoan shows degrading behavior, he or she is identified as *tufanua* (ill-bred), the opposite of being *tamalii* (well-bred). *Tufanua* literally means "standing on land." It implies intrusion and trespassing, standing in the wrong place by using improper manners, etiquette, protocols, and actions. *Tufanua* is the antithesis of a person who exemplifies core values in *va* relationships. Nothing is worse than being labeled *tufanua*, and most Samoans strive ceaselessly to avoid this most devastating of labels.

This striving was also described by another participant, from the *faletua ma tausi* subgroup, Participant CVG027. She spoke of the importance of working hard to demonstrate her core values in her roles as a school teacher and secretary of her church's women's fellowship: "[My core values are] honesty, impartiality, respect, accountability, service, transparency and efficiency. The reason why I use them is because the work that I do includes all these values. If they [values] are not there, then it is just a waste of time working. You must stick by the values mentioned to direct your work." To explain why she works so hard to exhibit these particular values, she told a story about her evolution as a teacher, and how her profession obligates her to behave in a well-bred manner:

> It's been twenty years since I became a teacher in primary school . . . When I was young I always wanted to become a teacher. It seems like my dream has come true. . . eh? It wasn't easy being at Teachers' College because there are times you have to go out to do training. It seems as if this was where I learnt being a teacher. But it wasn't quite the same as the qualities you learn in your family. These are the principles you use in your work. If you learn love, honesty and respect in your family, you will also try and teach the children [in school] these values. Because it is not right if you want the children to be honest, have compassion and be respectful, but the teacher becomes the role model in *not* showing respect, love and honesty. In doing my job I prepare for each day's lesson. Within those preparations is respect and honesty. Because if they are not there, then it's just a waste of time. Maybe this is why I enjoy my job, because I do it out of honesty.

A key statement here is "If they are not there [her values], then it's just a waste of time." Participant CVG027's use of the phrase "waste of time" indicates her commitment to ensure that she is a teacher who teaches not only a body of knowledge but also values. If her students do not learn to embody these values in their behavior, they will become *tufanua*—ill-bred. Participant CVG027's narrative shows her own self-awareness of how fundamental these values are in becoming a well-bred person.

Tautua Fa'amaoni (Loyal Servant)

For participants from the *aumaga* (untitled men) subgroup, the value of *fa'aaloalo* (respect) was frequently coupled with the notion of *tautua fa'amaoni* (loyal servant). Everyone from this group explained their values in terms of their roles within their *aumaga* group. For example, Participant CVG031 is a young untitled man who works as a farmer on family land. This is the way he provides for his parents and siblings. He is single and very active in village affairs, especially in his duties as a *taule'ale'a*. He described his core values as follows:

> Know how to respect others. Be a loyal servant to others, like chiefs, parents, sisters and elders. Love through caring and sharing with others. In return, others will also respect you. I believe that life is like a circle; what I do today for others, one day others will do the same to me. Performing these values identifies my role as a *taule'ale'a* and my identity as a Samoan young man.

Here Participant CVG031 touches on the reciprocity implied in the moral imperative as an untitled man to show respect by being a loyal servant ("what I do today for others, one day others will do the same to me"). He also makes reference to the significance of his *va* relations of respect with his parents, older people, *matai*, and sisters. He sees it as his responsibility to uphold these relationships in order to reflect his identity as a *taule'ale'a* who is well-bred.

In the *matai* subgroup, as expected, *tautua* defined as "loyal servant" was routinely referenced, together with related concepts such as *nofouta* (being responsible) and *osiaiga* (caring for the family). Like Participant CVG031, Participant CVG073 is a farmer. He is also a fisherman and a *matai*. He shares values in common with the *taule'ale'a*, but articulated these in terms of his role as a *matai*, one who is equally passionate about his Samoan culture and his Christian beliefs:

> The values that I think of are the customs and traditions such as respect and service, because no one becomes a chief without serving. You don't become a chief if you have not served! The reason why you become a *matai* is due to the fact that you have the ability, talents, and because the church, family and village have faith in you. These are the means of blessings for a *matai*; it is to serve the church. These values show that you are a person capable of becoming a *matai*.

Participant CVG073 reiterates the importance of being a loyal servant as the basis for becoming a *matai*—not only service to family and village, but also to the church. This confirms our earlier findings that the church has been internalized as a core institution of the *fa'asamoa*, so intertwined with Samoan culture and everyday life that there is a triad of contexts for *tautua*—family, village, church. To be a loyal servant is to serve all three.

Table 5.2 Core Values of Nongovernmental Organizations Group

pulega lelei (good governance), *fa'aletagata* (humanity), *saolotoga* (independence), *maopopoga* (unity), *aoao* (universality), *ofo* (voluntary [service]), *fa'amaoni* (honesty), *galulue fa'atasi* (team work), *fefa'asoaa'i* (sharing), *aiga* (family), *aganu'u* (culture), *tapuaiga* (religion), *faiganu'u* (community), *fa'asaoina o ola* (saving lives), *soalaupule* (dialogue), *auaunaga mo tagata* (customer service), *tapena lelei* (well-preparedness), *fa'atuatuaina* (trust), *mamalu* (dignity), *mafaufauga* (being considerate), *malamalama* (understanding), *onosai* (patience), *aufa'atasi* (cooperation), *mautinoa* (confidence), *to'afilemu* (calm), *e o latou* (belonging), *autasi* (consensus).

NGO GROUP CORE VALUES

Although the core values presented by the NGO group (see table 5.2) were those they held personally, they also clearly influenced the way they conduct themselves in the workplace.

Alofa and *Tautua*

Participant NGO010, who is the deputy CEO of an NGO, highlighted the paramount importance of the values of *alofa* (love) and *tautua* (service) in her work. These she sees as essential to both the *fa'asamoa* and the Christian faith, both of which are of great significance not only for her but also for the clients in her NGO. In her view, both *alofa* and *tautua* are essential in any attempt to make Samoa a violence-free society (the aim of her NGO). She states,

> I think the issue discussed is evident in the vision of this organization, which is leading Samoa towards [being] a violence-free society. We deal with issues of domestic violence and abuse within families. . . . When we talk about issues like these, they originate from within families. You know the foundation of Samoan families is Christianity and culture. We look at the foundation of Samoan families, and when we do our programs we look at a return to this basic foundation: a solid foundation of Christianity and Samoan culture. If we can solve and confirm these solid foundations, then we will have families free from violence and abuse. The most important value that we practice in this organization is love, as well as service. When we perform our tasks, we perform them out of love.

Honesty, Team Work, and Sharing

Another participant from the NGO group also spoke about her values in the context of the work she does. Participant NGO020 is the coordinator of a special education program. She spoke of the importance of honesty, team work, and sharing in her NGO.

> A lot of it has to do with honesty, and a lot of team work, and the value of sharing.... Because we deal a lot with children, the major understanding is that we open ourselves up for intrusion, intrusion of a lot of disabilities with a lot of love.... But born with this is compassion and passion... and that [is] especially for the children and families we deal with. In my relationship with the public, that stands as the core with the public. If we don't have that love, then I don't think it would work. We always have challenges, but I got into it because of my love for it.... I think of all the values to be integrated here, it comes down to that [love].

What is most important about Participant NGO020's statement is that the core values she most relies on in her dealings with the public through her work (honesty, team work, and sharing) are all held together by *alofa*. As she puts it, "If we don't have that love, then I don't think it would work."

CHURCH GROUP CORE VALUES

The core values articulated by the participants in the Church group are summarized in table 5.3.

An Interweaving of Values

Although *alofa* (love) was the most commonly mentioned value among Church group participants, *amiotonu* (justice) was also frequently mentioned, alongside *fa'aaloalo* (respect) and *fa'amaoni* (honesty). Participants' narratives from this group included perspectives from both the more conservative and the more liberal factions of the churches and religious groups in Samoa.

Table 5.3 Core Values of Church Group

tatalo (prayer), *fa'aolataga* (salvation), *fa'amalosiau* (empowerment), *alofa* (love), *amiotonu* (justice), *fa'aaloalo* (respect), *maopoopo* (unity), *tulaga tutusa* (equality), *saolotoga* (freedom), *aloe se mai le ava malosi ma fualaau fa'asaina* (abstinence from alcohol and drugs), *aoaiga* (chastity), *tapuaiga* (religion), *au tasi* (consensus), *fa'amaoni* (honesty), *usita'i* (obedience), *tausiga* (caring), *agalelei* (kindness), (dialogue), *tautua* (service), *lotomaualalo* (humility), *fefe'asoaa'i* (sharing), *fa'amagaloga* (forgiveness), *alofa* (compassion), *so'otaga* (relationship), *talitonu* (trust), *fa'atuatua* (faith), *fa'apaiaga* (sanctification), *papatisoga* (baptism), *taua o le Tusia Paia* (importance of the Bible)

For Participant CRG048, who belongs to a small religious group that is not mainstream, *maopopoga* (unity) and *fa'atauaina le tasi o tapuaiga* (oneness in religion) were named as important values. She articulated her values in the following way:

> Unity, justice, equality, freedom from prejudice, recognizing the oneness of religion, the oneness of humanity, the importance of education for all, spiritual solutions to economic problems, living a life based on spiritual practices and morality, abstinence from alcohol and drugs, chastity, religion as a way of life. Because these are the teachings from Bahá'u'lláh[33] (whose name means The Glory of God), and we believe that he is the Messenger of God for this age, and that he has revealed the teachings from God that humanity needs for its current stage of development.

Participant CRG048 is unique among research participants in that she belongs to the Baha'i faith. Although it is not a Christian church, it seeks to unite people of all religions. It is notable that the values she espoused are congruent with other values identified in this study, with the addition of several distinctive Baha'i values, such as reliance on "spiritual practices, abstinence from alcohol and drugs, and chastity." Although she represents a religious minority in Samoa, and in other comments expressed a sense of discrimination and defensiveness for that reason, her values nonetheless cohere with the pervasive Samoan-Christian values that characterize Samoan society.

Another in the Church group, Participant CRG009, is a leader of one of the mainline churches. He spoke of the importance of understanding that all core values are of equal standing. In his view, one is no more important than the other; they "must not contradict" because they share with each other the ultimate purpose of ensuring a public expression of theology that reflects the goodness of God and the *fa'asamoa*:

> They [values] should be at the heart of public theology. All values are interrelated. They nourish each other. Make sure they don't contradict each other. I would not place values on a scale, as if there is a time one value is useful and another is not. In order to develop a public theology that is relevant to Samoan life, we need to make sure the core values don't contradict each other.

Participant CRG009 is one of the few participants who spoke easily about public theology. This is not surprising given his level of theological training. His insistence that all Samoan-Christian values are of equal value reflects the interrelatedness that defines what it means to be Samoan.

Another Church group participant, Participant CRG045, spoke directly about *fa'aaloalo* (respect) and *soalaupule* (dialogue) as core values, but these two values were interlinked with other values. He explained *fa'aaloalo* with reference to *alofa* in particular, but also *amanaia* (acknowledgment) and *aua le vaai maualalo* (not looking down on someone):

> The word *fa'aaloalo* originates from the word *faalo*, meaning salute. The police's salute to the Head of State is an act of high respect. But it is a respect that calls for recognition and love towards the other. You should regard the other in high respect and must not look down on him or her. If you do that, then you are not doing what Jesus has asked you to do, [to do to the other] just like you want the other person to do to you. Love embraces respect. . . . Beyond respect is love.

A key point in Participant CRG045's narrative is that there can be no genuine respect if one party looks down on the other. There is a kind of relational equality implied here, even though he acknowledges the reality of hierarchy in Samoan society, as seen in his reference to the "police's salute to the Head of State." It is also noteworthy that he defines *respect* in explicitly Christian terms (it is "what Jesus has asked you to do"), and that it exists because of love. *Alofa* is what creates respect.

Participant CRG045 went on to explain that *soalaupule* is something that everyone contributes to equally; it is based on the principle that everyone involved in the dialogue has equal rights to voice their views. The value of having *tulaga tutusa* (equal rights) is that it ensures balance and fairness, which in turn safeguard harmony and peace: "Dialogue is about equality of all people, and equality of sharing in order to arrive at a good and happy ending. The root word of dialogue is *fa'asoa*, to share. Sharing between people shows the sharing of authority and power." This description by Participant CRG045 further nuances the importance of mutual respect, and situates the "equal sharing" of *soalaupule* within the frameworks of both *fa'asamoa* and Christianity.

Lotomaualalo (Humility)

Like a number of other participants, Participant CRG045 paid special attention to the value of *lotomaualalo* (humility). His identification of humility relates to a common Samoan phrase which he used in his *talanoa*, *O lalo a e saili ai malo* ("It is down below that we seek victory"). A theologically trained participant from the Church group, Participant CRG006 offered a theological perspective on the meaning of humility. Like many other participants, he drew on his own personal experience in his family to illustrate the point he was making. He came from humble beginnings, from a family with few economic resources. From this background he learned to appreciate humility as a core value:

As a young person, the core values that I use are humility and honesty, in order for me to connect with other brothers and sisters in this field. There is a reason why I use these values. Firstly, it is something I learned in my family. My family did not begin in a good way, I mean financially. It was a poor family and my parents were poor as well. But being poor did not stop my parents from putting us into school. The uttermost concern of my parents was for their children to have a good future. I have seen with my own two eyes my mother's tears [at the effects of our poverty]... . My father is not the kind of person who shows sad feelings. He tends to hide his feelings about his children. I witnessed my whole life, in the words and actions of my parents, what it is like to be humble. For example, if we are advised about our relationships with people, we often hear words like "it's good to be a coward because you get to live longer. . . . Don't act like children who are well off; don't you know we are trying to develop our poor family." The words bring out the true thoughts within our parents for us to be humble. The words also bring out the feelings of knowing how to be honest in the responsibilities we carry out for the family, in order for us to reach a good ending.

Although it may seem rather shocking that this participant's parents advised him to "be a coward," what he seems to be saying is that, despite the poverty he experienced growing up, his parents insisted that it was preferable for him and his siblings to exhibit humility than to be like those who flout their prosperity. The honesty they were taught entailed an acceptance of the reality of their situation—it was better to be honest about their poverty than to pretend they were better off than they were.

GOVERNMENT WORKERS AND POLITICIANS GROUP CORE VALUES

The underlying value system of the Government Workers and Politicians group, summarized in table 5.4, is influenced by the Samoa Public Service Values specified in Section 17 of the Public Service Act of 2004. This code

Table 5.4 Core Values of Government Workers and Politicians Group

alofa (love), *fa'aaloalo* (respect), *amiotonu* (justice), *soalaupule* (consensual dialogue), *tautua* (selfless service), *fesoasoani atu* (helping out), *fa'amaoni* (honesty), *le fa'aituau* (impartiality), *mafai ona tali atu* (accountability), *leleifa'afo*e (efficiency), *fa'amaoni* (integrity), *so'otaga lelei* (good relationships), *agava'a* (professionalism), *fa'atuatuaina* (loyalty), *le fa'aituau* (fairness), *faiga ma pulega manino* (transparency), *tuto'atasi* (self-sufficiency), *galulue fa'atasi* (cooperation), *fa'apaaga* (partnership), *fa'atalatalanoa* (being consultative), *lotomaualalo* (humility), *tulaga tutusa* (equality).

of ethics spells out the moral values that all government workers are expected to exhibit. There were overlaps between this government sector code of ethics and the values participants in this group held personally, which also have commonalities with secular values such as accountability, transparency, and good governance.

Government-Imposed Values

According to the Public Service Act, every employee, including all Heads of Departments, must uphold the following values in their work:

1. *Fa'amaoni* (Honesty) is acting honestly, being truthful and abiding by the laws of Samoa;
2. *Le Fa'aituau* (Impartiality) is providing impartial advice, acting without fear or favor and making decisions on their merits;
3. *Auaunaga* (Service) is serving the people well, through faithful service to the Government;
4. *Fa'aaloalo* (Respect) is treating the people, the Government, and colleagues with courtesy and respect;
5. *Faiga ma Pulega Manino* (Transparency) is taking actions and making decisions in an open way;
6. *Mafai ona tali atu* (Accountability) is being able to explain the reasons for actions taken and taking responsibility for those actions;
7. *Lelei fa'afoe ma le taunuuga lelei* (Efficiency and Effectiveness) is achieving good results for Samoa in an economical way.[34]

Public workers generally accept and attempt to abide by these values, including Participant GM065, who commented, "As a public servant we are obliged to [follow the] public servants' core values. The values stipulated are honesty, impartiality, service, respect, accountability, efficiency and effectiveness, so those are the core values that each employee of government is supposed to execute in normal duties every day."

However, Participant GM065 voiced a concern that such a code is not merely a guideline but is mandatory, which means that the state is imposing itself onto its workers in such a way as to dictate government workers' behavior. She implied that a kind of moral dictatorship may be imposed, and that this does not necessarily encourage workers to embrace these values based on their own sense of moral agency.

Another Government Worker participant, Participant GM064, an assistant CEO of a government ministry, reflected on the contribution of the Samoan constitution, as well as the law as set out in the Public Service Act (2004), in identifying what core values meant for him as a public servant. He saw these legally imposed values as being more foreign (Western) than distinctively

Samoan, yet he accepted that they are meant to be in the service of the common good: "In the constitution, [which guides] the public sphere, and the [guidelines in] the Public Service Act of 2004, we recognize values such as impartiality, good governance, good and solid advice; we also recognize [the promotion of] social and ethical morale, in order to provide good service to the public."

Overall, public service workers seemed to accept that there is a need for an explicit code of values at the governmental level, although there was some ambivalence about whether their imposition "from above" inculcates these values in an authentic way, and about the extent to which these are "foreign" rather than "Samoan" in the way they are framed.

Tuaoi (Boundaries)

For Participant GM005, who has held leadership positions in Samoa's parliament and also in his *aiga potopoto* (in a way that has national significance), the value of *tuaoi* (designated boundaries), which is related to self-respect, is of central importance:

> The important thing in the life of the Samoan is boundaries; one aim of the boundaries is to protect your properties . . . but the most important thing to protect is your self-respect. It is you respecting yourself. This was what I was raised on . . . my father would send me to be with the elders there. The elders get angry if you just wait for food, or admire food and properties of other families. . . . You should think of something to reciprocate what has been given.

In identifying the theme of *tuaoi*, Participant GM005 echoes the significance of the concept of *va*. *Va* relationships acknowledge the sacredness of relational boundaries that function to protect one's "right relationship" with God, family members, persons in authority, neighbors, and the whole of creation. The importance of these relational boundaries has been described in depth by Falelua Tuala, whose discussion of *tuaoi* focuses on the importance of boundaries of respect between parent and child, brother and sister, and human beings and God.[35] These boundaries provide guidance both in the cultivation of self-respect and in respect for others.

A COMMON THREAD: *ALOFA* AND THE INTERLINKING OF VALUES

The importance of the interconnectedness of all core values, mediated through the central value of *alofa*, was clear in the contributions

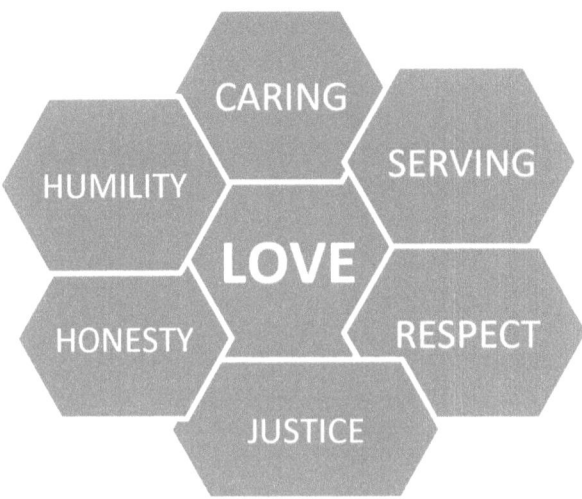

Figure 5.1 Values Flowing from *Alofa*.

of participants in all four groups. This was highlighted, for example, by Participant GM079, a political leader, who stated that in order to have respect and honesty, there must be love: "At the center of these two values [respect and honesty] is love." Although this appears to contradict the view expressed previously by Participant CRG009, who argued that all values have equal standing, the larger point made consistently by participants was that *alofa* is the lifeblood that infuses all Samoan values. This is visually depicted in figure 5.1 below.

This way of describing values is something of a deviation from the sociologist Max Scheler's view that values exist in a hierarchical order, which occurs because we prefer "one given value to another."[36] Participant GM079, like numerous other participants, saw *alofa* as being at the center of all values, as depicted in figure 5.1. Rather than ranking these values in a hierarchical order, in which one can "pick and choose" values depending on personal preference, Samoan values exist in an interconnected matrix, with *alofa* at the center and all other values both emanating from *alofa* and overlapping with each other. Samoans cannot choose one of these values and neglect the rest.

Love seeks many interrelated channels of realization. It is not surprising that a frequently quoted biblical passage in Samoa is 1 Cor 13:4–7: "Love is patient, love is kind. Love is not envious or boastful or arrogant or rude. It does not insist on its own way; it is not irritable or resentful; it does not rejoice in wrongdoing, but rejoices in the truth. It bears all things, believes all things, hopes all things, endures all things." Both in the Christian faith and in the Samoan psyche, love is the most essential characteristic of the human soul, and it has many facets and forms of expression. It is the core principle on which both the gospel and the *fa'asamoa* are founded.

INFLUENCE OF GLOBALIZATION ON SAMOAN VALUES

Our elaboration of Samoan values would not be complete without an acknowledgment of the impact that globalization is having on the Samoan value system in the contemporary era. Anthony Giddens defines *globalization* as "the intensification of worldwide social relations which link distant localities in such a way that local happenings are shaped by events occurring many miles away and vice versa."[37] More specifically, it is "the development of an increasingly integrated global economy marked by free trade, free flow of capital, and the tapping of cheaper foreign labor markets."[38] What this has meant, in practice, is that a small group of wealthy corporations and global financial institutions has come to control the world's economies, to the detriment of small, vulnerable nation-states and their resources.

A good example of the far reach of globalization is the "Great Recession" beginning in 2008 that affected many regions of the world. Although it originated in America, its devastating effects were felt across the globe. Samoa was not exempt from the effects of this global financial crisis. The decline in remittances from relatives living overseas (which in island states like Samoa is often the greatest source of GDP) is just one example of how Samoa and other Oceanian nations were negatively impacted.

A Pacific Islander who has written extensively about the impacts of globalization in Oceania is Aisake Casimira, Director of the Institute for Mission and Research at Pacific Theological College in Fiji. His social analysis makes cogent connections between the ideology and policies associated with globalization and the negative impacts experienced by the small island states in the Pacific region. These range from environmental degradation due to resource extraction by foreign corporations to the pressures exerted on developing nations to accept the "structural adjustment programs" of international financial institutions such as the International Monetary Fund and the World Bank, in order to receive loans—a trade-off that only further impoverishes these nations.[39]

Drawing on Manfred Ernst's earlier research on the interplay between globalization and Christianity in Pacific island nations,[40] Casimira issues a challenge to the churches of the region. Given the increasing devastation wrought by the onslaught of globalization in Oceania, "the churches are challenged to discover new forms and expressions of witness and service relevant to the context of Pacific peoples. The current system of neoliberal capitalism needs to be constantly and concretely analyzed, and rejected and resisted as a matter of faith."[41]

A more optimistic assessment of the impact of globalization, focusing specifically on Samoa, is Cluny and La'avasa Macpherson's *The Warm Winds of Change: Globalisation in Contemporary Samoa*. The authors make a case for Samoa's resilience in adapting to the changes wrought by globalization, stating, "Rather than depicting these changes as "loss of tradition," we have focused instead on the "dynamism" inherent in social organization. . . . We have refrained from judgments of whether change is 'good' or 'bad' for the village."[42] While Samoans' sense of agency is certainly something to be cultivated, it is important not to underestimate the almost incalculable power of those forces whose globalization agenda is undermining small nations like Samoa. In addition, public theology demands of us that we do, in fact, make judgments about whether the effects of globalization are "good" or "bad."

Participant GM005 made the observation that, although Samoans continue to treasure their foundational values, these are now constantly being undermined by Samoa's entrapment in globalization. He argued that Samoans can and must find a way to adhere to their own truth in the midst of their global interconnectedness, and in order to do that they must search for this truth through *alofa* (love) and *amiotonu* (justice):

> Samoa's indigenous reference is considered, but what Samoa must remember is that it cannot be separated from the world; we are connected and are mingling together. It [our challenge] is not only the search for wisdom but something [that can be] upheld by everyone. Because if we work to search for the truth . . . the truth is based on love and justice.

Participants in the Government Workers and Politicians group, who are perhaps more exposed to globalization because of their public roles and associations, were understandably more aware than other groups of the ways in which globalization is negatively impacting the *fa'asamoa*, particularly in terms of the erosion of the sacredness of the *matai* system. They decried the fact that formal Western education and material wealth are now often considered more important criteria for one's selection as a *matai* than *tautua*. In Samoa today, almost every person who holds a leadership position in government or educational institutions has a *matai* title. Some have not served their *aiga* and do not even have the ability to speak the formal Samoan language properly.

A Samoan public theology of values must take into account the ways in which Samoans are being influenced by the foreign value system that accompanies globalization. Globalization is not values-neutral. It emanates from the ideology of Western neoliberal capitalism that values individual effort (the "rags to riches" myth), unrestrained corporate greed, and the maximization of profit above all else. In this ideology, peoples and societies are viewed as commodities to be exploited so that their resources and labor can be used for the benefit of the few who run the corporations, financial institutions, and military-industrial complexes that control the world.

Even some forms of institutional Christianity, especially as constructed in the West, have at times unquestioningly adopted the neoliberal globalization project, investing their wealth in the very corporations and financial institutions that prop up the globalization agenda. At the same time, the influence of these so-called "established" churches of the West is declining as Christianity's center of gravity shifts to the Global South.

None of globalization's values sits well with Samoan or Oceanian values, yet Pacific Islanders are nonetheless being impacted by these foreign values, through the media they consume and the materialism they embrace. Although the impacts of globalization are not a focus of this work, it is worth noting that any public theology for Samoa must include critical awareness and critique of how Samoan-Christian values are being eroded by the values that undergird globalization.

FINAL THOUGHTS

Based on the contributions offered in this chapter, it is evident that the research participants were able to speak honestly about their core values, which were shaped, first and foremost, within the foundational settings of family, village, and church, but which were also influenced by their experiences in broader economic, professional, and political spheres. These are all settings involved in the shaping of what constitutes core values in Samoa today.

When I arrived at Participant GM078's office, I was mindful of the fact that I was meeting a highly respected person, in terms of his status in Samoan society. I knew that I should therefore greet him using the appropriate protocols of the Samoan culture and formal language. I was quite surprised by his response. His way of making me feel welcome was to ask his secretary if she could make me a cup of tea. It was a genuine sign of his hospitality and was rooted in the values he highlighted in our *talanoa*. My status as a pastor's wife had a direct impact on his approach to me. He used the term *faletua* (pastor's wife) several times in addressing me. According to Participant GM078,

> Ever since I started in the job I am in now, I remember my parents' words while working in the public service; they weren't with me when I became Minister but were with me when I was working in the public service, up to when I became CEO. . . . I adopted their basic values and I was never wrong in my attempt, and I always try [to practice these values]. Sometimes it's hard to do. Firstly, they

[my parents] wanted me to be respectful and show my respect at all times. . . . And I accepted that from the beginning. It didn't matter how great was the range of my knowledge of the subject we discussed, in my relationships with people I respected each person. And I knew the importance of this value. Secondly, [the value of] honesty [is crucial]. I am not saying I am not honest, but I try in the ways that I can to practice it. There are times that I am tempted, but I try to stick to focusing my mind and my decision on honesty. . . . If there is something hindering that, then it means it's done for a justified reason. Especially in my work, I face people every day, and what we do is offer help for the good of the public. There are times [when there are] things like money used to corrupt the person from the truth. I know there are many situations like that in my work, especially situations in the past. Because there are lots of business people with wealth. There are also many opportunities [when] they challenge your honesty. But I am satisfied and happy that I am safe from it [dishonesty]. I don't know, because God judges! We only try in the things we do. But I use this honesty [as a core value]. If you use these values, you will get back to love. Because you cannot say you are polite to a person but you don't do a loving deed for that person; that is love. Honesty is like that too. . . . The core of these two values [respect and honesty] is love. The end of all these things is the good for all people.

As with so many other research participants, at the heart of Participant GM078's cherished values of respect and honesty is *alofa*. Moreover, his discussion of core values, like so many other participants, led, implicitly or explicitly, to the essence of Samoan identity (*fa'asinomaga*). Participants in all four groups expressed themselves in strikingly similar ways in this regard. Regardless of their social location or status, their sense of identity was rooted in the same core values, if with slightly different emphases.

The underlying values of *alofa, tautua, amiotonu, fa'aaloalo, and soalaupule* have been part of Samoa's oral traditions since time immemorial, passed down from one generation to another. Over time these values have incorporated new emphases as new environments and associations have influenced Samoan life. Despite these external influences, the core values that were elaborated by participants in the four groups are indicators of how the Samoan worldview continues to be shaped by *aganu'u, agaifanua*, and *fa'akerisiano*.

NOTES

1. See, for example, Tui Atua Tupua Tamasese Efi, "*O Le E Lave I Tiga, Ole Ivi, Le Toto, Ma Le Aano:* He Who Rallies in My Hour of Need is My Kin," Paper Presented, *New Zealand Families Commission, Pasifika Families' Fono*, Wellington, NZ, November 3, 2009, 5–9; and Efi, "More on Meaning, Nuance and Metaphor."

2. Huffer and So'o, "Consensus Versus Dissent," 281–304.

3. See Frank Smith, *The Johannine Jesus from a Samoan Perspective: Toward an Intercultural Reading of the Fourth Gospel* (PhD Thesis, University of Auckland, 2010).

4. Fineaso T. S. Fa'alafi, *Carrying the Faith: Samoan Methodism, 1828–1928* (Lufilufi, WS: Piula Theological College, 2005), 127.

5. Fofo I. F. Sunia, *Lupe o le Foaga Vaega Muamua* (Tafuna, AS: Matagaluega o A'oga, 1997), 169.

6. G. B. Milner, *Samoan Dictionary: Samoan-English, English-Samoan* (Auckland: Polynesian Press, 1993).

7. See George Pratt, *Pratt's Grammar and Dictionary of the Samoan Language* (Malua, WS: Malua Printing Press, 1911).

8. See Sualii-Sauni, "Le Matuamoepo: Competing Spirits of Governing."

9. Feiloaiga Taulealeausumai, "The Word Made Flesh: A Samoan Theology of Pastoral Care," in *Counselling Issues and South Pacific Communities*, ed. Philip Culbertson (Auckland: Accent Publications, 1997), 161–88.

10. Laufai Sauoaiga, *O le Mavaega i le Tai: The Will by the Sea* (Apia, WS: Methodist Printing Press, 2000), 14.

11. Upolu Vaai, *A Theology of Giving* (BD Thesis, Piula Theological College, 2001), 4.

12. Iosefa Lefaoseu, "*Fa'aaloalo* as a Model for the Church Ministry," *Class Presentation*, Piula Theological College, November 11, 2001.

13. This sense that the act of respect will be reciprocated at some point, despite having no expectation of this happening as a direct result of one's own action, is also seen in other Oceanian cultural traditions, such as the gifting of a *tabua* (whale's tooth) in Fiji. This most sacred sign of respect in Fijian culture is given with no expectation of receiving a *tabua* in return, yet Fijians know that at some point this same sign of respect will be shown to them. If you are given a whale's tooth, you will in turn give it away at some point to someone else, and in this way the limited numbers of whales' teeth continue to circulate throughout Fiji, as they have for generations. See Steven Hooper, "'Supreme Among Our Valuables': Whale Teeth (Tabua), Chiefship and Power in Eastern Fiji," *Journal of the Polynesian Society* 122, no. 2 (June 2013): 103–60.

14. Unasa Felise Va'a, "Samoan Custom and Human Rights: An Indigenous View," *Victorian University of Wellington Law Review* 40 (2009): 245.

15. Tui Atua T. T. T. Efi, "Sufiga O Le Tuaoi: Negotiating Boundaries—from Beethoven to Tupac, the Pope to the Dalai Lama," Paper Presented, *Samoa Conference II*, National University of Samoa, Vaivase, Samoa, July 5, 2011, 5–6.

16. Ibid.

17. Ibid.

18. Ibid.

19. Cluny Macpherson and Laavasa Macpherson, "Churches and the Economy of Samoa," *The Contemporary Pacific* 23, no. 2 (2011): 308.

20. See, for example, Cluny Macpherson and Laavasa Macpherson, *The Warm Winds of Change: Globalisation in Contemporary Samoa* (Auckland: University of

Auckland Press, 2010); Cluny Macpherson and Laavasa Macpherson, "Churches and the Economy of Samoa," *The Contemporary Pacific* 23, no. 2 (2011): 304–37; Maria Kerslake, *Maloafua: Structural Adjustment Programmes—The Case of Samoa* (PhD Thesis, Massey University, 2007); Latuivai Latu, *Fetausia'i: A Servant Leadership Paradigm for the Mission of the Methodist Church in Samoa* (MTh Thesis, University of Otago, 2017); and Alec Thornton, Maria T. Kerslake, and Tony Binns, "Alienation and Obligation: Religion and Social Change in Samoa," *Asia Pacific Viewpoint* 51, no. 1 (April 2010): 1–16.

21. Pratt, *Pratt's Grammar and Dictionary of the Samoan Language*, 239.
22. Ibid., 287.
23. Ibid., 295.
24. Alexander Fala and Katie Fala, "Bio-ethics and the Samoan Indigenous Reference," in *Su'esu'e Manogi—In Search of Fragrance*, ed. I'uogafa Tuagalu, Tamasa'ilau Sualii-Sauni, Tofilau Nina Kirifi-Alai, and Naomi Fuamatu (Le Papaigalagala, WS: Centre for Samoan Studies, National University of Samoa, 2008), 354.
25. Fa'alepo A. Tuisuga, *O Le Tofa Liliu a Samoa: A Hermeneutical Critical Analysis of the Cultural-Theological Praxis of the Samoan Context* (PhD Thesis, Melbourne University of Divinity, 2011), 15.
26. Seresese Tapu Vaaimamao, *Justice and Righteousness: A Comparative Study of the Word Pair in Amos with its Application to the Life of Communalism in Samoa* (MTh thesis, University of Otago, 1998), 99.
27. Ibid., 100.
28. Efi, "*O Le E Lave I Tiga, Ole Ivi, Le Toto, Ma Le Aano.*"
29. Tui Atua T. T. T. Efi, "A Wedding, a Party and Samoan Funerals: Pacific Leadership and Cultural Competence," in *Su'esu'e Manogi: In Search of Fragrance*, ed. I'uogafa Tuagalu, Tamasa'ilau Sualii-Sauni, Tofilau Nina Kirifi-Alai, and Naomi Fuamatu (Le Papaigalagala, WS: Centre for Samoan Studies, National University of Samoa, 2009), 124.
30. See Reinhold Niebuhr's description of *agape* in *Faith and Politics*, ed. Ronald H. Stone (New York, NY: George Braziller, 1968), 84.
31. Alessandro Duranti, "Language and Bodies in Social Space: Samoan Ceremonial Greetings," *American Anthropologist, New Series* 94, no. 3 (1992): 670.
32. Efi, "*Fa'asamoa* Speaks to My Heart and My Soul," 55.
33. Bahá'u'lláh, born in Persia (present-day Iran) in the nineteenth century, founded the Baha'i faith in 1863, claiming that it was the fulfillment of Christianity, Islam and other religions. In his writings he outlined a framework for developing a united global civilization that would integrate the spiritual and material dimensions of life. See Peter Smith, *An Introduction to the Baha'i Faith* (Cambridge: Cambridge University Press, 2008).
34. Government of Samoa, *Public Service Act 2004 (No. 14)*, Section 17, accessed July 2015, https://www.mof.gov.ws/LinkClick.aspx?fileticket=XgYGI2Kivls%3D.
35. Falelua Tuala, *A Theological Reflection of Tuaoi in the Search for Peace and Harmony in the Samoan Society* (BD Thesis, Piula Theological College, 2008), 5–9.

36. Max Scheler, *Formalism in Ethics and Non-Formal Ethics of Values*, trans. Manfred Frings and Robert Funk (Evanston, IL: Northwestern University Press, 1973), 26.

37. Anthony Giddens, *The Consequences of Modernity* (Cambridge, MA: Polity Press, 1990), 64.

38. *Merriam-Webster Dictionary* (2018), s.v. "Globalization."

39. See Aisake Casimira and Anna Anisi, "An Historical Overview of Ecumenical Formation and Development," in *Navigating Troubled Waters: The Ecumenical Movement in the Pacific Islands Since the 1980s*, ed. Manfred Ernst and Lydia Johnson (Suva, FJ: Pacific Theological College, 2017), 13–50.

40. Manfred Ernst, ed., *Globalization and the Re-Shaping of Christianity in the Pacific Islands* (Suva, FJ: Pacific Theological College, 2006). See especially Ernst's "Introduction to Globalization," 40ff. There he summarizes four themes of globalization: "1. The expansive conquest of developing countries through Western neoliberal economics [that has] undermined and marginalized traditional cultures . . . ; 2. The global environmental devastation caused by climate change . . . ; 3. The internationalization of undesirable developments in the form of speculative capitalism, unemployment, feminization of poverty, [and] trafficking of people, drugs and arms; and 4. Increasing inequality and lifestyle disparities . . ." Cited in Casimira and Anisi, "An Historical Overview," 28–29.

41. Casimira and Anisi, "An Historical Overview," 30.

42. Macpherson and Macpherson, *The Warm Winds of Change*, 4.

Chapter 6

Talanoa about Public Theology

Chapter 1 introduced public theology based on literature largely from Europe and North America, with some contributions from Asia, Africa, and Oceania. The core concepts discussed in chapter 1 will be brought to bear in this chapter in conversation with insights gleaned from fieldwork, specifically the participants' narratives around the following themes: *what public theology is; the relationship between core values and public theology; the avenues for theologians to participate in public life; the training of theologians; theology's influence on public life;* and *the role of public theology in Samoa.*

TALANOA ABOUT WHAT PUBLIC THEOLOGY IS

Some of the perspectives shared by participants in this study are unlikely to align with the way public theology has been articulated in the West. The public theology that emerges from these participant narratives exhibits distinctive contextual priorities and emphases. This was something I had anticipated in pursuing a topic such as public theology in Samoa, but my expectation had to be confirmed by fieldwork, particularly in light of the dearth of literature on Samoan public theology.

Research participants' perceptions of what they understood public theology to be are a valuable repository of insights, even though they were largely unfamiliar with the term "public theology." Once it was translated into Samoan and a summary explanation given, they began to relate it to their own experience. Since the subjects of this study are "the public" in whose interests public theology exists, important knowledge can be gleaned from their experiences as Samoan citizens. Their narratives can thus reliably illustrate some of the key aspects of a public theology that is contextually relevant for Samoa.

The Importance of Christian Roots

Research participants first began to speak more easily about public theology when they made connections with the gospel and the practices of the New Testament church—with which they were very familiar, as active church members who read the Bible and hear it preached regularly. Once they traced the call for Christians to engage with the world to the New Testament, and recalled that Jesus's own ministry took place in public, public theology began to make sense.

The Book of Acts was referenced, for example, which contains many illustrations of such engagement by the early Christians in their local contexts. A theologically trained research participant recalled that the Apostle Paul demonstrated his own public witness while waiting for Silas and Timothy in Athens, citing Acts 17:16–18a: "While Paul was waiting for them in Athens, he was deeply distressed to see that the city was full of idols. So he argued in the synagogue with the Jews and the devout persons, and also in the marketplace every day with those who happened to be there. Also, some Epicurean and Stoic philosophers debated with him."

Paul based his "debating" in Athens on his convictions about God's inbreaking in the world, centered in the transformative power of God in the incarnation of Jesus. Paul was willing to enter into dialogue with whomever he encountered "in the marketplace," including Greek Epicureans and Stoics. Using rational debate, a style of communication which the Greeks valued, Paul countered their claims with Christian claims, doing so in a way that took their Athenian context seriously.

Several research participants also had no difficulty recalling that the early Christians in the Book of Acts ministered to the most vulnerable in society— the poor, the outcast, the widows, and orphans. Moreover, the early church reached beyond its Jewish roots to embrace "the other" in the form of other ethnicities broadly defined as Gentiles. In so doing, they became a multicultural church, where "Jew and Greek" were one. These early Christian communities grappled with what it meant, in their social context, that not only different ethnicities but "women and men" and "slave and free" were one in Christ (Gal 3:28). In short, Christians were not meant to be isolated from the world but were called to be an inclusive Body of Christ in the world.

By recalling the witness of the early church, then, several research participants made sense of public theology by connecting the Christian story to their own contextual realities. For example, because Participant CVG023 represented the church, he framed public theology within his biblical understanding of the church's public witness. Participant GM079 likewise asserted that because "Jesus' ministry did not take place behind closed doors" but was enacted in public, we should do the same. References to New Testament stories were scattered throughout participants' narratives. Knowledge of their Christian roots assisted them in making the leap to situating public theology in the Samoan context today.

The Importance of Relationality

Participant CVG024's hunch about what public theology might be is as follows: "Isn't it the connection between you and the other, or the way we view God's work in public?" Here public theology is envisaged as a relational concept, an understanding shaped by the participant's relational identity as Samoan and Christian. When Participant CVG075, from the Village group, began to speculate about what public theology might be, it was clear that her views were influenced by her background as a woman, a *matai*, a doctor, and a well-respected member of her church and community. Her involvement in these contexts led her to interpret the term in her own way. According to Participant CVG075,

> [Public theology] is . . . everyday theology that relates to the life of people. [It is] making a difference in people's lives, using theology as a guide. . . . It helps people to be on the right path when faced with difficulties in life. It is a type of theology that promotes good life for all people. Yes! It is the practical application [of the Gospel] to make a difference in the quality of life of the people. That is basically the core of it. . . . It is the most practical theology, if there is such a thing, because it will make a difference in order to connect sacred things to the life of the public. Public theology is very relevant and very down to earth, very relevant to the lives of people.

Participant CVG075's account identifies ordinary people as the subjects of public theology. The notion that public theology must be an "everyday theology that relates to the life of people" and "a type of theology that promotes good life for all people" resonates with the Samoan concept of the relational self, and with public theology's commitment to the common good.

The Importance of Praxis

Participant CVG025 related her sense of what public theology might be to her own experience. She is a talented woman in her late thirties, married with three children, employed as a secretary, and also a tailor. She was educated overseas, and this was evident in her knowledge of public issues, but her greatest passion is helping others in the Samoan context. Her definition of *public theology* was influenced by her faith and her activism in her community. In fact, she grounded her understanding of public theology in her community, by relating an interesting story:

> A woman in my village came to me to ask for my help in sewing her children's white clothes for White Sunday [Children's Sunday]. Apparently this woman had been to another tailor, but that tailor told her it's $30 for each outfit. This woman has seven children. When she approached me, I felt love in my heart. I had to help her. So I offered to sew her children's clothes for free, because she is poor. I didn't only sew for her but I also gave her food from my fridge. This is public theology to me. I have put my faith into practice.

Participant CVG025's narrative made it clear that her faith is centered in helping those in need. Her instinctive view of public theology as an *activity* is indeed one of the distinctive features of public theology, as it is concerned with how beliefs are put into action for the common good. Public theology for this participant meant putting her Christian faith into practice in situations of need. It is faith in action. Participant CVG025's story also highlights the problem of poverty as a critical social issue in Samoa.

From the Government Workers and Politicians group, Participant GM078 spoke of *public theology* in a similar manner, defining it as a way of doing theology that involves concrete responses to the needs of others:

> Public theology is an interpretation and giving a name to what we are doing....
> It is actually an effort, an attempt to put together the meaning of what we are doing in our daily lives and what we are supposed to be doing in our daily life to guide people [toward what is] good. Whatever we're doing, there should be principles and guidelines to act out our relationships of respect with people, in order to arrive at good decisions. What is a good decision? It's what our Lord requires us to do. We won't be able to understand good decisions if we don't follow them. Jesus came to make good what is bad. This is the guiding principle for our actions, and this is important. Public theology is what you do in the open, to others, through your values and your activities.

Participant GM078 envisioned public theology as moral actions that are a reflection of how people are meant to relate to one another, following the pattern of Jesus, who "made good what is bad." Making such relationships the foundation of public theology is viewed as a practical realization of the values Jesus exemplified in his own ministry.

The Importance of Addressing Social Problems

Participant NGO025 from the NGO group spoke of public theology as a way for Christians to engage with the public to address critical social problems. The participant is a single woman in her early thirties who is very passionate about her work. She framed public theology in the context of the work she and her colleagues do in their NGO. It was formed in 2005 through the initiative of a young female lawyer who saw the need to establish such an organization to deal with the increase in cases of rape, family violence, and other incidences of violence. The motto of this NGO is "we support, we help, we care, and we are your family." Participant NGO025 located public theology in this context:

> In terms of what we do, during our home school program, we ... talk about what love is, [about] Jesus. ... We talk about self-respect ... about patience, behavioral issues. These are not your average mainstream students. Also, within our own office we have different pastors coming in to do our cleansing during the week, where we have them come and talk to us about ... what God has given to their hearts to share with us, to keep us motivated to carry out the work that we do and to give us the Word for today, for the week. ... When we have people rush in about different things [problems], we stick to what Pastor or Father has said earlier. In dealing with the problems, we deal with them with the mind of Christ. We have to deal with them with compassion. We have to look at it from both sides, from the offender and the victim. ... That is basically the way we run [our NGO]: first is God and then everything else falls in line. ... Just as our country is founded upon God, so is [our NGO].

Participant NGO025 compared her organization's services to Jesus's own ministry, where Jesus went out and ministered to the most vulnerable in his society. Jesus's ministry was focused on the "least of these," and that is also the focus of this woman's NGO. She construed public theology through this lens, as a healing and pastoral process, in which she and her co-workers relate to the public by being interpersonally engaged with many sectors of society, including not only victims and perpetrators of violence but representatives of the churches, government, and the media.

Another participant from the NGO group, Participant NGO011, is a female CEO and also someone with theological training. She articulated public theology in the light of her theological understanding and her experience in civil society: "It [public theology] is how you see the gospel in light of the suffering and social problems that are taking place today. How do you apply it [the gospel]? How do you apply your faith, ... how do you see the ultimate good alongside what's happening today? It is putting your faith into practice." For Participant NGO011, public theology is a call to Christians to directly address issues affecting people's everyday lives and society as a whole. It is a faith response to situations of suffering in society.

Participant NGO023, like Participant NGO025 above, explained public theology in terms of the work her organization does to ease people's suffering. Her account again underlined the belief that addressing people's needs is at the very core of public theology.

> All I know is that it [public theology] has something to do with practicing your spirituality openly. For instance, in the context of [her NGO], public theology to us is explained in the work that we do to help the community, [for example] in terms of supplying blood, as well as helping any person in need... The way we interact with people in general is one way of demonstrating our public theology. [Our organization] emphasizes the importance of all of humanity, and public theology is our way of showing that emphasis.

Participant NGO023 identified public theology as a practical theology. At the core of this practical emphasis is Samoan Christians' calling to help others because we all share a common humanity.

From the Church group, Participant CRG006, who belongs to one of the smaller denominations not represented among the mainline churches, likewise presented a broad understanding of public theology as a response to the social issues that are important in Samoan society. He stated that if public theology "arises out of public issues and anything that involves the public, in a societal setting, in a larger picture, then I would assume that there is a theology there to be understood. . . . I assume that it is a theology that involves the lives, the interactions and the interrelations of society in the public view." Here public theology is a theology of connection and response. Rather than seeing public theology as emanating from scripture or the church, Participant CRG006 envisions it as arising out of social situations themselves. In this sense, his understanding is similar to liberation theology, which also finds its starting point in experience.

The Importance of Connecting the Sacred and the Secular

Some of the Church group participants brought explicitly religious insights to bear on their articulation of what public theology might be. Participant CRG048 explained public theology as "applying spiritual principles to the needs of society." Another participant from the Church group, Participant CRG003, explained public theology by defining *public* and *theology* separately, in order to arrive at his own working definition:

> My personal understanding of public theology is based on the two words, public and theology. The word public refers to something that is not private,

not isolated or contained. . . . Public is something that is open. And the other term is theology, which is the combination of two Greek words: *theos* and *logos*. *Theos* means God. And *logos* is word. Theology is a word that relates to God. So public theology in my understanding is the public word of God, or a public word for God, or about God. So anything that is proclaimed publicly about God, or God speaking publicly, or a Word from God that is not isolated is public in my understanding. For example, when . . . God speaks to us from the Bible, . . . that is public theology. [When] we have worship in church, or open prayer, in conferences or meetings, if we speak about God in the open, that is public theology.

In Participant CRG003's framing of public theology, he gave specific examples of possible contexts where Christians' professions of faith could take place "in the open," such as worship services, public prayers, or his church's annual conference. These contexts were front and center because of his own experience as a church minister, and his views reflected the ethos of his church.

TALANOA ON THE ROLE OF CORE VALUES IN PUBLIC THEOLOGY

The participants in this study overwhelmingly interpreted public theology through the lens of Samoan and Christian core values. These values were explained by the research participants in somewhat differing but compatible terms. For instance, there were those who saw public theology's task as supporting relational and natural principles which are already widely embodied in the Samoan way of life and are deemed essential if society is to be cohesive and strong. Others highlighted Samoan-Christian values as powerful forces for the common good in contrast to individualistic Western values. The mutually reinforcing contribution of core Samoan and Christian values, according to the vast majority of participants, is the foundation upon which any public theology for Samoa must be constructed. The role of these values in constructing a public theology in Samoa is summarized through representative participant narratives.

The Role of Honesty and Humility

Participant GM079 is a politician who was elected to parliament in the 2011 election. Becoming a politician was not easy as he had to face an election bribery charge, but he won because he and others believed in his honesty and innocence. Before becoming a member of parliament, he was in charge of a tertiary institution. He is a deeply religious man who is passionate about his Christian faith and grateful to his parents for the way they had raised him.

This man described public theology as the movement of Christian and Samoan values into the everyday life experience of people in society. He recognized that the church should have a public voice in matters affecting the lives of the Samoan people. Like several other participants, Participant GM079 asserted that Jesus' ministry did not take place behind closed doors, but was enacted in public. The two most important values highlighted by this participant were honesty and humility, and he argued that public theology must be grounded in these values in order to be called an authentic public theology. In Participant GM079's words, "Honesty and humility are very important in dealing with people. If the person's life is based on these values, this will also be his or her public theology."

The reason honesty and humility are a prerequisite for public theology is that they are essential in the building of "right relationships." The implication is that the function of public theology is to build right relationships, not only between individuals but in society as a whole. Voicing a similar perspective, Participant CRG060 offered the following observation:

> There is a big connection between honesty and humility and the understanding of public theology. Humility and honesty can guide people's lives in order to connect with others through love. A person who has a proud heart does not feel love for others, especially those with low standing and economic situation, unless he or she comes down to where these people are. Because this kind of person will always strive to achieve his or her own ambitious goals and does not consider the feelings of those below him or her.

A key point in this narrative is the conviction that it is the values of honesty and humility that will enable Samoans to get rid of their "proud hearts," and only then will they be free to "come down to where these people are" (the poor, those with "low standing"). It is only when one joins those of low standing that one's heart can be opened to express unconditional love, which is the calling of public theology.

The Role of Values as a "Ticket"

Participant CRG010 explained the role of core values in public theology by referring to these values as the "ticket" one uses to gain entry to the public sphere: "Values can be used in your community and outside your community. There is no difference. They are useful, workable, and applicable within your church and outside your church. They are the ticket that allows one to journey outside of where one is, where one stands." Participant CRG010 uses the imagery of the "ticket" to speak of the efficacy of Samoan-Christian core values as a means of reaching out to others. Lifting up these values will push Samoans to show concern for the injustices in society, providing a point of entrance to the door that "allows one to journey outside of where one is" toward places of need. This suggests that the role of values may be to push Samoans out of their comfort zones, in order to meet others at the point of greatest need.

TALANOA ON AVENUES FOR THEOLOGIANS TO PARTICIPATE IN PUBLIC THEOLOGY

In responding to questions about the ways in which theologians in Samoa might be able to enact a public theology, the research participants began with their own interpretations of the term "public theologian." These interpretations ranged from referring to public theologians as church ministers to anyone performing the role of Christian witness in public, though the majority saw public theology as the prime responsibility of clergy and theologically trained persons.

The research participants identified the following avenues through which persons might function as public theologians: *mass media, preaching, public forums, public awareness, education, fa'asamoa, village council meetings,* and *public policies.* These were considered to be crucial avenues through which Samoan public theologians might enter into public debates and attempt to influence public policy, or initiate other responses to social issues.

Naming these themes is an essential first step, but understanding how they function in the Samoan public sphere is the main concern of this study. Participant CRG006 described how challenging this task is in the Samoan context, where "theologians and ministers are separated from public issues," and he urged them to "go out into the streets":

> I think it is very difficult for a theologian to enter into a public debate. In the Samoan culture and the way we live, theologians and ministers are separated from public issues. I think the easier way is through the media, through the newspapers, television and other [forms of media]. There are not that many opportunities. I think it is necessary for public theologians in the church to make more of a public stand, to be heard, make rallies and actually go out into the public and raise their opinions instead of just discussing it between colleagues, which would not reach the public at every level. If public theologians want to be heard, they should go out into the streets, to the villages, and make a stand.

Mass Media

Participant CRG006's comment above is in line with the sentiments of a number of other research participants who expressed the view that making use of the media is a significant avenue through which to enact public theology in Samoa. As Participant GM054 commented,

> One way to voice the concerns [of public theology] is through the media, [for example,] in the newspapers. When issues arise, they [theologians] should make comments about them. They should not shy away or be discouraged because of nasty comments of people against their comments. I think it's naïve to think that what you say will not be responded to. Another way is the traditional way, through sermons and public devotions on the radio and TV. Theologians should be prepared to be critiqued by others. That way they will advance their message.

Participant GM054 made specific reference to newspapers and sermons or devotions on radio and television as avenues for public theology engagement. The *Samoa Observer* newspaper has a specific section for spiritual reflection in the form of sermons, but this section includes sermons prepared by only one church minister.[1] The various organs of mass media are utilized to a much greater extent by NGOs.

Participant NGO010 also made a strong case that Christian spokespersons should make use of mass media to further the causes of public theology:

> Theologians can participate in public debates through the media. They can take part in public debates on issues affecting the lives of the public. Five years ago, we as public theologians [in her NGO] started to look at new ways of engaging the public in our programs. We went out into the villages and churches to raise the awareness of the public on how people are affected by violence and abuse.

The appeal to mass media shared by these research participants mirrors the increasing significance of all forms of media in recent years around the world. There is general agreement in sociology and social theory that the function of mass media is to build, renew, and increase knowledge of one's own context and the world at large, and to convey that knowledge broadly across all sectors of the society.[2]

The sources of information available to the public have certainly exploded in recent years, with instant online access to information from around the world, and a global embrace of online "social media." Yet while the internet has democratized the sharing of public information, its platforms for information-sharing and self-expression have come with their own perils.[3] Samoa has jumped on the social media bandwagon in recent years, but it is not yet clear how the internet might be a viable platform for public theology.

What is clear is that, in this study, there was broad consensus among research participants concerning the importance of mass media as an avenue for advancing the agendas of public theology. Of all the avenues identified, mass media was by far the most frequently mentioned, and observations about the use of media were strikingly similar among representatives of all four groups.

Yet this desire for public theologians to engage in public theology through the media is far from the current reality in Samoa, as theologians and clergy seldom use the media to advance social causes. Some churches have policies that forbid their ministers to participate in public debates or even to express views on social issues in public. Some villages also have rules that forbid their people to discuss certain issues in public. The likely punishment for breaking such rules is banishment from the village.

Moreover, the media is not always an effective mouthpiece for public theologians, as media outlets are sometimes controlled by the government. In Samoa the television service was until recently owned by the state, and as a result the government had the sole right to dictate what was screened on air. This meant that all programs had to be in line with the policies of the government. Today, however, with the media becoming more privatized, there are fewer restrictions on media access, and this may open up new possibilities for theologians wishing to engage in public theology.

Preaching

Samoans are accustomed to pastors preaching on the radio or on television, as well as in churches. Yet Participant CRG003 critiques their ineffective use of this platform:

> The only way that I know that Samoan theologians can participate in public theology is through the pulpit. We are so silent about public issues—for example, the land issue, the casino issue. It's true that there is the National Council of Churches, but the establishment of the casino has already been passed. But the voice of the church is not strong. There are not many avenues in which the church can participate in public theology.

This is a pessimistic assessment of the clergy's willingness to use preaching to address social issues. They are perceived to be "so silent" and to have a voice that is "not strong." Participant CRG003 represents the Church group, yet has little faith in its leaders' commitment to use the one platform that is respected and recognized throughout Samoa—the pulpit—to speak into the public square.

One participant expressed the view that since public theologians by definition must be clergy, they should *only* address social issues from the pulpit, avoiding other public platforms. However, only a few participants from the Church group and the Government Workers and Politicians group supported this idea. Participants in the Village group were less likely to agree with restricting preachers in this way, except for Participant CVG035, an untitled man. Although he did not specifically mention preaching, he was clear in his minority-of-one opinion that ministers should stay out of public witness altogether: "I don't think theologians should participate in public theology. They should concentrate on the Bible and looking after the parish. If they want to participate in public debates on public issues, then they should leave the church and become a politician."

This restriction disregards the public relevance of theology and the inherently public nature of theology. If theology is to have any bearing on the common good, any notion of containing it within the church walls must be discarded, and this was the view of the vast majority of research participants. They were broadly in agreement that theology must be publicly accessible and publicly relevant. Most participants felt that social issues affecting the well-being of society should be addressed by clergy. This can certainly take place through preaching in the pulpit, but the church's proclamation of Good News for the world must also be heard beyond the church walls.

Public Forums

In Samoa today, clergy are often at least nominally represented in public forums, since the church occupies a pivotal place in Samoan culture. The problem is not that there is a lack of formal representation by clergy in such public consultations, but that their presence is over-spiritualized, typically restricted to offering public prayers or devotions. Indeed, the mention of public forums as an avenue for public theology in all four participant groups typically entailed a critique of the current situation.

It was lamented, first, that the majority of the public are left out of public discourse, with only a very select few engaging in public forums. Public forums are mostly attended and dominated by those with status, power, prestige, and higher education. Second, several participants argued that the fact that theologians or clergy may be invited to such forums does not mean that they offer much to the discussion. This was noted by Participant GM079: "There are lots of opportunities given to theologians and churches to participate in the discussion of public issues. Whenever there's a new policy there is an opportunity given to the public, meaning the church and any concerned citizens, to voice their opinions. Yet I've been to a number of public discussions and the church ministers do not say anything."

This was a common complaint—that Samoan theologians and clergy all too often "do not say anything" or make superficial comments when attending public forums. This silence could be interpreted as a sign of their being supportive of the status quo, or not understanding the matter under discussion, or being silenced by the restrictions of their churches.

Education

A few participants, from the Village and NGO groups, named education as an avenue through which theologians could engage in public theology, while the Church and Government Workers and Politicians groups made no mention of this avenue at all. This general lack of support for the efficacy of education, according to the participants who did mention it, is related to widespread public condemnation of the current state of education in Samoa. This came to a head around the issue of school violence occurring in Apia. As a result of one of these incidents, a nineteen-year-old student who attended the senior college of one of the mainline churches was charged with murder.[4]

Such incidents require critical reflection on what is wrong with education in Samoa today.[5] Tofilau Ivara, in a letter to the *Samoa Observer* newspaper, located the root cause of the problem within the school environment itself. If schools are the cause of the problem, then a critical review of the causes of their shortcomings is required. There appears to be widespread agreement that schools are failing in the practical application of Samoan and Christian values that promote peace, love, and respect for others. Dialogue among all stakeholders in education about this problem could itself be a practice of public theology, and should include representatives of the churches.

It is also important to note that public theologians can engage in educational activities beyond the confines of formal education—in much the same way that Freire envisioned conscientization as an ongoing dialogue between teachers and learners in a variety of informal settings. Chapter 8 will suggest several ways in which this kind of dialogue might be encouraged by those in leadership in the churches, with particular reference to the problem of domestic violence.

Public Awareness

Research participants from the Village, Church, and NGO groups identified the promotion of public awareness as an avenue through which public theologians might enact public theology. Interestingly, public awareness was not mentioned by the Government Workers and Politicians group, even though their work in the public sphere would benefit from greater public awareness. According to participants from the Village group, public awareness is important in empowering people and enhancing the public's knowledge about their political, social, and economic situations, with the aim of finding solutions to social problems.

Participant NGO011 gave an account of her NGO's current public awareness initiative to inform the Samoan public about the social and political realities in Samoa, and the reasons this is so important: "There is not enough information given to people, and therefore they are not able to weigh the pros and cons [of particular social issues]. I want to tell the people that they have the power." By raising public awareness, knowledge is planted in people's minds. This, in turn, empowers them to make decisions for themselves and to participate with greater confidence in public discourse and action.

It is also interesting that both the Church and NGO groups displayed the same concern for raising public awareness, despite the differences in their settings. Raising public awareness does not generally happen within the churches, but is instead most often witnessed in the work of NGOs. The NGO011 organization has as one of its major priorities informing the public about pressing social issues.

Another NGO, *O Le Siosiomaga* (OLSSI), raises awareness about environmental concerns, which are often neglected in the wider public sphere. OLSSI promotes balance and harmony in creation, monitors the state of the environment in Samoa, disseminates information so as to create public awareness, and promulgates sound principles and practices for the purpose of promoting conservation and sustainability. Because this organization's work is grounded in Christian and Samoan values, it may be seen as a practice of public theology. Yet theologians and church ministers are largely absent from this important public awareness work. They need to learn from the philosophies and practices of such NGOs.

Fa'asamoa

Given its centrality in Samoan life, it is not surprising that many research participants referenced *fa'asamoa* as an avenue through which theologians can enact public theology. In the Village group, participants spoke of *fa'asamoa* as a potent pathway for the enactment of public theology. Participant CVG031 maintained that, in order for clergy or theologically trained persons to enact public theology, they must always take into account the importance of the *fa'asamoa*.

> [The public theologian] should feel the essence of our *fa'aaloalo* as a unique aspect of our daily living before making any judgments. Must spend more time

in the society or experience the community setting in the villages and make comparisons to urban community settings. Should have a sound knowledge of our *fa'asamoa*, language and work. Never assume any points of view without consulting with others. Must share ideas with others before entering public debates.

This comment prioritizes the cultural identity and social location of the theologian. One must fully understand one's culture in order to participate in public theology, and this necessitates having a real presence in whatever setting is at stake, understanding the values that underpin *fa'asamoa*, and practicing *soalaupule* ("never assume any points of view without consulting with others").

An NGO participant, who is involved in both NGO programs and ecumenical programs, spoke of the importance of public theologians explicitly connecting the *fa'asamoa* to theological concerns as they speak into the public square: "There are many ways by which our local theologians can do this [enact public theology]. For example, if they want to know more about the public . . . , they must consider our own Samoan cultural values in relationship to God. How do Samoans understand God? What is God to Samoans? How does culture value God?"

Participant NGO017's statement reinforces, again, the close relation between the Samoan culture and the Christian gospel, and the need to have a deep understanding of that connection in order to do public theology effectively. This is one of the few participants to ask such explicitly theological questions—the implication being that Samoans' perceptions of how God relates to the world are relevant to the social issues being addressed by public theologians.

Village Council Meetings

As noted earlier, in the *fono* (village council) the *matai* sit together and make decisions concerning affairs of the village. The *fono* is the sole source of legitimate political authority within the *nu'u*. The way Samoans conduct their lives is directly influenced by the way the *fono* perceives their behaviors. Some research participants identified village council meetings as an avenue through which theologians might participate in public theology, but only in the Village group. This is not surprising considering that the *fono's* oversight is front and center in their everyday lives. The other three groups did not appear to have considered the village council as a likely setting for the enactment of public theology, perhaps because the *fono* is a closed group comprising only chiefs, mostly male.

Despite this drawback, there should ideally be a space for public theologians in village council meetings, so that they can offer theological contributions in relation to issues of public concern. Realistically, however, allowing those who are most likely to be considered public theologians (clergy) access to village councils would be a direct challenge to the commonly held notion that "men of God" should limit their ministries to spiritual concerns and not venture into the political realm. (This is an ironic prohibition, of course, since village and national political leaders exert so much influence in the church.)

The reality is that, in the prevailing protocol, pastors and *matai* each have their own domains, and although pastors may at times intervene in village crises, village councils are restricted to *matai* and not open to other voices. They are not considered to be a venue for hearing the voices of "the public," especially women, youth, and children, who are silent or absent in most public discussions.

At the same time, pastors can work together with experts to facilitate informed sharing on selected public issues at the village level. This is a role that is urgently required, in the view of Participant CVG074:

> It should be allowed within the state or within the village to have this voice [of public theologians] as a [form of] advice. Ah! If they [theologians] know of any public gatherings happening, they should attend and offer their advice. Because their advice and participation is regarded as the will of God that must be done. The voice and contribution of theologians should be regarded as the missing voice that should be included in the discussion of every public issue.

Participant CVG074 is a chief who does not participate in his village *fono* because he believes there is a great deal of injustice and corruption in his village. Nonetheless, he appeals to *matai* as persons who should be enacting public theology at the village council level:

> Within the village, the *matai* should rely on God's guidance. He should not rely on his knowledge. Because in most of the villages, there is a lot of injustice. So the *matai* has to rely on God for courage to speak out against the injustice he sees, because it is not God's will. He should speak the truth regardless of the consequences. The role of the *matai* in a village is to speak the truth and to do justice.

Participant CVG074's call for *matai* themselves to act as public theologians reflects his passion for God, truth, and justice. (This is clearly shown in his repeated use of these three words.) The failure of some *matai* to live out their own core values should provoke other *matai* to play a public theology role in village council meetings. There are, of course, dire consequences that *matai* could face for acts of dissent, including banishment.

This highlights the risk entailed in bringing a public theology voice to bear in the village context. Even when injustices or abuses of power occur in the *fono*, its decisions remain final and unquestioned, and typically pastors do not challenge them. However, as noted previously, pastors have occasionally been known to intercede to save victims from banishment. Such rare interventions are acts of public theology, but they are a reminder that being a public theologian in the Samoan village setting may involve risks and sacrifices.

Participant CRG010 identified the village, community groups, the circle of chiefs, the church, and governmental and nongovernmental organizations as some of the avenues he believes theologians should work through in order to enact public theology at the village level. This made sense to him because these are existing structures, often functioning in cooperation with each other already: "The village and its various spheres, like the *matai*, the church, the government, and organizations have a significant contribution [to make]. The theologian can connect with these spheres in order to understand the issues affecting the lives of the general public."

Public Policy

Although only a small number of participants named public policy advocacy as an avenue for public theology enactment, this does not diminish its importance as a path theologians might take to engage in public theology. Public policy was only mentioned by participants in the Government Workers and Politicians group. Participant GM013 made the following comment:

> I think there are so many ways [theologians can be involved in public policy]. They can debate issues in terms of new legislation, they have an avenue through the submission of public submissions to provide their views on issues. [Regarding] how church leaders [responded] in the context of the casino issue, they made their submissions to the select committee reviewing the laws.

There are several crucial points which should be highlighted in relation to public policy. First, there is a general lack of awareness among the Samoan public about public policies that have a direct or indirect bearing on their well-being. Second, there is a lack of transparency on the part of the government in publicizing policies for the general awareness of the Samoan public. Third, and perhaps most importantly, there is a relationship waiting to be initiated and encouraged between church and state. Rather than the state assuming the sole prerogative to determine public policies, church and state in Samoa need to work together for the common good.

Some Government Workers would welcome greater participation from representatives of the churches in the development and implementation of public policy. In Participant GM085's view,

> This is a very important factor, because our role is to prepare guidelines for the development of Samoa. These guidelines are discussed with the public, and the other group whose opinions we seek is the church. We ask for their contribution to the issues that we are working on, because we believe that the church or the gospel has a lot to offer in reducing the problems faced by people in Samoa. So this is why it is important, because this is the channel through which we will get the input of public theologians about the issues. This will help us in developing guidelines for the good welfare of the people.

Participant GM085 seems to be almost pleading for what she calls the churches' "contribution to the issues we are working on." Because of the churches' assumed Christian concern for the well-being of all, the implication is that Samoan public theologians have no alternative but to respond to public policy issues. They must have the audacity to address the government where necessary, and to articulate people's plight at the stage of public policy development.

In so doing, public theologians must not simply call on the government and wait for the government to act; they must also be involved proactively in the process of policy-making. Samoan public theologians must push the government to ensure that all citizens can live in safety, security, and justice. This includes protecting the interests of the least advantaged citizens and ensuring that everyone has a permanent stake in their society.[6]

This engagement in the process of creating just public policies is already visible in the work of NGOs, an example being NGO011, which makes important and critical contributions to government policy submissions as a matter of course. Yet this NGO's "out front" approach has made it very unpopular with the current government. As a result, NGO011 received an eviction letter from the prime minister, ordering it to vacate the government land where its office was based. This came about as a result of the appearance of the CEO of NGO011 on the Campbell Live television news program in New Zealand, where she commented on the misuse of the 2009 tsunami recovery funds and the prime minister's autocratic leadership style. She stated publicly, "He's [the prime minister] a dictator and a one-man party state." The dire consequences of her speaking out show the risks entailed in speaking truth to power.

Christians' calling to address the needs of everyone, especially the most vulnerable and disadvantaged, clearly includes public policies. Moltmann's challenge to Christians to embody Christ's Kingdom in the world means that the marginalized in society become the center of our attention, because the Kingdom of God is for them. This vision of social justice can be a source of empowerment for public theologians as they fight against unjust social structures and policies.

TALANOA ON THE TRAINING OF THEOLOGIANS

It was apparent from *talanoa* responses that most participants viewed theological education through their observations of the graduates of theological schools (the clergy). In Samoa, theological training takes place almost exclusively within the confines of denominational theological schools. These theological institutions have strict rules and regulations that guide the behavior of their students. The teaching staff (mostly clergy) are governed by the policies of their churches.

There are currently six established theological institutions in Samoa: Malua Theological College (Congregational), Piula Theological College (Methodist), Moamoa Theological College (Roman Catholic), South Pacific Nazarene Theological School (Nazarene), and the non-denominational Congregational Church of Jesus Theological School and Rhema Bible Training Centre. While the first five training institutions admit only candidates who will go on to become church ministers or catechists in their denominations, the Rhema Bible Training Centre is open to anyone who feels called to study the Word of God; this makes it the most popular theological institution, because it is open to women and laity.

The responses provided by research participants reflect what they think theological training should be, as well as their firsthand experience of church ministers who have graduated from theological institutions. Their assessment of theological training is summarized in terms of three themes they highlighted in their responses: *conservatism, gender inequality,* and *authoritarianism.*

The Problem of Conservatism

Conservatism is defined as "a general preference for the existing order of society, and an opposition to efforts to bring about sharp change."[7] The excerpts below, from members of all four participant groups, identify the theme of conservatism as one of their main concerns in relation to theological training. Participant CVG076, from the Village group, underlines this concern:

> All I know is that it [theological training] is geared towards producing future ministers, but I think the training needs to change in order to conform to the

changes in society today. Some theological schools are still *very conservative!*[8] And as a result they produce conservative ministers who are *not flexible* in their ministry but only believe that what they say is divinely given by God, and it should be the only way!

Participant CVG076 expressed strong views about the effects that conservatism has on current and prospective church ministers. One of these effects is a lack of flexibility among ministers, a characteristic that has contributed to some of the problems facing churches in Samoa today. Clergy take for granted their high status as ministers and the respect bestowed upon them by the public. They therefore see no reason to dialogue with parishioners or even to listen to their pleas.

Participant NGO015 underscored several points related to the problem of conservatism in theological training. For example, conservatism is considered the norm in the various denominational settings. Those who pursue theological training within the denominational system are locked up in that system. They have no freedom to do what they believe is just, as they are accountable to the institutional authority that has been legitimated by church structures, exemplified by the church hierarchy. Consequently, there is a lack of vision and openness, as noted in the narratives below. Participant NGO015 made the following observation:

> People who are trained in theology understand it very well, but it is very difficult to connect it to the everyday life because it is like a job: if you don't do it, you don't get paid, but if you do it differently from the normal way then you can be questioned by your [church] authority. . . . People taught in theology know exactly what they should do, but they are accountable to higher authorities, especially the constitution and standard protocols of the church. They *have to be careful about what they do.* Their imparted knowledge depends on the status quo of the church! . . . The training of public theologians has not changed at all. Because *there is no future vision!*

In examining Participant NGO015's account, the problem of inflexibility is clear. Flexibility is important because it gives people the space to reflect and act on issues as they arise, whether in the family, church, village, or nation. This is related to another significant concept expressed by Participant NGO015, namely *tofamamao*, or "long-term vision based on wisdom and knowledge." It is also associated with *tofaloloto*, which is "knowledge and wisdom that has critical depth."[9] Participant NGO015 was concerned about the lack of *tofamamao* among those involved in theological training.

Participant GM013 had the following to say about the state of theological training in Samoa:

My understanding of it [theological training] is that this is the *theological orientation from the past*, and it is still being done today. . . . The reality is that the church is *very behind in its development*, because [the view is that] the beliefs that our ancestors held should still be continued for us today. You know, the world continues to evolve, our culture continues to evolve because if it doesn't it is not culture at all. And so we also need to adapt to change [with the] times. When we adapt, we adapt by way of learning, by way of how we approach issues and challenges in life. And I think in our world, where life is not easy and things are difficult, where times are not the same [as they once were], we need to be resilient, we need to build resilience so that both women and men . . . are the same. We need to adapt to the changing times.

Based on her observations of those who have received theological training in Samoa, Participant GM013 concluded that such training is outdated, as evident in the conservative attitudes within the churches. She thus posed a challenge to the church to be more flexible in order to have relevance in the face of social changes and stresses.

The Problem of Gender Inequality

Another interesting critique of theological training raised by some research participants relates to the lack of gender equality in the churches. As noted previously, women are not allowed to become candidates for ministry in the theological colleges. As seen in the comments above, Participant GM013 fervently called for theological institutions and the churches they represent to uphold the equality between men and women, as they are both created in the image of God.

However, because of the conservative beliefs that govern church policies and general cultural thinking, the churches' traditionalist attitudes on gender persist, marginalizing women in terms of theological education and ministry. Gender inequality prevails in church thinking due to the theology that is preached by ministers, who are echoing what they themselves were taught during their theological training.

This concern was raised by Participant NGO070 and Participant GM079. Participant NGO070 made this comment: "I believe that the [theological] training is still the same [as it always has been]. However, I think it needs to accommodate the needs of both men and women. I have witnessed that . . . the primary focus of theological training is men. And *women are seen as shadows of men*." Participant GM079 reinforced this view, stating with great passion, "And another thing is that it's about time we have some women ministers! I don't know why it [the church] is *slow to admit women into the ordained ministry*, but I think *they should be included*! All I want to see in the graduates is to be humble in their calling!"

Participants NGO070 and GM079 were unafraid to touch on this most sensitive issue in the life of the Samoan churches. Women typically make up around 60 percent of the active membership of many congregations. Yet their dedication and service as the "backbone" of the churches is not enough to grant them their God-given place in the ministry of the church simply because Samoan churches continue to operate on the basis of the biblical and cultural ideology of patriarchy.[10]

Clear evidence of this is illustrated in the following conversation recorded by a Samoan woman who was ordained to ministry in New Zealand, after which she visited a church in Samoa. It begins with the words of the minister:

"Excuse me, you are sitting in my place. This is the
place set aside for ministers only."
"What made you think I am not a minister?"
"Because you are a woman, dear. You will never be a minister, you will
fall in love and follow your husband. The church structure will not
allow it. You are a woman and you are young. You cannot make a final
decision for a parish like ours. We want a man to be our minister. A
man is stronger. We are comfortable with a man. You are destructive to
the church and too radical. There is no need for you to study theology
because your husband is the only one who can minister. There is no need
for you to be forward about women's leadership in the church."[11]

This conversation illustrates the attitudes that have been internalized by most Samoans. These attitudes have, over time, become norms that control church structures and teachings. Such views hinder the recognition and utilization of women's God-given gifts. Those research participants who called for women to be included in theological education and ministry highlighted the need to learn about the societal and church structures that restrict women, to understand how they have come about, and how to take steps to be in solidarity with those who are working for change.[12] Thankfully there is a growing awareness, as evidenced by the research findings of this study, that women's voices are essential for the viability of a Samoan public theology.

The Problem of Authoritarianism

Speaking more broadly about the rules-bound nature of theological education in Samoa, Participant CRG010 shared from his experience as a former seminary theology lecturer:

> There is little change. The training is mostly branching towards the *old system of doing theology*. There is a culture that should be changed, because it is a

hindrance in the shift from traditional to public theology. For example, [consider] the relationship of respect. If it is used appropriately it is good. But if not, then it has a damaging effect; that is where theology is locked up. Even when knowing the truth, because of the relationship of respect, justice is ignored. . . . This means *nobody is allowed to question* a decision made by church authorities. Everything runs smoothly if *it's just yes and no*. Do not question anything. Our system should be revived. I marked a thesis on spirituality that recommended the usage of John Wesley's model for [the participant's church]. It is good but very hard. We should explain the theology. Another door is through our preaching; believe me . . . , 90% of our preaching is theological and there is less practical understanding. The pastors cannot redefine their theology in order to apply it to everyday life. Theology must be applied to the grassroots level. . . . We need to work on ways to simplify the theology for the public. *Theology needs to touch the ground.*

Several key concerns are identified in Participant CRG010's narrative. For example, he reveals the misuse of the relationship of respect, whereby *fa'aaloalo* in the church is conceived vertically, in that seminarians and parishioners must pay respect to church authorities but not the other way round. This relational imbalance challenges us to recall Tui Atua's depiction of *fa'aaloalo* as *alo mai* and *alo atu,* which connotes the reciprocity of "face meeting face." If this does not happen, the basis of a mutually respectful relationship disappears and *fa'aaloalo* is no longer there, only *tufanua* (being ill-bred).

Participant CRG010 described how this system is self-perpetuating, because those who are theologically trained themselves become authoritarian when they achieve status and power. As seminary students and junior ministers, "nobody is allowed to question a decision made by church authorities. Everything runs smoothly if it's just yes and no. Do not question anything." When they gain seniority, they turn the tables.

Participant CVG074 reflected on the attitudes of these ministers: "Some ministers tend to think that because they are ministers, therefore people should obey their instructions. They seem to be using the wrong approach, *a very authoritarian approach.* I believe that public theologians and the public should work together." Here Participant CVG074 identifies one of the most serious shortcomings in the Samoan churches today. Because of their high status and authority in society, many church ministers have become distant from the realities in which the poor and the marginalized live. Their attitudes and actions justify some of the criticism against church ministers as not having humility and respect for others but as thinking only of themselves. This separation is an obvious impediment to the doing of public theology.

Based on these observations by research participants and my own observations as an insider researcher, it is clear that the actions and attitudes displayed by church ministers are the fruits of how they were trained in their theological colleges, as well as their own socialization within their families and villages. Unless theological training is critically reviewed so as to better reflect Samoan and Christian core values, authoritarian attitudes and behaviors will continue to have a negative impact on the churches and public life in Samoa.

TALANOA ON THE ROLE OF PUBLIC THEOLOGY

In their reflections on the role of public theology in Samoa, research participants highlighted several themes that arise from their own experiences: *embodying the value system*, *providing solutions to problems*, and *connecting the religious and secular spheres*.

Embodying the Value System

One of the most obvious themes on the role of public theology in public life, a theme that dominated the contributions of the research participants, was the continual referencing of Samoan and Christian values. This bolstered our separate findings that the Samoan value system, in its ideal form, has many parallels with the core values of the Christian faith, and should be the bedrock of public theology. Several research participants expressly described these underlying values as fundamental to the well-being of Samoan society:

Participant CVG028 stated, "I think the role of theology, to my understanding, is to contribute and maintain the value system of Samoa as reflected in its motto, 'Samoa is founded in God.' If we maintain this, then we become a good society and we nurture good people and good generations in the future." Participant CVG029 made a similar comment: "Public theology will reinforce the value system, which is lacking with the public [today]. It reminds people that God is a public God, and created everything to be good and people according to God's good image."

Participant GM012 further elaborated on the role of public theology in relation to Samoa's core values: "It [public theology] perpetuates the values, . . . the teachings, and the application of all the values. And the other role of public theology is to push people to know that, whatever they do, there are principles and values they have to consider first of all. [They must ask] if these values are wrapped in their actions, whether their actions reflect these values and principles . . . and also [whether our values] enhance love among people!"

Several themes are noteworthy in these comments. First, if Samoans embody their core values, then "we become a good society" which lives up to its national motto of being "founded in God." Second, living out our values will remind Samoans that "God is a public God," whose compassionate love for all we should emulate; after all, we are made in God's "good image." Third, public theology "pushes" Samoans to "wrap up" their values in their actions in a way that will "enhance love among all people." This is a call to embody *aga tausili* through our actions.

Providing Solutions to Problems

Research participants frequently stressed that public theology should provide practical solutions to social problems. With the increase of such problems in Samoan society, especially under the influence of globalization, concern is mounting regarding finding ways to deal with social ills such as the increase in poverty, crime, and violence.

Interestingly, a large number of female participants, particularly in the Village group, saw public theology as an attempt to find practical solutions to specific problems, as a practical theology that "helps [people] to be on the right path when faced with difficulties in life." This sentiment was echoed in the statements of Participant CVG021, a housewife who described the role of public theology as enabling those facing difficulties to cope. She related a story of violence against women and identified it as one of the issues that public theology might be able to address in her own village. She states, "If there are such problems in my family, that is where the role of public theology is helpful. It brings peace in my family."

This view was supported by Participant NGO010, speaking from the perspective of her NGO. As it responds to the social problem of violence, especially domestic violence, it does public theology by relying on the "solid foundation of Christianity and Samoan culture. If we can . . . confirm these solid foundations, then we will have families free from violence and abuse. The most important value that we practice in this organization is love, as well as service. When we perform our tasks, we perform them out of love."

This narrative is a microcosm of what a values-centered, problem-solving public theology might look like in the Samoan context. Participant NGO010's organization addresses a specific social problem—family violence and abuse—and attempts to provide solutions to this problem by applying the values that flow from the "solid foundation of Christianity and Samoan culture" to tangible responses to the social problem of violence. She ends by affirming that "the most important value . . . is love."

Connecting Church and Society

A number of participants characterized the role of public theology as providing a link between church and society. Participant CVG075 of the Village group shared the following observation:

> Today there is a big gap between the clergy and the secular [arena], but public theology can become the link [between the two]. It also helps to inform people about public issues affecting their lives. It promotes understanding among Samoan people. One friend of mine said that if you want to make a difference in your religious life, you should hold the Bible in one hand and your newspaper in the other, [so that you can know] what's happening in your country, what is really affecting the poor and vulnerable in your community. I strongly believe that public theology will make a difference, but it will take time and a lot of work and hope in God's spirit, considering the conservative culture existing in the CRG [the Church to which Participant CVG75 belongs, one of the mainline churches in Samoa].

Participant CVG075 acknowledged that there is presently a "big gap" between the religious and the secular in Samoa, but suggested that public theology could be the "link" that connects these two spheres. One way for this connection to occur is through public theologians making people more aware of the "public issues affecting their lives." Implicit in this remark is the belief that people will listen to public theologians because (as she seems to assume they will be clergy) they are already highly respected and will thus have the ear of the people. Yet she acknowledges that this may still not be easy, because of the "conservative culture" in her church.

Participant CRG010, a liberal-minded pastor and theologian, used an interesting image to connect the religious and the secular: "Public theology will be able to unite the political, cultural, the religious spheres. It can be the belt that fastens everyone together." The assertion that public theology should be the "belt" that binds people together across religious and secular spheres implies that this binding together will force us to interact with people we may not otherwise listen to. Such encounters recognize and lift up the often unheard voices of the marginalized. In Samoa, as Participant CVG075 pointed out above, this would mean recognizing and embracing the poor and the vulnerable in society. Participant NGO017 used a similar image, describing public theology as a "binder that can bind the hearts of all Samoans into unity."

TALANOA ON ENACTING THEOLOGY IN PUBLIC LIFE

The findings of our research reveal a conviction that theology should have a discernible influence on public life. This is an essential component of theologizing if Christians are to participate in God's mission of abundant life for all. We saw this claim first in our review of key public theologians, where Moltmann described public theology as "being involved in the public affairs of society," and Forrester insisted that public theology entails contributing to "public discussion" that leads to action for the common good. Research participants highlighted several central themes related to ways that public theology can influence public life in Samoa: through *enacting core values, communicating values effectively, enactment by the laity,* and *enactment by the clergy.*

Enacting Core Values

Samoan core values were perceived by the vast majority of participants in this study as ideally having a crucial influence on public life. This theme was highlighted explicitly in all four groups, although their foci varied according to their respective groups. Research participants typically appealed to specific values, such as love, service, respect, peace, humility, or honesty, which they believed should be brought to bear on specific needs in public life. Participant NGO011 states that

> if [public theology is] based on values such as love and honesty, I believe there will be a big change in our common life. When I look at Japan, they have a lot of trust in each other. In a store they only have one person to look after the shop, because they have the understanding and trust in people who come to the shop. And they believe that everyone will come through the till to pay. It's not like Samoa, where we have three or four people to look after the shop [to guard it] from thieves. If everybody has these values [of love and honesty], it will also be reflected in public life.

Participant NGO011 brings into her narrative her understanding of the reality of the Samoan social context. She speaks as a Samoan and a Christian, and believes these interwoven value systems must be manifested in behaviors that are demonstrated in the public sphere; if not, then they are not values at all. She implies in her story that if the core values of love and honesty were being actualized as they should, there would be no fear of criminal activity and lack of public safety in Samoa today.

Research participants were drawn to their core values as the platform from which to influence public life because these values are internalized as the embodiment of Samoan identity. If these values are at the heart of what it means to be Samoan, then of course they should be discernibly enacted in public. However, because as human beings we are imperfect, these values which are so central to Samoan identity can also be disregarded or abused.

For example, several research participants noted the misuse of the value of respect when it becomes vertical and non-reciprocal, such that the respect of ordinary people for those in authority (chiefs, pastors, politicians) is not reciprocated by the powerful.

Communicating Values Effectively

Effective use of language is crucial in communicating Christian values in the public sphere. This necessitates an examination of the language that public theologians use in public, in terms of its accessibility and communicability.[13] Drawing on Habermas's three functions of language (reproducing culture and keeping tradition alive, social integration, and socialization[14]), it is clear that language is not neutral, but an essential conveyor of human values. This is especially true in Samoan culture where, as noted in chapter 3, what Samoans say, and how they speak, is critically important in the communication and safeguarding of the core values of the *fa'asamoa*.

Several research participants spoke of the necessity for values to be communicated in the public sphere in a way that speaks to people's lived experience. From the Church group, Participant CRG048 spoke with conviction about the potential for a positive influence of public theology if it is "translated" properly into the everyday lives of the Samoan people: "In Samoa, theology should have a huge influence on society because almost everyone goes to church at least once every Sunday . . . so the public are getting a significant amount of religious teachings every week. However, this religious teaching often doesn't seem to be translated into true Christian living, based on the eternal spiritual truths."

In Participant CRG048's view, theology should ostensibly have a huge influence on Samoan society, because "almost everyone goes to church"—hence the public are "getting a significant amount of religious teaching every week." Yet this nearly universal church attendance has not guaranteed that Samoans will behave in accordance with Christian-Samoan core values. Part of the blame for this disjunction is the poor "translation" of the Christian faith. Participant CRG048 seems to suggest that the problem of the language used in church is that it remains abstract, such that insufficient connections are made with church members' everyday realities and their calling to respond as Christians to those realities. Words proclaimed from the pulpit are not galvanizing listeners into social witness. Everyone goes to church, yet there is widespread violence, crime, and other social problems.

A common perception among research participants was that public theology should be "translated" into publicly accessible language so that social issues can be accurately understood and a pathway to solutions can be found. This means that the language of faith cannot be restricted to the religious sphere of church worship or family devotions; it must have public resonance and relevance. This point is made explicit by Participant NGO010: "In terms of influence, I see the importance of language. . . . What I mean is that theology influences public life by means of the language people use in the way they interact with one another." Participant NGO010's concern is not surprising given the public nature of her NGO's vision and work. She is accustomed to communicating in the public sphere about the relationship between values and social realities.

While public theologians in the West are concerned with how explicitly "theological" their language should be in a secular environment, this is not an issue in Samoa, where everyone uses the language of faith. The issue in Samoa is the *application* of the language of faith in relation to social problems. It is also important to restate that most public theology discourse in the scholarly literature, which has generated its own "language," has emerged from and is based on Western perspectives. While Western scholarly contributions are valuable, the challenge of this study is to construct a public theology from within the Samoan worldview, as it is embodied in the Samoan language and thought forms.

Public Theology Enactment by the Laity

Two levels of public theology enactment were highlighted by research participants: enactment by the laity and enactment by clergy. Although the majority of research participants believed that doing public theology is the role of clergy, there were others who believed that they (as laity) were also doing public theology, in terms of the roles they play in their families, villages, churches, and workplaces. Participant GM012 reflected on her public theology role as an executive officer:

> I participate in debates that discuss the issues in my area of work, and at the same time I also take part in other issues that I am passionate about, especially issues that affect the well-being of people. So I participate in public forums that discuss public issues. Another way is to participate in discussions within your church parish or religious gatherings in order to help people out, but also as a way of explaining things to people and listening to what they say in regards to such issues.

Participant CRG046 is a woman in her late fifties, active in her faith community, and in a nongovernmental organization. She saw public theology as a way to connect her religious values with the social realities impacting Samoa, in order to "help humanity and create a better society." She welcomed opportunities to engage in public discourse about current issues facing society, but bemoaned the marginalization of her own minority faith community by the mainline churches. She suggested that her lay-led faith community could easily be present in social spaces in which policies could evolve on issues such as governance, the environment, climate change, human rights, education, and the equality of men and women.

In order for the laity to engage in public theology effectively, there must be a new collaborative learning relationship between clergy and parishioners, based on a dynamic and critical reflection on the implications of the Christian faith for the larger society. For this to happen, clergy must not only be more engaged learners themselves but must actively disciple and equip the laity. Members of a parish cannot be expected to live out a life of public Christian witness without being prepared for such witness. I therefore concur with Neil Darragh's call for clergy to re-envision their calling as *enablers* whose calling is to equip *citizen theologians*:

> There is one implication of a commitment to public theology that is not often acknowledged. This is that a first call on anyone claiming to do public theology is to enable others to do it. . . . Christian theology is unlikely to be a significant voice unless it increases the number of citizen theologians, members of society who are able to do theology well. This is not primarily an argument for more theology students in academic institutions. . . . It is an argument for democratizing theology itself, for opening up access to Christian resources by demonstrating how the interaction between Christian sources and public forums can be accomplished. . . . Public theology is best carried out by reflective Christians who see themselves as both theologians and citizens.[15]

Public Theology Enactment by the Clergy

The role that clergy play in Samoan communities is important in terms of how theology could potentially be enacted in public life. This is reflected in the majority of participants' view that pastors logically ought to be public theologians. This is based on their understanding that clergy are the representatives of God in society. They are the ones who are supposed to mediate God's intentions for and relationship with the world. Yet this ideal is contradicted by the widespread belief (among the public at large) that church ministers should only concern themselves with church matters.

Despite this stereotype, it is also true that Samoan church ministers are generally regarded as public spiritual leaders. If this is so, then surely church ministers should not limit their responsibilities to the pulpit and parish affairs. They are involved in public occasions to offer prayers and devotions, but they should also be making meaningful contributions to panel discussions, public forums, and other public settings designed to promote the betterment of Samoan society.

The widely respected leadership role of clergy also suggests that they should be willing to "do their homework," as one participant put it, to gain an accurate and in-depth understanding of the situations their parishioners and communities inhabit. Clergy must be willing to speak to the situations which people in their communities are actually facing, pointing the church toward God's desires, and helping people to engage with one another, with their local communities, and with the larger society in new ways.

Research participants spoke with clarity about the calling of the clergy to both practice and call forth in others a Christian influence on public life. This was revealed particularly in the narratives of participants from the Church group and the Government Workers and Politicians group. For example, in the view of Participant CRG060, a pastor now teaching in a theological college, theology should influence public life through all aspects of the pastor's work, including preaching, leading bible studies, and devotions, as well as outreach done by the church in public. This is an assertion that clergy have an imperative to do ministry in a variety of settings, and this requires a critical awareness of their social location and the courage to be proactive in the public sphere.

Participant CRG006 is a young pastor and theologian whose vision of public theology is summed up in his expression, "knowing God in public." He envisioned public theology as the primary role of a minister, and argued that it must be enacted in ways appropriate to the minister's context. He suggested that pastors make use of the media through sharing theological insights on specific issues, or even preparing sermons that are made available to the wider Samoan public. This is a laudable ideal to which clergy should aspire but, overall, this study revealed a widespread critique that there is an observable lack of interest in enacting public theology on the part of clergy. This may be attributed to their rigidly prescribed roles (which do not extend to public life), and to the conservative views most churches hold with regard to public issues.

NGO workers were the most adamant in their critique that church ministers are not performing their role as public theologians. They complained that church leaders are largely silent on the critical issues affecting the well-being of the Samoan people. The church leaders' persistent silence, according to some of these participants, could either mean that they are supporting the injustices in society, or that they are ignorant of the realities affecting their church members and society in general. Participant NGO011 states this clearly:

> Did you read Sano's article in the *Sunday Observer*? He depicts three characters, and one of the key characters is the church. It tells the story of a man who

hanged himself. When the church saw him, they moved away. But when he had a lot of money, he was well respected and became a strong church-goer! It implies that you are strong if you have a lot of money. Then you have a strong faith. It's like the entry point into the church is you have to have a lot of money. But when the man hanged himself, the minister didn't even look for him. You must question the church out of your love for God.

Participant NGO011 is a woman holding a prestigious position in a nongovernmental organization. She has used her position to fight for the good of Samoan society. For this reason, she has been strongly criticized by the government. In fact, her ongoing battle with the present Samoan government has made her popular with the poor while being unpopular with the government. She is not waiting for church ministers to do public theology, as she moves into the gap created by their inattention and inaction.

Participant GM013 strongly supported the crucial role of church ministers in public theology. She noted that ministers already occupy positions of moral authority because of their perceived calling as representatives of God, such that anything they say will be seen by the people as God's Word. However, the problem, in her view, is that they have become too materialistic. The majority of church ministers in mainline denominations receive large amounts of money from parishioners, live in large houses built by their parishes, and may own expensive vehicles and freehold land. As a result, they are not able to have a prophetic voice in Samoan society; instead, they foster the kind of religion that Karl Marx famously referred to as the "opiate of the people." According to Participant GM013,

> I think there are so many ways [ministers could do public theology]. They can debate issues in terms of new legislation, as they have an avenue through the submission of public submissions to provide their views on issues. Some church leaders did this in the context of the casino [bill]; they made their submissions to the select committee reviewing the laws. I think they also have an opportunity where they can either have that voice publicly or through the media. You know, I am also thinking that they also have a chance where they can actually engage . . . the particular sector of society in things that [affect them]. They have an opportunity to engage with them. They may approach the people, or they may be invited to speak on particular topics. But they are cowards! [interviewee laughs]

These kinds of responses, derived from participants' personal experiences, point to a crucial factor that impinges on the church's public witness in Samoa today. People have internalized an idyllic myth about the importance of the church and the clergy in Samoa, but lurking beneath this myth lies the peril of complacency and a reluctance to engage in self-criticism that prevents the church from being true to its mission as the Body of Christ on earth. For one to engage in public theology, one must have the courage to speak and act against all forms of social injustice. For Samoan clergy, this will necessarily entail enduring criticism and even the loss of power and status, which they loath doing. Perhaps this is why Participant GM013 says, "they are cowards!"

FINAL THOUGHTS

This chapter has identified ways in which public theology can be framed and enacted within the Samoan context. It has discussed various understandings presented by participants in each of the four research groups, and highlighted the significance of core values in the process of defining and constructing a public theology for Samoa. In principle, every Christian in Samoa appropriates the Christian message in his or her own life as part of religious and cultural socialization, but the issue is how this faith should be lived out in the public sphere.

The themes elaborated in this chapter have revealed an urgent need for religious language to be translated in the public sphere in ways that make Samoa's core values understandable and relevant for all Samoans. The church's failure in this regard makes it clear that any construction of a Samoan public theology must entail a revisiting and reappropriation of the core values all Samoans hold dear. In this light, a variety of avenues by means of which public theologians could enact public theology in Samoa have been explored, in relation to themes identified by research participants.

At the heart of any viable Samoan public theology lies the imperative to creatively appropriate the compatible values of Samoan culture and Christianity for enactment in the public sphere. Such a public theology is inherently practical—it offers solutions to real social problems and makes connections with the various spheres of Samoan society. Christian theology's necessarily prophetic, practical, and pastoral stance in society is the bedrock of this public theology.

This chapter has also discussed various avenues of public theology enactment, with a particular focus on the widespread failure of the clergy and theological institutions in this regard. Taken together, the rich contributions of research participants have revealed the present context and future hopes for a public theology in Samoa. Chapter 7 proposes a framework for this public theology.

NOTES

1. This minister used to be a minister in the Methodist Church of Samoa, but was expelled for publicly speaking out on issues involving the abuse of power by leaders in the MCS.

2. Wilhelm Graeb, "The Influence of Communications Technology and Mass Media in Modern Society: A Challenge for Public Theology," in *Pathways to the Public Square: Practical Theology in an Age of Pluralism*, ed. Elaine L. Rowlands and Anna Graham (Piscataway, NJ: Transaction Publishers, 2005), 129.

3. In some countries, for example, there is virtually no regulation, such that "anything goes" online and it is difficult to discern fact from fiction. In other contexts, the internet is over-regulated, dissenting or controversial You Tube channels and Facebook pages are shut down, and censorship prevails. A recent critical analysis of the impact of the internet on Pacific Islanders' cultural values is Cresantia Koya-Vaka'uta, "The Digital *Va*: Negotiating Socio-spatial Relations in Cyberspace, Place and Time," in *The Relational Self: Decolonising Personhood in the Pacific*, ed. Upolu L. Vaai and Unaisi Nabobo-Baba (Suva, FJ: Pacific Theological College and University of the South Pacific, 2017), 79–101.

4. Jasmine Netzler, "Student in Samoa Charged with Murder," *Samoa Observer*, September 14, 2012, n.p. "The young man from Saleaumua is alleged to have stoned a 22-year-old after a dispute while drinking near the school grounds some two weeks ago. The victim was rushed to hospital after the incident but died the next day."

5. Efforts such as control measures enforced by police, banning of interschool sports events for nearly a year, and reconciliation through a renewed emphasis on Christian principles have been made to try to resolve the erosion of discipline and respect which has undermined education. See Tofilau Lupematasila Nanai Misa Fa'amanu Ivara, "School Brawls and Fights Exasperating," *Samoa Observer*, August 5, 2012, n.p.

6. Jonathan Boston, "Christianity in the Public Square," in *Voices for Justice: Church, Law and State in New Zealand*, ed. Alan Cameron and Jonathan Boston (Palmerston North, NZ: The Dunmore Press, 1998), 18–20.

7. *The New Dictionary of Cultural Literacy* (2002), s.v. "Conservatism."

8. All words in italics in the ensuing sections are the author's.

9. These understandings of wisdom are elaborated in Maiava Carmel Peteru, *O Le Tofa Mamao: A Samoan Conceptual Framework for Addressing Family Violence* (Wellington: Samoan Working Group, NZ Family and Community Services, 2012).

10. Mercy Ah Siu-Maliko, "Women in Acts and in Oceania," in *A Commentary on Acts*, ed. Yon Gyong Kwon (London: SPCK, 2012), 160.

11. Marie Ropeti-Iupeli, "A Biblical Basis for the Ordination of Women in the Pacific Churches," in *Weavings: Women Doing Theology in Oceania*, ed. Lydia Johnson and Joan Filemoni-Tofaeono (Suva, FJ: Institute of Pacific Studies, University of the South Pacific and SPATS, 2003), 133. For other reflections by Samoan women on the issue of women's ordination, see: Roina Fa'atauva'a, "Precedents for Samoan Women's Ministry: Samoan Women—Caught in Culture Change," *Pacific Journal*

of Theology II, no. 7 (1992): 15–30; Feiloaiga Taule'ale'ausumai, "Herstory: The Struggle of Pacific Women in Ministry," *Pacific Journal of Theology* II, no. 7 (1992): 31–34; and Marie Ropeti-Iupeli, "A Pacific Woman's Journey in Ministry," *Pacific Journal of Theology* II, no. 7 (1992): 34–38. From the wider Pacific (Melanesia/ New Caledonia), see Tamara Wete, *Women and Ministry in Melanesia: A Kanak Perspective* (Dunedin, NZ: Manahine Press, 2007).

12. Ah Siu-Maliko, "Women in Acts and in Oceania," 161.

13. Marshall, "What Language Shall I Borrow?," 16–17.

14. Jürgen Habermas, *Moral Consciousness and Communicative Action* (Cambridge, MA: Polity Press, 1990), 25.

15. Neil Darragh, "Doing Theology in Public: An Engagement with Economic Rationalism," *International Journal of Public Theology* 4, no. 4 (2010): 392–93.

Chapter 7

The Contours of a Samoan Values-Centered Public Theology

With the theoretical foundations of public theology and the core values of Samoan society established, this chapter shifts to a reflection on the shape of a Samoan public theology of values. To set the stage for this discussion, the first section provides a personal reflection on the possibility of a Samoan public theology, assessing the likely subjects, elements, and nature of such a public theology. The next section brings together the contributions to a Samoan public theology gleaned from this study. These reflections provide a framework for a praxiological demonstration of this public theology in chapter 8 around the social issue of domestic violence.

A PERSONAL REFLECTION

Prior to fleshing out the parameters of a Samoan public theology, it is important to revisit several crucial concerns related to the nature of public theology itself. For example, if public theology is targeted toward religious leaders, then the academic discipline of theology is front and center, because it is targeting those in positions of leadership in the church. But if the focus of public theology is the plight of those in society who are marginalized (the subjects of all forms of liberation theology), then such groups and individuals will play a key role in shaping and informing public theology. If the focus is on the marginalized, then the subaltern subject is "the other" who suffers, including women and children.

This fundamental concern for the other is essential, and it pushes us toward the contextual nature of public theology. In constructing a public theology in Samoa, a basic question to be addressed is: *What are the fundamental interests of the Samoan public, especially those "others" who are suffering?* In

Samoa there are people who are poor and those who are rich. There are those who have jobs and those who are unemployed, both young and old. There are those struggling in villages and those struggling in the town areas. There are men and women, young people and children, and "others" outside the mainstream, such as homosexuals and those who have been banished from their villages for deviating from the established norms. All of these categories of people collectively represent a visual image of the Samoan public. They are the face of the Samoan public square.

Public theology is about finding ways in which the Christian faith has relevance in this public space. In Samoan society, public theology's actors and actions occur in the contexts of the church, village, government, and civil society. I maintain that any meaningful Samoan public theology must speak to and have relevance for all Samoans, in all of these contexts, because it is centered in a God whose love embraces all of creation. God's compassionate care extends to all people and sectors of society, and public theologians are agents of that compassionate care.

There is also a need to acknowledge that there is not one theological voice that will appeal to everyone, because of the multiple identities Samoans hold on the basis of their gender and their social, political, educational, economic, and religious locations. It is therefore possible that there could be a number of theological voices speaking into the public sphere, and some of these voices will be painful to hear for certain groups in Samoan society. Public theology is offered as an agent of healing and reconciliation for everyone, but not all Samoans will embrace this offer, depending on their status and social location. What liberation theology refers to as Jesus's *preferential option for the poor* (which includes all who are oppressed) will necessarily be a "thorn in the flesh" for those who exercise power in an oppressive way.

Support for the church having a moral responsibility to enact public theology is confirmed in the views of the research participants in this study. Although this may not be evident in reality, because of the conservative stances of some church leaders and the rigidities of church traditions, what participants have proposed is a re-construal of what the Samoan church ought to be. This re-envisioned church would incorporate several constitutive elements of a public theology: "Human dignity founded in God and human community; vocation in service of neighbor and the common good; the sufficiency and sanctity of creation; and empowering people and communities."[1]

In a context like Samoa, where people share the same core religio-cultural values, the process of constructing a coherent public theology based on these four presuppositions depends very much on how public theology engages the three publics proposed by Tracy: the church, the wider society, and the academy. In preparing the church to engage with public issues, Katie Day asserts that there must be a correspondence between church and public on such issues at all levels of society, from local congregations and communities to the level of national policy-making.[2] Following Tracy, Day suggests that "synapses need to be in place so that the data coming from the social realities experienced on the local level are related to the construction of theological reflection by clergy and academics, and they in turn can enter into critique and advocacy of public policies."[3]

A number of the research participants in this study exposed examples of the Samoan church's failure to live out its public witness by searching for "synapses" or points of contact with the public, to the extent that many clergy and their respective denominations do not seem to believe that an essential part of their calling is to address social issues affecting people's lives. A related concern is the privatization of social problems in Samoan culture, wherein these problems are hidden within families to "save face" and avoid public shame. Our case study of domestic violence is one of the most glaring examples of this culture of shame and avoidance.

In this environment, it is imperative to take on board Day's crucial comment that "we can learn something about how public theology is constructed by looking in the negative space where it is not."[4] The absence of public theology tells a great deal about the way things are, about actual priorities and underlying assumptions; it also goads us to reflect on how things ought to be. In pursuing the theme of negative space, the focus of this study must be on the churches in Samoa.

In constructing a contextual public theology for Samoa, Samoan Christians must therefore reflect critically on how to bear witness more authentically to the ideals of their Christian-Samoan values. These values are still considered national treasures, and many Samoans would agree with Mata'afa Keni Lesa, editor of the *Samoa Observer* newspaper, who asserts, "The truth is that what's keeping this country peaceful and stable are its core cultural values and Christian beliefs. We should never let go [of them]."[5] Fa'afouina Iofi affirms this widely held belief that "Samoan cultural values can be integrated with Christian understanding to help Samoans affirm the best in their cultural heritage. This will encourage them to make a relevant contribution toward the enrichment of life in the communities and churches to which they belong."[6]

This assertion is broadly affirmed in theory, but there is a wide gap between theory and praxis. The essential role of Samoan cultural and Christian values in guiding its national life must be more visibly reflected in Samoans' behavior and relationships with each other, in the various spheres of Samoan society. Lesa's claim above, that it is these values that are keeping Samoa "peaceful and stable," only has validity if Samoan society is indeed peaceful and stable. Given the prevalence of violence and crime, including domestic violence, one has to question how well these core values are actually being lived out.

As this study has made clear, public theology is not simply quoting from the Bible or making surface comments about social justice that do not reflect deep analysis or result in public witness. To implement a Samoan public theology, Samoan theologians and concerned citizens must work together to critically examine the many problems that are causing a fraying of our social fabric, drawing on contributions from pertinent secular disciplines and theological and cultural wisdom.

The role of the church in particular must be analyzed critically in terms of its calling to be an agent of God's empowering and reconciling love. Since the church is a very powerful institution in Samoa, and thus hypothetically a natural agent to implement public theology, it must be called anew to contribute to the proclamation and embodiment of a message of hope and action for the flourishing of all Samoans.

TOWARD A SAMOAN PUBLIC THEOLOGY OF VALUES

Public theology as it emerged in the West cannot be adapted wholesale in the Samoan context. In its inception, public theology was "fashioned partly in reaction to a trend in the United States to interpret faith in terms of individual piety and salvation, to essentially privatize it."[7] This privatization had engendered a "hands-off" response by many Christians to social concerns, despite the gospel imperative to be "salt and light" to the world.[8] Public theology also developed "at a moment of crisis in American life,"[9] a crisis described by Robert Bellah as "the inability of people to find a language, a moral tradition, which adequately conveys the nature of social existence."[10]

In the Samoan context, in contrast, there are strong ethical values that are still collectively affirmed in both private and public spheres, as this study has shown. At the same time, my research indicates a breakdown in the living out of these core values. Otherwise we would not be confronted with the social reality the country faces today. This is a reality in which there are daily reports in the media on the ill effects of social problems such as corruption and other injustices perpetrated by public servants, politicians, village leaders, and church leaders; high incidences of violence, especially domestic violence and abuse; one of the highest rates of suicide in the world;[11] and banishment of individuals and families from villages. All of these social problems, and others such as poverty and crime, are serious and increasing.

These social realities necessitate a questioning of the efficacy of Samoan agents of socialization—*aiga* (family), *nu'u* (village), *lotu* (church), and *aoga* (school)—in communicating and upholding Samoan-Christian core values. This dire situation requires an urgent theological response from Samoan theologians, clergy, and citizens, to initiate dialogue on the social problems that plague the nation. As Fa'alepo Tuisuga correctly states, "Social issues [in Samoa] emerge as challenges to the church, which unfortunately has failed either to respond sufficiently or remains totally mute when the people and the government desperately need her theological stance and input in their search for help."[12]

As this study has argued, public theological discourse on issues that impinge on the common good in Samoan society must be grounded in the ethical framework embedded in the Samoan-Christian core values of *fa'aaloalo, alofa, tautua, amiotonu,* and *soalaupule*. An authentic Samoan public theology must be committed to the practical application of these values around issues of concern in Samoa's spheres of family, village, church, and society. Drawing on Freire's understanding of conscientization, such a public theology necessarily relies on open, inclusive dialogue, critical consciousness, social analysis, and a commitment to work with others as subjects rather than objects.[13]

In promoting dialogue around the common good of Samoan society, public theologians must engage in a critical analysis of context, including the following themes: *the relationship between church and state, the relationship between fa'asamoa and the Christian faith, the enactment of core values, the role and vision of the church, theological training, social policies,* and *the role of the media.*

CONTEXTUAL CONSIDERATIONS

The case has been made throughout this work that public theology is contextual theology, as it encompasses the totality of situations and circumstances that color and shape every theological response. *Context* refers to the situations out of which theology emerges.[14] A synopsis of key facets of the Samoan context highlighted in this work reminds us that

- 99.8 percent of the population belong to a church.
- Samoa's cultural values have over time found parallels in the Christian faith.
- Both cultural and Christian core values are grounded in relationality and are interconnected.
- Those who assume leadership roles on both local and national levels are also leaders in the church, and thus exercise great influence over what the church does and does not do.
- Samoa's constitution is ostensibly based on Christian principles.
- The unquestioned authority of church ministers has contributed to authoritarianism and a reluctance to take risks or unpopular positions in the public sphere.

These contextual factors are all relevant in the development of a Samoan public theology, and must be subject to the questioning that is inherent in the cultivation of a critical consciousness (following Freire). In the cultivation of critical consciousness, those engaged in public theology look beneath the surface of cultural assumptions, as this study has attempted to do.

Church and State in Samoa

This study has made it clear that church and state are indeed intertwined in Samoa, even though clergy are expected not to speak out or get involved in addressing social or political problems in the public sphere. Secular leaders in the social, political, educational, and economic life of Samoan communities and the nation are, as we have seen, also leaders in the churches and show respect for church leaders.[15] As Cluny and La'avasa Macpherson have noted, "Many national politicians, civil servants, and senior *matai* (titleholders) are also officeholders in their congregations. Their involvement in church ensures a secular awareness of, and political support for, the church's aspirations."[16]

This closeness between political leaders and the church both influences church politics and, on a surface level, means that clergy are included in consultations around public issues. Yet, as a number of our research participants have pointed out, this "inclusion" of church representatives in government consultations has, to date, been largely superficial. As one participant wryly put it, "they do not say anything."

In defence of the symbiotic relationship between church and state, Fepa'i Kolia, former secretary of the Samoa National Council of Churches, made the following comment:

> Since [Samoa's] independence in 1962, the church and state have worked side by side to develop the Samoan people. Government leaders are often church leaders as well, which therefore reinforces the mutual beneficial relationship between these two important sectors of society. Hence, democracy, culture and Christian values have integrated well in a manner that is acceptable to the local community.[17]

I argue, however, that this relationship is not as "mutually beneficial" as this portrayal suggests. The reality is that this cozy relationship sometimes leads to collusion between church and state in the concealment of injustice and corruption. It is a relationship of convenience that preserves the status quo. This collusion must be addressed and challenged.

Fa'asamoa and the Christian Faith

It has been acknowledged in this study that Samoa has unique cultural characteristics that distinguish it from many other contexts, even within Oceania. Because Samoa's culture came to be anchored in the Christian faith, Christianity occupies a prominent position in Samoan cultural and public life. All spheres of Samoan life claim to be grounded in Christian values. The constitution of Samoa upholds the crucial role of the Christian faith in shaping the lives of Samoan people, so much so that in the preamble of the Constitution of Samoa the following words are clearly stated:

I LE SUAFA PAIA O LE ATUA, LE E ONA LE MALOSI UMA LAVA,LE E ALOFA E FA'AVAVAU,

  ONA o le pule aoao i le Lalolagi e i ai lea i le Atua na o Ia, e afio i mea uma lava ma o le pulega e fa'aaogaina e tagata o Samoa i totonu o tuaoi na fa'asinoina mai i Ana Tulafono o se tofi paia tuufa'asolo;

  ONA ua fa'aalia e Taitai o Samoa le tatau ona avea Samoa ma Malo Tutoatasi e fa'avaeina i luga o talitonuga fa'a-Kerisiano ma tu ma aganuu a Samoa.

  IN THE HOLY NAME OF GOD, THE ALMIGHTY, THE EVER LIVING,
  WHEREAS sovereignty over the Universe belongs to the Omnipresent God alone, and the authority to be exercised by the people of Samoa within the limits prescribed by His commandments is a sacred heritage;
  WHEREAS the Leaders of Samoa have declared that Samoa should be an Independent State based on Christian principles and Samoan custom and tradition.[18]

As noted previously, all public occasions and celebrations typically begin with a formal devotion conducted by a village pastor. Villages in Samoa, especially in rural areas, still observe evening curfews where all families are expected to conduct prayers and devotions in their homes. These quiet times are well policed by village chiefs and untitled men, as a sign of respect to God. This is one of the many traditions which reinforce the assumed adherence to the Christian faith in Samoan society. Yet the critical consciousness that is essential for any effective public theology requires us to question the meaning of this assumption in the present Samoan social reality. How does our social life actually demonstrate that we are a nation "founded in God"?

Churches in Need of Vision

The conservative nature of many of the mainline churches in Samoan society, as confirmed by a number of research participants, has resulted in the church becoming an institution that supports the status quo. This is evident in the church's silence on social problems such as domestic violence. This silence means turning a blind eye to the suffering of the most vulnerable members of society.

If the church is to participate in public theology, it must, in the first instance, be open to becoming better informed by sources of expertise on specific social issues. This includes proactively seeking out contributions from secular fields such as sociology, psychology, and other relevant disciplines. Their contributions can then be analyzed and strengthened by insights from scripture and theology. Armed with this broad-based knowledge, the church can then wholeheartedly embrace its social mission. This will enable the church to speak and act regarding all matters that negatively impact the lives of its people, instead of merely parroting what government leaders expect the church to say (or not say).

Prior to speaking and acting, however, the churches need to reflect more critically on their vision, which is to respond to God's call to "provide for the common good and the flourishing of all people." This is an ecumenical vision that should bring all Christians together in meaningful dialogue and action, as proposed by Kamu.[19] This call to Christians to promote the common good brings to mind the VAGST (Value Added to Goods and Services Tax) Protest in 1995, in which some clergy marched with other protesters across the capital, Apia. As a consequence of this protest, the participating ministers belonging to one of the mainline churches were given a stern warning from their church leaders that they were not to meddle in public affairs, which are the concern of politicians.

This view remains the norm today. If a church minister gets involved in public matters, he is not only given a warning but is advised to leave the church and become a politician! This mentality disregards the urgencies of Samoan social realities. For example, the draconian tax scheme which precipitated the 1995 public protest was negatively affecting the well-being of the most vulnerable in Samoan society. Suffering members of the public, and the courageous clergy who marched alongside them, protested because the VAGST created heavy financial burdens, adding to the already high cost of living. The effects of the VAGST are still negatively impacting the lives of Samoans today.

A Samoan public theology calls upon the church to move away from its culture of silence and institutional materialism and focus instead on the well-being of its members and society at large. The critique of the church's materialism came through very clearly in my field research, in comments such as Participant NGO011's statement that "the church is making physical developments and expensive church buildings its priority, at the expense of parishioners." A number of research participants described the church and its ministers as being "too materialistic" and thus insufficiently focused on the well-being of others, including their own financially struggling members.[20]

The Need to Revamp Theological Training

Since public theology is an unfamiliar concept in Samoan society, there must be a beginning point for its orientation. This is the role of theological education. Samoan theological schools must be the breeding ground of public theology, and public theology must become a cornerstone of their training. Institutional resistance to public theology must be addressed as a reality that impinges on the ability of the churches to have a viable public witness.

One of the more revealing discoveries in my field research was the widespread criticism of the training provided by theological institutions. The churches clearly need to review the curriculum of their theological schools so as to include courses in public theology and social ministries, including the church's ministry around gender issues. Theological training must also more effectively analyze and inculcate core Christian-Samoan values for the holistic development of church leaders. In support of this concern, Kamu makes the following assertion:

> The Church needs to consider training which will provide the necessary education for the whole person. This means the message of the Gospel must no longer be confined to the realm of the spirit; it must encompass the whole person, every aspect of life, including the environment. The Gospel encompasses the whole of God's creation and the involvement of the Church in politics and social issues, affecting the lives of the people, should reflect that fact.[21]

If future ministers and theologians are trained to "be involved in social issues" and to participate in the life of the community, church members may in turn become more appreciative of the practical outworkings of theology. In addition to curricular changes, theological schools need to rethink the practical component of theological education, placing ministers-in-training not just in parishes but in secular settings, such as NGOs, community organizations and schools. Expanding theological education in this way can help to raise consciousness about what it means to embody core values in secular as well as ecclesial contexts.

Some research participants in this study exhibited an astute awareness of the need for changes in theological education. As Participant NGO007 commented, "I think it needs to accommodate the needs of both men and women. . . . It seems like the primary focus of theological training is men. And women are seen as shadows of men." Participant GM079 made the observation that "there is no humility in those coming out of theological schools." Both of these sentiments need to be taken to heart if there is to be an effective public theology in Samoa.

The Church and Social Policies

The church can only make constructive contributions to the development of just social policies if its representatives offer comprehensive, balanced, and well-nuanced proposals to address policy concerns. It is evident from the responses of research participants that the voice of theology is generally absent when it comes to discussions of social policies, even though churches are free to put forward submissions in regards to specific government policies.

It is imperative, therefore, for public theology practitioners to approach social policy dialogues with clear objectives. As noted earlier, in addition to insights from theology and scripture, any Christian response to social policy discussions must also be informed by knowledge from broader spheres of inquiry. These contributions will enrich the quality and outcome of these discussions.

In Samoa, as we have seen, "the church is embedded in the *matai* system and, in this regard, the church is well positioned to influence all aspects of village life and broader public policy-making."[22] Yet if the church is to use this influence in a positive way, it must move beyond mere attendance by some ministers at public forums discussing government policies. The failure of church ministers to make well-informed contributions to such discussions was heavily criticized by some research participants. They were adamant that ministers need to "do their homework" so that they can offer a constructive contribution to the shaping of public policies.

Revisiting the Use of Media

Effective use of all forms of mass communication is an important factor in the development of a Samoan public theology. This was highlighted more than any other avenue for enacting public theology by the research participants. Yet it is clear that this means of furthering public awareness is underutilized and, more importantly, that there are barriers imposed on the use of the media to voice opinions on social issues. For example, after Samoa's national election in 2011, some people were banished from their villages because they discussed election matters with the media.

It has also been noted that there are often church policies that prevent ministers from speaking publicly on issues of social concern. Unless these policies are revisited by the churches, the rich possibilities of the media will be wasted. My research has revealed that NGOs are far more adept than the churches in using media to increase public awareness of issues and policies affecting Samoan society. There is clearly a need for collaboration among all concerned citizens to make social issues and policies more open for discussion, and it is obvious that using mass media is an important avenue for making this happen.

One of the fears associated with engaging in public conversations, especially in a homogenous society such as Samoa, is the uneasiness felt with the notion of one group or person imposing values on others, or even highlighting differences of opinion. Yet, according to Participant GM054, people should not be discouraged if a difference in opinion or criticism arises: "When issues arise, they [public theologians] should make comments about it. They should not shy away or be discouraged because of nasty comments of people against their comments. . . . Theologians should be prepared to be critiqued by others." Being open to public criticism will enable public theologians to become more welcoming to new insights and to engage in critical reflection in an effort to find ways to move forward.

FINAL THOUGHTS

This chapter has highlighted a number of key elements that are crucial to the practice of a Samoan public theology. It began with a personal reflection that tied together strands of knowledge from previous chapters, taking into account the distinctiveness of the Samoan cultural and Christian contexts. The contributions of research participants and Samoan scholars were evident in the call for an integration of Samoan and Christian core values as the scaffolding upon which a Samoan public theology is constructed.

This study has also revealed that those engaged in doing public theology in Samoa must be willing to reach beyond the comfort zones of their usual domains of activity (whether as clergy, politicians, villagers, *matai*, or members of civil society) so as to engage in dialogue together. It is only such cross-fertilization and mutually enriching dialogue that can lead to values-based responses to the social ills plaguing Samoan society.

This dialogue must entail critical analysis of the relationship between church and state, the relationship between *fa'asamoa* and the Christian faith, the church's understanding of its social witness (which necessitates a re-envisioning of its theological training), and its role in contributing to social policy. If the Samoan people—"the public"—are indeed the subjects of public theology, then the task of developing this theological praxis must involve all sectors of society. The church must be animators, enablers, and facilitators, but all Samoans have a stake in the outcome of public theology.

NOTES

1. Len D. Hansen, ed., *Christians in Public: Aims, Methodologies and Issues in Public Theology*, Beyers Naudé Centre Series on Public Theology #3 (Stellenbosch, SA: Sun Press, 2007), 11.

2. Katie Day, "The Construction of Public Theology: An Ethnographic Study of the Relationship between the Theological Academy and Local Clergy in South Africa," *International Journal of Public Theology* 2, no. 3 (2008): 367.

3. Ibid., 368.

4. Ibid., 372.

5. Mataafa Keni Lesa, "Those Evils Are Already Here," *Samoa Observer*, March 8, 2013, n.p.

6. Fa'afouina Iofi, *Samoan Cultural Values and Christian Thought: An Attempt to Relate Samoan Traditional Values to Christian Understanding* (PhD Diss., School of Theology at Claremont, 1980), 32.

7. Bradstock, "In Search of the Good Society," n.p.

8. Ibid.

9. Himes and Himes, *Fullness of Faith*, 5.

10. Robert Bellah, Richard Madsen, William M. Sullivan, Ann Swindler, and Steven M. Tipton, *Habits of the Heart: Individualism and Commitment in American Life* (Berkeley, CA: University of California Press, 1985), 20–21.

11. See "Suicide Rate in Pacific Islands Among Highest in the World," *Pacific Islands Report*, August 15, 2015, http://www.pireport.org/articles/2015/08/15/suicide-rate-pacific-islands-among-highest-world. The incidence of suicide in Samoa is more than double the global average. Concentrated among youth ages fifteen to twenty-nine, identified causes include the "shame culture" (e.g., young girls becoming pregnant out of wedlock, young men failing at school, etc.), and social pressures such as unemployment. See also Jemaima Tiatia-Seath, "Negotiating Personhood in Light of Pacific Suicide Prevention," in *The Relational Self: Decolonising Personhood in the Pacific*, ed. Upolu L. Vaai and Unaisi Nabobo-Baba (Suva, FJ: Pacific Theological College and University of the South Pacific, 2017), 79–101.

12. Fa'alepo A. Tuisuga, *O Le Tofa Liliu a Samoa: A Hermeneutical Critical Analysis of the Cultural-Theological Praxis of the Samoan Context* (PhD Thesis, Melbourne University of Divinity, 2011), 212.

13. See Ah Siu-Maliko, "Conscientization and Pacific Women." 64–84.

14. Gerhard Sauter, *Protestant Theology at the Crossroads: How to Face the Crucial Tasks for Theology in the Twenty-first Century* (Grand Rapids, MI: William B. Eerdmans, 2007), 86.

15. Macpherson and Macpherson, "Churches and the Economy of Samoa," 305.

16. Ibid.

17. Fepa'i Fiu Kolia, "The Church and Development," in *Samoa National Human Development Report: Sustainable Livelihoods in a Changing Samoa*, ed. Unasa Felise Va'a, Le'apai Lau, Asofou So'o, and Telesia Lafotanoa (Apia, WS: Centre for Samoan Studies, National University of Samoa, 2006), 147.

18. "Preamble," *Constitution of the Independent State of Samoa, 1960: Consolidated Acts of Samoa, 2008*, ed. Legislative Drafting Division (Apia, WS: Government Printing Office, 2008).

19. Kamu, *The Samoan Culture and the Christian Gospel*, 162.

20. A recent sociological study concluded that "the monetisation (cash-infused conditions) of church membership in Samoa is creating a material as well as spiritual dilemma for those who are struggling to cope with increasing hardship while meeting church and kinship obligations." Alec Thornton, Maria T. Kerslake, and Tony Binns, "Alienation and Obligation: Religion and Social Change in Samoa," *Asia Pacific Viewpoint* 51, no. 1 (2010): 7.

21. Kamu, *The Samoan Culture and the Christian Gospel*, 171.

22. Thornton, Kerslake, and Binns, "Alienation and Obligation," 6.

Chapter 8

Case Study for a Samoan Public Theology

Domestic Violence

Domestic violence is a serious problem in Samoa. Social attitudes tolerate the abuse of women in the home, and such abuse is common.[1] The growing numbers of named cases of domestic violence, and many other cases which are not reported, should make domestic violence a priority in Samoan public discourse. Samoan public theologians have a responsibility to translate the Samoan-Christian values of love, respect, selfless service, consensual dialogue, and justice in terms of the way Samoans should be living out their daily lives. Clearly this will mean an unequivocal condemnation of domestic violence, honesty about naming its causes, and a commitment to its eradication.

DEFINING THE ISSUE

The term *domestic violence* was first used in the early 1970s to name men's violence and abuse toward a female adult partner. Since the 1970s, there has been an enlargement of focus in research on the nature, causes, scope, and effects of domestic violence. This has been due mainly to the growth and prominence of the women's movement worldwide, legislation in many countries that has tackled the destructive impacts of domestic violence, as well as the significant numbers of women who were subjected to this type of violence in intimate relationships[2] who have increasingly given voice to their experience.

Because of the complex factors involved in domestic violence, researchers have devoted considerable attention to defining its parameters. Ellen Pence and Michael Paymar[3] and Audrey Mullender and Catherine Humphreys[4] define *domestic violence* as physical, emotional, and sexual abuse. Intimidating actions, belittling, harassment, and threatening also constitute violence against women. The sociologist Liz Kelly provides the following comprehensive definition:

> It is now widely accepted that domestic violence involves a variable combination of physical and sexual assault, alongside forms of psychological and economic abuse. The most important point to remember about domestic violence is that this is not about a fight, a single or occasional incident—although these do happen and may themselves constitute criminal offences. Domestic violence is an ongoing pattern of violence and abuse, often described as violence within a pattern of coercive control. It is a situation of repeat victimization where the victim is vulnerable precisely because in the majority of cases she shares her home with her attacker and has feelings of loyalty and even love towards him.[5]

One of the basic principles entailed in doing public theology is a commitment to an interdisciplinary approach to analyzing the issue being discussed. To fulfill that purpose, I wish to draw on the following frameworks to gain a better understanding of domestic violence: *sociological theory, feminist theory, social learning theory, psychological theory,* and *human rights.*

Sociological Theory

Sociological theory has "been much concerned with and broadly effective in analyzing social conflict, but much less so [on] the specifics of interpersonal violence, domestic violence or violence in intimacy."[6] Sociological theories of domestic violence assume that men behave violently in relationships as a response to stress from environmental factors. These influences include unemployment and discriminatory class structures, for example.[7] In the sociological theory framework, "Social stress (producing frustration) and socialization (which condones the use of violence) are singled out as the two main factors producing an environment conducive to the use of violence . . . men are under great pressure in the modern world and women's striving for equality has somewhat displaced men's sense of identity."[8]

Certainly social stress is a very real factor in Samoan society today. I have noted in this study the impact that globalization has had and is having in terms of increasing income inequality, desire for material goods, and environmental stress. Gambling, alcoholism, suicide, and violence are all consequences of this social stress. However, women experience these social stresses as well as men, and yet there is no reported increase in incidents of women committing acts of violence. Moreover, not all men who experience extreme social stress commit acts of violence against women. It is likely that the second factor mentioned above, socialization, is the more critical influence in Samoa, as men are socialized to believe that violence against women is tolerable in certain situations, and women are socialized to believe that such treatment at the hands of men is normal.

Feminist Theory

Feminist theory regarding domestic violence emphasizes gender and power inequality in opposite-sex relationships. It focuses on the societal messages that sanction a male's use of violence and aggression, and the proscribed gender roles that dictate how men and women should behave in their intimate relationships.[9] Feminist theory sees intimate partner violence as the outcome of living in societies that tolerate aggressive behaviors perpetrated by men, while socializing women to be nonviolent.

The feminist perspective is well articulated by Pence and Paymar, whose research demonstrates how domestic violence is a result of the ideology of patriarchy. They conclude, "The feminist socio-political worldview accounts for violence by males in intimate relationships by linking violence and abuse, power and control in intimate relationships to the larger societal constructs of male privilege."[10]

Feminist theory characterizes domestic violence as a complex problem that is not only personal but systemic. Domestic violence happens not just because of personal flaws in individuals but as the result of socialization around male attitudes to women. Violence against women is thus "any male behavior which results from a patriarchal view of women as objects rather than subjects."[11] The objectification of women is a "given" in patriarchal societies, and Samoa is clearly a patriarchal society.

Social Learning Theory

Social learning theory has often been referenced to explain why domestic violence persists across generations. Drawing on F. M. Moghaddam, Rachel Taylor explains social learning theory's assumption that human behaviors become habitual by observing and imitating others in order to receive rewards or to avoid punishments.[12] In relation to domestic violence, such "violent behavior is learned in childhood by receiving readily available messages through observing behaviors of parents, fictional heroes on television, or violent people in the public who achieve power and control through behaving violently."[13]

One of the devastating effects of such social learning is that behaviors are passed down from one generation to another, in a "cycle of violence." Children who grew up viewing violence as part of their parents' relationship often become abusers themselves as adults, internalizing domestic violence as a practice that is not only acceptable but normal. Social learning theory is particularly relevant in a homogenous culture such as Samoa, where social conventions are universally shared and dissent from these conventions is not tolerated. Children learn and repeat the patterns of behavior they observe in the adults around them, and in a society that views husbands' dominance over their wives and wives' submission to their husbands as normative, these attitudes will naturally be passed down to younger generations. Breaking the cycle of violence in this kind of setting is particularly challenging.

Psychological Theory

From a psychological perspective, domestic violence "was initially predominantly viewed as a medical problem, suggesting that abusive men had some sort of illness that was causing them to behave violently toward their partners. This could relate [for example] to their excessive use of alcohol."[14] This view, while it may help individual men who receive therapy for their psychological problems, runs the risk of reducing men's accountability for their abusive behavior—they, in effect, become victims themselves.

Researchers have in fact found that psychological theories cannot account for all acts of domestic violence committed by men.[15] The Domestic Violence Prevention Unit in Australia found that there are significant numbers of domestically violent men who do not show signs of violent behavior in other social contexts (e.g., the workplace or public settings).[16] There are also many cases of violent men who have no discernible mental health conditions.

It is important not to dismiss the value of psychological theory, despite its limitations. The field of psychology has not been given prominence in Samoa, as it is considered a Western concept geared toward the individual. The idea of an individual talking to another individual privately about his or her problems is foreign to the *fa'asamoa*, where an individual's problems are the collective problems of the family, and where there is no concept of privacy as it is understood in the West. Pacific approaches to psychology are needed so that contextually relevant assistance can be provided to those with psychological problems.[17] This could be valuable for both perpetrators and victims of domestic violence.

Human Rights

Internationally, the problem of domestic violence is regarded as a human rights issue. It is a violation of women's human rights. While this is obviously the case, Abhinaya Ramesh provides an assessment of an often overlooked flaw in the human rights argument:

The development of the human rights movement . . . shows that rights are defined as "belonging to all human beings" irrespective of gender. However, though international law is gender neutral in theory, in practice it has constituted men and women into separate spheres of existence—public and private, respectively. Thus men exist as public legal entities that enjoy civil and political rights and, in a way, define the nature of rights discourse. Women's existence, on the other hand, is "privatized," and thus seen as existing outside the purview of the state's obligation. Often women's exclusion from human rights practice and discourse, their relegation to the private, has been justified on grounds of the social and cultural specificity of a region or a group. Thus, social and cultural norms, which become grounds for respective states' consistent relegation of women to the private sphere, result in international law either reinforcing or replicating exclusion of women's human rights abuses from the public sphere. The effects of this public/private divide in international law are more evident in domestic violence, which literally happens in private. Many laws are gender neutral; however, their application is gender biased.[18]

The separation between private and public is not helpful in dealing with the issue of domestic violence, because the relegation of women to the private domestic sphere has contributed to their being oppressed and abused. Their presumed inferiority is related to their lack of power in both the public and the private spheres, a reality not fully addressed by international human rights law.

Christians have a distinctive perspective on human rights. The creation of humankind "in the image of God" is, in fact, the foundation of all human rights, for human rights are located in the nature of God. In scripture the ways of God with humankind are described as "justice and mercy," and these qualities are required of both women and men as persons made in God's image. As Christopher Marshall puts it, "Rights are not reductions made on the basis of abstract notions of equality, freedom or justice. They are expressions of what God is like, as revealed in historical acts of deliverance. Rights represent the justice of God."[19]

It is this Christian perspective on human rights that should theoretically find acceptance and validation in Samoa, where biblical concepts of justice and mercy are embraced by almost all Samoans. Human rights discourse has not been prominent in the Samoan public sphere, but as a nation that belongs to the United Nations and other international bodies that value human rights, the time has come for Samoans to consider human rights, especially the Christian understanding of human rights, in their response to domestic violence.

Summary of Root Causes

In order to analyze the issue of domestic violence, it is imperative to be clear about its causes. Numerous contributing factors have been identified.

Perpetrators commit abuse "for many reasons, including external stressors such as financial problems, unemployment, extended family pressures, community violence, racism, personal addictions, insecurity, fear of abandonment, or jealousy."[20] But whatever its form and its contextual or personal particularities, violence against women has its roots in distorted power relations. Filemoni-Tofaeono and Johnson conclude that

> In every patriarchal setting—workplace, school, home, church, seminary, community, nation—it is women's lower status *as women* that makes them vulnerable to the violence that is the natural handmaiden of patriarchy. Rather than being merely the private moral failing of random individuals, violence against women is the natural outworking of a systematic and pervasive oppression of women.[21]

CONTEXTUALIZING DOMESTIC VIOLENCE IN SAMOA

The Present Reality

Domestic violence in the Samoan context refers in this study to violence and abuse committed by males against their female intimate partners. (For the purposes of this study, it does not address the equally serious problem of child abuse.) A 2007 study by the Secretariat of the Pacific Community (SPC) presented the following facts about violence against women in Samoa:

> 46% of Samoan women who have ever been in a relationship have experienced one or more kinds of partner abuse. The most common form of spousal abuse is physical abuse (38%), followed by sexual abuse (20%) and emotional abuse (19%). The kinds of abuse experienced by women include: being slapped or having objects thrown (35%); being punched (18%); being forced to have sex (17%); insults (14%); being coerced into having sex (11%); and being kicked, dragged or beaten (11%).[22]

Statistics provided by the World Health Organization indicate that women in Samoa experience both physical abuse (41 percent) and sexual abuse (20 percent), and more than 50 percent do not tell anyone about the abuse. Of those women who do not seek help, 86 percent stated that they thought such abuse was "normal" or "not serious."[23] Peseta Sio's 2012 research on domestic violence in Samoa underscored similar findings:

> Domestic violence victims were reluctant to report cases to the councils, and instances were also reported where cases had not received a fair hearing due to the fact that "some of these *matai* sitting there do this (domestic violence)" and

"they aren't going to judge another *matai*." Taking complaints to the police was not encouraged and some villages banned this. The fact that there are two status groups for women in Samoa—the sisters and the wives—also influenced domestic violence. Wives had no rights in their husband's village and were expected to serve their husband's family. . . . They were and are a highly vulnerable group.[24]

Finally, the most recent study on domestic violence in Samoa, published in 2017, reported that an alarming 60 percent of women between the ages twenty and forty-nine had experienced some form of abuse by an intimate partner.[25] The cumulative effect of these studies is confirmation of the Samoa Victim Support Group's reporting that "more than half of Samoan women are victims of domestic abuse. . . . And the abuse is getting worse."[26]

Certain sectors of the media have recently been more forthcoming in reporting some of the horrific stories of domestic violence happening in the ostensibly religious nation of Samoa. The following are but a few examples:

Story 1: "Incest and Abuse"

A man [was] found guilty of raping his 14 year old step-daughter. The man was sentenced to eleven and a half years in jail. Earlier this month, a 36-year-old father was jailed for 20 years for raping his 15-year-old daughter. In a similar case, a 46-year-old father was jailed for ten years for one count each of rape and carnal knowledge.[27]

Story 2: "Life of Fear"

Jane thought she had met Mr Right. He came across as charming, funny, and understanding. "He was everything I wanted him to be," she tells the *Samoa Observer*. But that was only to woo her. Mr Right, as it turned out, had an ugly side. Today, Jane has learnt her lesson the hard way. With bruises, cuts, and scars from several beatings to show for her love for Mr Right, she has a message for all mothers who are in abusive relationships. "Get out of it before it is too late," she says. "Find refuge while you can. I now understand how hard it is to be with a man who beats me like there is no tomorrow. It is very difficult and I want other women out there to make sure that if they are in this kind of situation for the first time, get out. It is not worth it."

Jane is a mother of a 14-month-old baby. The 21-year-old has been with her 35-year-old partner for three years. "He never showed any signs of jealousy before," she recalls. But one day, all that changed. "We went to his family to celebrate an elderly relative's birthday," she explains. "I think he was angry about me laughing with his male cousins. So he came to the back of the house where I was and punched the sides of my mouth several times."

As if that wasn't bad enough, Jane had to endure more punishment. "He threw a steel cup at me and it broke my leg. The cup caused a massive cut on my leg which I've never really recovered from." But Mr Right wasn't done. "He chased me around the house that night and eventually I jumped into one of the rooms and locked it. He broke the door, ran towards me and punched me several times on the head. I felt his teeth sinking into the left side of my face." Jane has the scars to prove the beatings.

But something even more painful came up. She has found out that Mr. Right was in a previous marriage. "There was a second incident on Monday last week," she says. "On the day of the second incident, a woman came over to the house to see him. She made several rude remarks to my face and then we fought. He came around and pulled my head back and beat me up." Jane says she never knew Mr. Right had been married. "'If I knew, I would never have dreamed of being involved with him. Now all I have are regrets. I live a life of fear. It's a constant worry."

Jane's mother also spoke to the *Samoa Observer*. She is devastated about what has happened to her daughter. By speaking out, they hope that someone else out there might be encouraged to speak up against such abuse. "Violence against women is more serious in Samoa than what people think," said the mother. "I have never been beaten by my husband. It hurts me to see how my child is being treated. I am only thankful to God that she's alive." She encourages women to seek refuge if their lives are in danger. Her daughter has lodged a complaint with the Domestic Violence Unit of the Ministry of Police and Prisons. Jane also plans to seek help from the Ministry of Justice Courts and Administration. [Note: Jane is not the woman's real name. The *Samoa Observer* is withholding the mother's real name and village to protect her from further abuse if her partner finds out.][28]

Story 3: "Enough Is Enough"
Lemalu Sina Retzlaff is a well-educated businesswoman and the first ever woman to become the president of the Samoa Chamber of Commerce. This [*Samoa Observer*] article records the story of Lemalu Sina Retzlaff's continued experience with domestic violence from her former husband Brian Lima, although they have been divorced for two years.[29] Lemalu Sina Retzlaff did something for women not only in Samoa but across the Pacific this year. She broke through a social taboo, talked about her life and how she lived with domestic violence. Lemalu stood up and said enough is enough—she was not going to live her life anymore as if spousal abuse was normal. By doing so, not only did she take her own life back, she gave hope and instilled courage in others to do the same. She took what was considered a "private matter" and made it a public one, because she felt that it was time for change. Time to say that no matter who you are or where you come from, domestic violence is never okay.[30]

The willingness of Lemalu Sina Retzlaff to allow the *Samoa Observer* to publish a photograph of her with black eyes as the result of domestic violence was extremely courageous and rare, given the culture of silence about such abuse in Samoa. The newspaper was also bold in its acknowledgment that violence against women "doesn't have any boundaries in terms of culture or religion; it can happen to anyone and I believe it does happen to women from all walks of life."[31] The newspaper goes on to assert that "in Samoa we need to talk about it [violence against women] a lot more. It exists but it is very much seen as a private matter."[32] This privatization of domestic violence has been noted by other Pacific Islander commentators, such as Akuila Yabaki, who writes that "Violence against women . . . has been seen as a personal and domestic problem, and thus privatized and individualized."[33]

In the search for the causes of this privatization of domestic violence, Peseta Sio's research underlines the "shame factor" in the way domestic violence is handled in Samoa: "The belief is still widely held that family differences, such as domestic violence, should be settled within the family. These are not a matter for public discussion given the 'shame' this could bring."[34] Incidents of domestic violence are swept under the carpet to protect family unity and honor, at the expense of the victims.

Moreover, the socialization highlighted in the previous section makes it difficult to hold men accountable for the violence they perpetrate. As Filemoni-Tofaeono and Johnson note, "The common response by men [when challenges to violence against women are raised] . . . is that it is 'our culture' that determines the clear gender role divisions, and that since culture is sacred it cannot be questioned."[35]

POWER IMBALANCE IN SAMOAN CULTURE

There is general agreement among those who have studied violence against women in Pacific Islands societies that it is premised on a natural law argument, which confines women to the domestic sphere while men "rule the world." Akuila Yabaki makes this case in his claim that "Traditional gender roles in Pacific societies have been premised on women's biological capacity to bear children, and a division of labor believed to be dictated by nature and divine decree. Violence against women . . . is a serious consequence."[36]

The cultural ethos that flows from this natural law argument means that gender relations in Samoa are "characterized by inequalities of power, opportunity and access to resources, (and) these relations are closely linked to cycles of violence that maintain low levels of status and high levels of victimization of women and girls."[37] The implications of this power imbalance for the issue of domestic violence are sobering.

The journal of the London-based Council for World Mission (inheritor of the London Missionary Society), *Inside Out*, reported the following interview from the *Samoa Observer* newspaper which portrays this power imbalance in stark terms:

Reporter: Do you think domestic violence is a problem in Samoa?
Man: No, it is not really a problem. Why beat your wife? They are useful to do the chores. But if the wife is wrong, she should be beaten, and if she is wrong again, she should be kicked out of the house.
Woman: No, it is not a problem here; if there is love and obedience, then there is [a] good relationship . . . [which will] work.[38]

This conversation epitomizes the reality of gender inequality in Samoa. The article concludes, "What this conversation highlights is the construction of the man as the 'head of the household' and the way in which such a conversation is predicated on the possibility of violence."[39] Such violence is a logical consequence of the imbalance of power between men and women. As one Samoan social commentator puts it, "Violence against women is the ultimate imbalance."[40]

Given this imbalance, violence is inflicted on women with impunity because of the Samoan myth that they are "the weaker sex" (*itupa vaivai*) while men are "the stronger sex" (*itupa malosi*). Within this social construction, Samoan women are socialized to be obedient to their husbands, as they were as children to their fathers, and to act in certain passive ways to avoid being beaten. Women internalize this submissiveness to avoid violence, although sometimes the violence is inevitable despite their best efforts. Men, in turn, are socialized to see women as possessions that they own, control, use, and may discard if they wish.

This ingrained attitude can be seen in the following exchange between a Samoan student and one of his lecturers at Pacific Theological College in Fiji after the lecturer visited the student's flat and found his wife with black eyes and bruises. The student admitted hitting her, but claimed that "it was his 'duty' to hit his wife after she 'talked too much' in the presence of guests in their home. According to his cultural worldview, a woman should be essentially in the background on such occasions, and certainly not speak out . . . in a way which contradicted her husband in front of others."[41] Here domestic violence was framed as a morally justifiable act in the interest of disciplining his wife.

Despite their pride in and loyalty to their Samoan cultural identity, which they share with men, Samoan women need to gain greater awareness of the inequality which plagues the gendered construction of their Samoan identity. The injustice of normalized domestic violence must be a catalyst for their struggle for recognition, respect, and rights as women of Samoa.

Using the Bible to Reinforce Patriarchy

The Bible has been used in Samoan churches to justify men's presumed superiority over women. This practice was also commonplace in churches in other parts of the world until fairly recently, as the patriarchy of the cultures depicted in the Bible, and male interpretations of the Bible over the centuries, were taken for granted in many cultures. It has taken female biblical scholars to point out the obvious problems in this stance. A pioneer in this regard has been Elisabeth Schüssler Fiorenza, who reminded Christians that the Bible has not only been "interpreted by a long line of men and proclaimed in patriarchal cultures, it was also authored by men, . . . [is] reflective of male religious experience, and . . . transmitted by male religious leadership."[42]

Samantha Gerson expands on why this has been problematic for women, writing that "For many years, the only voices that were heard when describing the experiences of biblical personalities were the voices of men. . . . Even passages about women were interpreted from the perspectives of men," and this has meant that biblical passages have been used to "justify women's subordination."[43] It would be foolish to think that this history has had no impact on how the church has viewed women; it has certainly had an impact on women in Samoan churches.

Prescriptions for male-female relationships in Samoan churches have been strongly influenced in particular by the patriarchal system that dominates the Old Testament. This is a result of missionary teachings, whereby the English missionaries in the nineteenth century placed strong emphasis on the Old Testament. The missionaries proclaimed a theology of patriarchy and unquestioningly promoted the biblical narratives that depicted the patriarchal culture of the Bible.

The missionaries also interpreted the Bible in line with the domestication and subordination of women which were typical of the Victorian England from which they hailed. Although Samoan culture was also patriarchal, missionary culture may have made it more so, as Samoan females were at least traditionally venerated in the brother-sister covenant.[44] Church teachings greatly restricted their influence and agency.

The ideology of patriarchy continues to shape Samoans' interpretation of the Bible. A literal reading of biblical passages is still used to justify men's dominance over women and their right to physically "discipline" women and children. In Samoan churches, "patriarchal interpretations of the Bible have been and remain unquestioned. The uncritical imposition of this approach to biblical hermeneutics . . . is a contributing factor to the problem of violence against women . . . [since] it is through the influence of this tradition that the inferior status of women has been reinforced."[45]

At the heart of this way of interpreting scripture is a patriarchal understanding of God. This is a Father-God who "is in control of everything . . . [and who] relates to his creatures by command and decree, expecting a response of submission and obedience."[46] In the "father-rule" that flows from this understanding, God is "Sovereign, King, Warrior, God of Power and Might . . . [who] cannot be imaged in the faces of women or children."[47]

Elizabeth Johnson makes the observation that "The way a faith community speaks about God indicates what it considers the greatest good, the profoundest truth. . . . The image of God shapes a community's corporate identity and behavior as well as the individual behavior of its members."[48] In short, our image of God has real-life consequences. As Johnson points out, the "patriarchal naming of God in the image and likeness of the powerful ruling man has the effect of legitimating male authority in social and political structures. In the name of the male Lord, King, Father God who rules over all, men have the duty to command and control."[49]

Although some Christian women, in Samoa as in other contexts, have countered that the masculinizing of the God of Scripture "does not adversely affect the way they experience God," most female biblical scholars "insist that this is where discussions of issues like violence against women must begin."[50] The reason for this is that "we have absorbed male language for God into our very selves . . . and when this is combined with images of authority such as Father, Lord and King, it is difficult to escape from the picture of God as a male authority figure."[51]

The men who have dominated biblical interpretation and church authority throughout the centuries have emulated this image of God in their teachings and church practices that have sidelined women from leadership and "voice" in the church. If God is a controlling male father-figure, then men must be like this masculine God. The question then becomes, to what lengths does their control go?

There are a variety of biblical passages which are used by Samoan clergy to justify this patriarchal theology that has unwittingly ended up condoning violence against women. For example, the standard interpretation of the second creation story in Gen 2:4–3:24 has been that the phrase "out of man woman was taken" means that women are secondary to men—an after-thought, an offshoot. This assumed "order of creation" places men in a position of dominance.

Likewise, 1 Cor 11:2–5[52] has been interpreted such that the words "the head of every man is Christ, the head of a woman is her husband" (vs. 3) have been accepted unquestioningly, forming the basis of a "headship theology" that compares males to Christ and relegates women to a lower status. A companion text used to shore up this view is Eph 5:22, "Wives, be subject to your husbands, as to the Lord" (often downplaying the previous verse, "Be subject to one another out of reverence for Christ").

This same language is found in Col 3:18 ("Wives, submit to your husbands, as is fitting in the Lord") and 1 Pt 3:1–6. ("Wives . . . accept the authority of your husbands," reminding them in vs. 6 that "Sarah obeyed Abraham and called him Lord.") Accepting the "headship" or "lordship" of men as normative today, of course, not only ignores the patriarchal first-century Palestine context in which these passages emerged but, more importantly, the gospel proclamation of the oneness of women and men in Jesus Christ (Gal 3:28).

Similar passages used by Samoan clergy to reinforce women's subordination to men emphasize the mandate for women to be silent in the church. 1 Tim 2:11–14 says, "Let a woman learn in silence with full submission. I permit no woman to teach or to have authority over a man; she is to keep silent. For Adam was formed first, then Eve; and Adam was not deceived, but the woman was deceived and became a transgressor." Similarly, 1 Cor 14:34–35 reads, "Women should be silent in the churches. For they are not permitted to speak, but should be subordinate, as the law also says. If there is anything they desire to know, let them ask their husbands at home. For it is shameful for a woman to speak in church."

Many female biblical scholars have in recent decades called upon the church to reject the patriarchal strands of scripture, as they are reflections of cultural norms in the Ancient Near East and first-century Palestine and not a reflection of the liberating gospel of Jesus Christ and the all-embracing love and justice of God. These include a growing number of non-Western scholars, such as the Mexican Elsa Tamez, who has asserted that "[t]he time has come to acknowledge that those biblical texts which reflect patriarchal culture, proclaiming women's inferiority and their submission to men, are not normative."[53]

Women's way of re-reading the Bible assumes a "critical stance, whereby the final form of the scriptures is opened up for questioning"; this is a "'self-conscious' reading of the Bible, in order to both engage the larger patriarchal context in its wholeness and also to discover alternative interpretations of biblical texts that uphold oppressive attitudes toward women."[54] This way of reading scripture highlights the common scriptural thread of God's unconditional love for all creation, wherein both women and men are created in God's image, and the liberating thrust of Jesus's ministry, which was directed especially to those on the margins of society, including women.

What is also distinctive about women's way of re-reading scripture is their situating the interpretation of biblical texts within the social realities of their present-day contexts. Writing from the South African context, Maretha Jacobs notes how, in women's biblical interpretation, "attention is not only paid to the biblical texts and their contexts, but also to their *impact*,"[55] especially their historically negative impact on women. She argues that biblical texts should be read in a way that links them to very real justice concerns in church and society today. This approach to biblical hermeneutics is in line with public theology's interest in the common good.

Female biblical scholars have vowed "to keep the prophetic and liberating story of God's concern for the oppressed and for the mending of creation alive among communities of faith by liberating the Word from its patriarchal bondage."[56] This re-reading of the Bible "with fresh eyes" is essential if the Samoan churches are to challenge the biblical underpinnings of their complicity in violence against women.

Domestic Violence and the Church

Anecdotal evidence suggests that village pastors in Samoa do at times attempt to protect female victims of domestic violence by offering them a safe house, or by intervening in domestic disputes.[57] However, Fairbairn-Dunlop and colleagues' research on domestic violence in Samoa found that "Domestic violence was not a priority on the agenda of the mainstream churches. . . . At the same time, churches were seen to be the agencies which should be playing a lead role in addressing domestic violence and abuse issues."[58]

This resonates with the findings in other studies from the region, which can be summarized as follows: "Most of the mainline churches in Pacific Island countries have not taken a proactive role to question or analyze cultural stereotypes, denounce gender inequalities or violence against women."[59] Because the churches of Oceania are themselves "thoroughly entrapped in patriarchy, it is no wonder that they teach women that they must respect and obey men at all times. . . . This is such a central understanding in these church traditions that it must be viewed as a significant contributing factor to the problem of violence against women."[60]

With respect to male-female relations, the Samoan churches are primarily concerned with maintaining traditional marriage. Marriages must be kept intact at all costs, regardless of the domestic violence that may be occurring within them. Even the churches' marriage vows "reinforce the understanding that the man is given the divine authority to rule over the woman, since the wife promises to obey the husband, but not vice-versa. Because he is given this divine sanction through the sacrament of marriage, it can never be challenged."[61]

It is not surprising, then, that in most cases the church is the last resort for women seeking help in situations of domestic violence. There are several reasons for this. First, these women have often internalized the belief that their abuse is their fault, or to be expected. Second, they feel that naming their abuse to their pastor will bring shame to their family. Third, there is a widespread belief that pastors do not always honor the need for confidentiality, and that gossip about their abuse will be broadcast far and wide. Finally, abused women feel that pastors all too often display a lack of sensitivity to their experience of abuse, counseling them only to become more obedient and submissive wives.

As a result of this tragic failure of the churches' pastoral care, women choose either to endure violence and remain silent or, in despair, to approach a nongovernmental organization such as the Samoa Victim Support Group (SVSG). The SVSG is the one shining ray of hope in darkness in Samoa in its efforts to come to the aid of abused women, to raise Samoan society's awareness of domestic violence, and to combat all forms of violence against women and girls.

Finally, mention must be made of the problem of the collusion of some Samoan clergy in the problem of violence against women. One of the reasons for church ministers' silence on this issue is that some clergy are themselves guilty of violent behavior toward women. Filemoni-Tofaeono and Johnson bring this mostly hidden reality to light: "The venerated position of male clergy [in Samoa] . . . undermines the ability of the church to address the problem of clergy abuse. . . . It is a well-known fact—though one almost never acknowledged—that there are ordained clergy who are themselves perpetrators of abuse against women. . . . These incidents are generally covered up by church authorities."[62] In short, the church is not only silent about domestic violence but is also complicit in it. It protects perpetrators and downplays or turns a blind eye to the domestic violence occurring in its midst.

APPLICATION OF CORE VALUES AS A PUBLIC THEOLOGY RESPONSE TO DOMESTIC VIOLENCE IN SAMOA

The problem of domestic violence in Samoa presents an opportunity "to rediscover our values—as people, as families, as communities of faith, and as a nation."[63] This is so because domestic violence in Samoa reflects a "profound values crisis"[64] among Samoans. It is a problem that requires a search for the common good and a reaffirmation of the value and dignity of all life, including all human life.

With my summary of relevant literature providing a framework for understanding domestic violence, within which the nature of such violence in the Samoan context has been described, I now examine how Samoan core values can contribute to a public theology response to this issue. To that end, it will be helpful to recall what has been learned about Samoan values in this study. As my research has shown, the core values embedded in the *fa'asamoa* cannot be separated from corresponding Christian values. This dual values orientation extends from the personal to the social sphere.

This work proposes that by reviving, reinterpreting, and applying the core Samoan-Christian values of *fa'aaloalo, alofa, tautua, amiotonu,* and *soalaupule*, Samoan public theologians and citizens can develop ways to initiate dialogue on and respond to sensitive social issues such as domestic violence. In these public dialogues, Samoan values will always be interrelated, such that each value supports, validates, and strengthens the others. The following sections suggest how a public theology response to domestic violence might be enacted through a reappropriation of each of the core Samoan-Christian values.

Alofa

Alofa, as we have seen, is much deeper than compassion or natural affection. It is an orientation toward the other which results in attitudes and actions that promote "right relationships." Mulitalo-Lauta highlights this understanding by citing the Samoan saying, *E le na'oupu ma tala, a'omea fa'atino e iloa ai le alofa*. ("It is not just words, but action and commitment which truly demonstrate love, compassion and concern for others.")[65] This resonates with the New Testament Greek understanding of *agape*—unconditional and sacrificial love that seeks to emulate the love of God and Jesus.

Alofa has much to offer to public discussions on domestic violence. We have seen that NGO010, the organization that addresses domestic violence in Samoa, explicitly appeals to the principle of *alofa* as being at the very core of their work. In order to combat domestic violence, *alofa* needs to be restored, first and foremost, within the primary agent of socialization, the *aiga*. To the extent that this happens, successive generations will continue to create a nonviolent environment within the family. This is how the cycle of violence in families can be broken, through reconnecting with the value of *alofa* that protects all *va* relationships in God's creation.

The Apostle Paul, in his advice to the church in Corinth, said, "Love is patient; love is kind; love is not envious or boastful or arrogant or rude. It does not insist on its own way; it is not irritable or resentful; it does not rejoice in wrongdoing, but rejoices in the truth. It bears all things, believes all things, hopes all things, endures all things" (1 Cor. 13:4–7). This is the foundation upon which *alofa/agape* must be built in intimate relationships.

How can this happen in the context of the widespread domestic violence which has become normative in Samoa today? The church must take the lead by initiating a multipronged approach to addressing this problem through reappropriating *alofa*. This approach could include the following initiatives:

- Representatives of NGOs and other professionals who have expertise in dealing with domestic violence could be invited to visit churches, where

workshops could be held that are open to the public. Information about the root causes of domestic violence and its devastating effects on victims could be presented in a non-threatening way, as a compassionate practice of *alofa/agape*.
- Courses in theological schools could intentionally examine the implications of the value of *alofa/agape* for social problems such as domestic violence. Students could explore the meaning of Christian marriage in this light, critically re-examining the effects of biblical passages that present women as submissive partners on Samoan marriages.
- Churches could sponsor public forums on the meaning and ramifications of *alofa* in contemporary Samoa, with a particular focus on what it implies in terms of intimate relationships. These could be advertised widely in the media, and representatives of government could be invited to reflect on how *alofa* could be better integrated into policies and laws relating to domestic violence.

Fa'aaloalo

Alofa is broadly linked to *fa'aaloalo* (respect), as highlighted in this work in the responses of many research participants and experts in Samoan culture. In the Samoan-Christian value system, showing love toward someone cannot be separated from showing respect. This is clearly articulated in Tavita Maliko's statement that "The action [of respect] denotes love and in effect defines the person."[66]

Like *alofa*, *fa'aaloalo* is a holistic principle and set of protocols that govern the observance of *va* relationships among people, with the environment, and with God. In human relationships, "*Fa'aaloalo* is accorded naturally to another Samoan because of that person's ethnicity, gender, *matai* status and background. It is regarded by Samoans as part of the elaborate etiquette which forms the basis of their culture."[67] Although it is often associated with respect for those in authority, *fa'aaloalo* ideally creates equality in relationships if used in its deeper meaning, which is *alo mai, alo atu* (I face you, you face me) or "reciprocal respect."

The concept of *fa'aaloalo* also features prominently in the Christian faith, which calls us to treat the other as we would like to be treated, the essence of the Golden Rule: "In everything, do to others as you would have them do to you" (Mt 7:12). Respect in the biblical tradition is grounded in the fact that all human beings—male and female—are created in the image of God, and are loved and valued unconditionally by God.

In relation to domestic violence, *fa'aaloalo* should be manifested in one's respect for the sacredness of the space between persons (*va*). *Fa'aaloalo* can never be used to justify domestic violence by men insisting that women obey them as a sign of respect. It can be strengthened and reinforced through practical steps such as the following:

- Churches could invite "exemplars of wisdom" (respected experts in *fa'asamoa*) to chair special *talanoa* where dialogues could be held concerning the true meaning of *fa'aaloalo* in Samoa today. Such dialogues could take place over a period of time so that all involved could have a solid understanding of what is entailed in *fa'aaloalo*. Participants could then apply what they have learned to the problem of domestic violence. They could ask questions such as, "What does it mean to enact *fa'aaloalo* in the context of marriage? How is respect best demonstrated between husbands and wives? What does reciprocity mean in marriage? How might the sacred covenant by which brothers must respect their sisters (*feagaiga*) be extended to apply to husbands' respect for their wives?"
- Theological schools could provide intensive refresher courses for clergy, where church ministers and theological students engage in theological reflection about the Christian interpretation of *fa'aaloalo*. Jesus' relationships with others could be studied as examples of Christian *fa'aaloalo*. Participants could then design action plans for their congregations around practical ways to foster *fa'aaloalo* in relationships within the *aiga*. These might include church-sponsored Marriage Enrichment courses or retreats for married couples.
- Churches could partner with NGOs and interested representatives of civil society to arrange public discussions of *fa'aaloalo* through special programs on television and on radio. Based on what has been learned in the *talanoa* in churches and theological schools, proposals could be shared about how to foster *fa'aaloalo* relationships in marriages and families, and how to strengthen social policies that protect women and children from abuse.

Tautua

Tautua for those affected by domestic violence is already manifested in the programs of organizations working to combat domestic violence in Samoa. But the church's role is also important, since part of the church's ministry is to provide pastoral care for both victims and perpetrators of violence. However, this has not happened thus far. The churches' pastoral care for those affected by domestic violence should be their *tautua* to those who are suffering from this trauma.

At the same time, theological reflection is needed to correct the misinterpretations of "selfless service" that have been detrimental to women. In this twisted version of Christian service, abused women "have been exhorted to accept their suffering in imitation of the suffering of Christ . . . [and] counseled to 'carry the cross they have to bear'."[68] This theological distortion of *tautua* has resulted in abused women being counseled by pastors to stay in abusive relationships as a form of *tautua* to their husbands.

While *tautua* functions well in terms of the service provided by untitled men to their *matai*, and by members of various groups within the *nu'u* based on their obligations within their respective groupings, it has been misunderstood within the institution of marriage. Here it seems to have been interpreted as sacrificial service by the wife to the husband, but not by the husband to the wife. To correct this imbalance, the following actions could be taken by public theologians:

- Theological schools can engage in creative theological reflection about the Christian meaning of sacrificial service. They can call on female theologians who have been trained in women's theology to assist them in revisiting biblical passages and theological presuppositions which have relied on patriarchy to teach that Christ-like service means that women must serve their husbands by sacrificing their very selves. Ordained ministers could be invited to join with theological students in *talanoa* exploring how self-sacrifice has been misconstrued so as to keep women subservient, thus opening the door to domestic violence.
- The results of these discussions could then lead to theological schools revisiting the way they teach pastoral care and counseling. Future and present ministers need to be retrained in terms of how they counsel both victims and perpetrators of domestic violence. New courses could be designed that incorporate a critique of how church ministers have contributed to domestic violence by counseling women to obey and serve their husbands, both because this is their "duty" as wives and as a way to avoid future abuse. Scholarship by women in pastoral care and counseling, particularly those who address violence against women, needs to be front and center in the curriculum of these new courses. Women should be included as students and presenters in these courses.
- Broader public discussions also need to take place around the connection between *tautua* and domestic violence. Experts such as physicians, counselors, and representatives of NGOs can join with church members and ministers to explore what can happen when women's *tautua* to their husbands is misused. Victims of domestic violence who are willing to speak out can be invited in public forums to explain how their belief that they must serve their husbands contributed to their husbands believing that they could demand such service and had the right to "punish" their wives through abuse if this service was not to their liking.

Soalaupule

In all relationships there will be differences of opinion. There are no perfect relationships, but the foundation of maintaining healthy relationships is honest, open dialogue. This is the contribution of *soalaupule* to a public response to domestic violence. The Samoan practice of *soalaupule* is inclusive in its positive intent, which is to foster the sharing of ideas. Of course the cultural understanding of *soalaupule* has been constructed in relation to the *fa'amatai*, which assumes respect for hierarchy, rank, and status. This means that honest questions need to be raised about how *soalaupule* should be enacted in marriage relationships.

As Huffer and So'o remind us, "*Soalaupule* also implies *alofa*. The fact that one has been asked to be part of the decision-making process means that someone cares about one's participation and the interests that one might have in the issues that will be discussed."[69] Jesus in his own ministry utilized this value to enhance his disciples' maturity and to reach out to those who were oppressed in his own society (e.g., Zacchaeus [Lk 19:1–10], the Samaritan woman [Jn 4:1–29], and the young lawyer [Lk 10:25–37]), with the aim of effecting their liberation. How might *soalaupule* be brought to bear on the problem of domestic violence?

- Since *soalaupule* is highly valued and well understood by all Samoans, opportunities must be created to enable such dialogues to take place around the issue of domestic violence. These can be initiated by a small group of animators joining together to strategize about the best ways to structure such dialogues. These "prophets" within each of the spheres of Samoan society (church, village, state, academy) would begin by networking—enacting their own *soalaupule*—to brainstorm about the best way to enable such *soalaupule* to take place in the public sphere.
- Because women—particularly victims of domestic violence—may not be comfortable sharing openly about this issue in the presence of men (especially since the village councils where *soalaupule* typically takes place are male-dominated), it may be wise for the *talanoa* to take place initially in women-only and men-only gatherings. Here the "prophets" will again serve as animators, creating the conditions that encourage the open sharing of experiences and ideas around the issue of domestic violence.
- The intention of this *soalaupule* is to allow and encourage the free exchange of opinions which will lead to positive suggestions on how to combat domestic violence. A goal would be to move toward the time when women and men together could discuss the causes of and solutions to domestic violence.
- The church has a special role to play in initiating public *talanoa*, through educational events or media programs, about how *soalaupule* should be

enacted within the marriage relationship itself. Key questions could be: "What does *soalaupule* imply in terms of how husbands and wives communicate with each other? Are they practicing *soalaupule* if husbands are permitted to order their wives to do certain things, while wives can only silently obey?" Clergy who join the ranks of "prophets" can challenge their parishioners to apply *soalaupule* to the marriage relationship through sermons, Christian education, and participation in public forums.

Amiotonu

Because love and justice are intimately intertwined in the *fa'asamoa* and in the Christian tradition, they are essential values that must be brought to bear on the problem of domestic violence. Research has shown that domestic violence, though it may have a variety of proximate causes, occurs because of the unequal power relations endemic to patriarchy. No matter which causes predominate in any given situation, domestic violence is evidence of a lack of justice.

Justice must be seen in the light of God's attributes. If human relationships are rooted in God's justice, men and women will relate to one another by adopting the language and practices of love and justice which are at the very heart of the gospel. This study has highlighted a number of examples of the understanding of justice that permeates scripture, centered in a covenantal relationship with God that flows outward to embrace the fair treatment of all, especially society's most vulnerable.

In relation to domestic violence, the value of *amiotonu* challenges Samoans to work toward establishing ways to combat domestic violence because it is a denial of God's justice. This could be enacted in the following ways:

- The value of *amiotonu* highlights the prophetic role of the church in calling on those who have power and authority—particularly *matai* in the village setting and policy-makers in government—to safeguard the rights and safety of the victims of domestic violence through the enactment of just laws and policies. Here again, the "prophets" who have become allies in proactively working for justice around this issue (ministers, theologians, village and town activists, NGO representatives, progressive politicians, and members of civil society) must gather together to examine existing policies and laws and propose ways of strengthening them.
- The "prophets" who are spearheading this effort should make full use of the media and public forums to dialogue around the meaning of *amiotonu* in relation to domestic violence. They must explore with the public questions such as: "What does justice mean for the victims of domestic violence? What does it mean for the perpetrators? How can perpetrators

be held accountable for their abuse of women while still being treated with Christian love?"

- Theological schools must intentionally revisit the value of *amiotonu* in their training of future ministers. In their biblical studies and pastoral care courses, they must focus on questions such as: "What is God's justice? How can biblical understandings of justice be applied to domestic violence? How should we counsel victims and perpetrators of domestic violence in terms of the understanding of *amiotonu* as a value that upholds the dignity of all people?"

FINAL THOUGHTS

Christian theology does not lack grounds upon which to stand against domestic violence. In fact, in the biblical concept of *shalom* (peace) we encounter a vision of a society without violence or fear. This vision is realized in the promise in Lev 26:6, "I will grant peace in the land, and you shall lie down, and no one shall make you afraid." Commentaries on the concept of *shalom* speak of a profound and holistic experience of well-being—"abundant welfare"—with connotations of justice for all.

In *Until Justice and Peace Embrace*, Nicholas Wolterstorff describes *shalom* as a harmonious and responsible relationship with God, other human beings, and creation.[70] A theology of *shalom* should be offered to the Samoan people as a theological gift to bring about justice, restoration, and healing in relationships where domestic violence has occurred. This theology is especially relevant given the communal self-understanding of Samoans, where the priority is to maintain peace, harmony, and stability.

In the process of naming the church's failure to address domestic violence, opportunities arise to discuss what it would be like if the church embraced its calling to respond to domestic violence as healers. The Samoan Ombudsman, Maiava Toma, challenged the church to rediscover this calling in a sermon on the Good Samaritan, proclaiming, "Surely the time has come for local congregations and for national churches to cross the road and to give of their time and resources to aid victims of violence within our churches and communities."[71] Toma further called for the church to be "a safe place for women to come and tell their story and to seek comfort. They should not be told to go home, to pray more, to submit more, and to turn the other cheek."[72]

If the church were to engage in serious theological reflection about domestic violence, taking on board insights from other relevant disciplines, it would surely be able to become an agent for healing for all those who are affected by domestic violence. This chapter is a challenge to the church to do just that.

NOTES

1. Mata'afa Keni Lesa, "Domestic Violence, a Coward and Speaking Up," *Samoa Observer*, February 18, 2014, n.p.

2. See Jung Young Lee, *Marginality: The Key to Multicultural Theology* (Minneapolis, MN: Augsburg Fortress Press, 1995); Rebecca S. Chopp, *The Power to Speak: Feminism, Language, God* (New York, NY: Crossroad, 1991); and Stephen B. Bevans, *An Introduction to Theology in Global Perspective* (Maryknoll, NY: Orbis Books, 2009), 13.

3. Ellen Pence and Michael Paymar, *Educating Groups for Men Who Batter: The Duluth Model*, 2nd ed. (New York, NY: Springer, 1996).

4. Audrey Mullender and Catherine Humphreys, *Domestic Violence and Child Abuse: Policy and Practice Issues for Local Authorities and Other Agencies* (London: Local Government Association, 1998).

5. Liz Kelly, "The VIP Guide: Vision, Innovation and Professionalism in Policing Violence against Women and Children," *Report Produced for the Council of Europe Police and Human Rights Programme*, 2000, 2.

6. Jeff Hearn, "The Sociological Significance of Domestic Violence: Tensions, Paradoxes and Implications," *Current Sociology* 61, no. 2 (2013): 153.

7. Rachel Ann Taylor, *Professional Perceptions of Domestic Violence: The Relationship between Causal Explanations and Views on Prevention and Intervention* (MCJ Thesis, Edith Cowan University, 2006), 31.

8. Ibid., 32.

9. Pence and Paymar, *Educating Groups for Men Who Batter*, xii.

10. Ibid., 3. Cited in Alan Edwards and Susan Sharpe, *Restorative Justice in the Context of Domestic Violence: A Literature Review* (Edmonton, AB: Mediation and Restorative Justice Centre, 2004). Their research also debunks the myth that domestic violence only happens among poor and uneducated people or in unstable families.

11. Joan A. Filemoni-Tofaeono and Lydia F. Johnson, *Reweaving the Relational Mat: A Christian Response to Violence Against Women from Oceania* (London: Equinox Press, 2006), 9.

12. Taylor, "Professional Perceptions of Domestic Violence," 31. See also F. M. Moghaddam, *Social Psychology: Exploring Universals Across Cultures* (New York, NY: W. H. Freeman, 1998); and "Domestic Violence," *Report Prepared for the Australian Institute of Criminology*, 1998.

13. Taylor, "Professional Perceptions of Domestic Violence," 31.

14. Ibid.

15. Ibid.

16. Ibid.

17. A recent contribution to the development of the field of psychology in the Pacific is Linda Waimarie Nikora, "Pacific Indigenous Psychologies—Starting Points," in *Relational Hermeneutics: Decolonising the Mindset and the Pacific Itulagi*, ed. Upolu L. Vaai and Aisake Casimira (Suva, FJ: Pacific Theological College and University of the South Pacific, 2017), 143–50.

18. Abhinaya Ramesh, "Why Is Domestic Violence a Human Rights Concern?," *Journal of Association for Women's Rights in Development* 110 (December 2008), accessed June 2014, http:www.eurowrc.org/06.contributions/1.contrib_en/51cor.

19. Christopher D. Marshall, *Crowned with Glory and Honour: Human Rights in the Biblical Tradition* (Kitchener, ON: Pandora Press, 2001), 116.

20. Michael Thomas, "Treatment of Family Violence: A Systemic Perspective," in *Family Intervention in Domestic Violence: A Handbook of Gender-Inclusive Theory and Treatment*, ed. John Hamel and Tonia L. Nicholls (New York, NY: Springer, 2007), 433.

21. Filemoni-Tofaeono and Johnson, *Reweaving the Relational Mat*, 11. Italics in original.

22. Secretariat for Pacific Community, *Annual Report* (Noumea, NCL: SPC, 2007), 14. Cited in Maiava Carmel Peteru, *Falevitu: A Literature Review on Culture and Family Violence in Seven Pacific Communities in New Zealand* (Auckland: Ministry of Social Development, 2012), 31.

23. Sophie Budvietas, "Enough Is Enough," *Samoa Observer*, December 18, 2013, n.p.

24. Peseta Betty Sio, "O Le Tofa Mamao: A Samoan Conceptual Framework for Addressing Family Violence," Paper Presented, *Auckland Regional Network Meeting—Family and Sexual Violence*, Western Springs, Auckland, NZ, September 10, 2012, 7.

25. Ministry of Women, Community and Social Development, Government of Samoa, *Samoa Family Safety Study* (Apia, WS: MWCSD, 2017), 3.

26. Samoa Victim Support Group, "Stop the Violence against Women," accessed August 2018, http://www.victimsupport.ws/stop-the-violence-against-women.html.

27. Sarai Ripine, "60-Year-Old-Father Jailed for Raping Daughter," *Samoa Observer*, March 20, 2013, n.p.

28. Jasmine Netzler, "Life of Fear," *Samoa Observer*, November 3, 2012.

29. Budvietas, "Enough Is Enough."

30. Sophie Budvietas, "Lemalu Sina Retzlaff Breaking the Silence," *Samoa Observer*, January 1, 2014.

31. Mata'afa Keni Lesa, "Domestic Violence, a Coward and Speaking Up," *Samoa Observer*, February 18, 2014, n.p.

32. Ibid.

33. Aquila Yabaki, Paper Presented, *Pacific Regional Workshop on Strengthening Partnerships for Eliminating Violence Against Women*, Pacific Forum Secretariat, Suva, Fiji, February 17–19, 2003.

34. Sio, "O Le Tofa Mamao," ii.

35. Filemoni-Tofaeono and Johnson, *Reweaving the Relational Mat*, 51.

36. Yabaki, Paper Presented, *Pacific Regional Workshop*.

37. "Overview of Efforts to Eliminate Violence Against Women in the Pacific," in *Strengthening Pacific Partnerships for Eliminating Violence Against Women: A Pacific Regional Workshop Report* (London and Suva, FJ: Commonwealth Secretariat, UNDP/UNIFEM/Pacific Islands Forum Secretariat, 2003), 82.

38. Cited in David G. Hallman, *Spiritual Values for Earth Community*, Risk Book Series (Geneva: WCC, 2000), 33.

39. Ibid.

40. Jason Brown, "Lack of Hard Facts Holding Women Back," *Samoa Observer*, March 8, 2014, n.p.

41. Lydia F. Johnson, *Drinking from the Same Well: Cross-Cultural Concerns in Pastoral Care and Counseling* (Eugene, OR: Wipf & Stock Publications, 2011), 30.

42. Elisabeth Schüssler Fiorenza, "The Will to Choose or Reject: Continuing our Critical Work," in *Feminist Interpretation of the Bible*, ed. Letty Russell (Philadelphia, PA: Westminster Press, 1985), 130.

43. Samantha Gerson, "Feminist Biblical Interpretation," *Capstone Project* (Spring 2014): 1–2, accessed August 2018, https://www.artsci.uc.edu/content/dam/artsci/departments/Judaic%20studies/Docs/Capstone_Final.pdf.

44. The interplay of nineteenth-century British patriarchy and Pacific Islands patriarchy has been noted by another Polynesian woman theologian, Lousiale Uasike, whose Tongan culture shares many affinities with Samoan culture. She describes how the Victorian missionary culture bolstered existing patriarchal island social structures, noting that "the Christianity that was brought to Tonga arrived in patriarchal form, and this comfortably reinforced the existing Tongan patriarchy." Lousiale Uasike, *Women in Transforming Mission: The Wesleyan Authority of Experience and Women Doing Theology in Tonga* (DMin Diss., San Francisco Theological Seminary, 2014), 128.

45. Filemoni-Tofaeono and Johnson, *Reweaving the Relational Mat*, 96.

46. Brian Wren, *What Language Shall I Borrow? God-Talk in Worship: A Male Response to Feminist Theology* (London: SCM Press, 1989), 56. At the top of this patriarchal pyramid is "Yahweh . . . Just below 'Him' are males, who are the 'heads' of households and societies. Their characteristics and prerogatives mirror those of the patriarchal God."

47. Rosemary Ruether, *Women-Church: Theology and Practice* (San Francisco, CA: Harper & Row, 1985), 70.

48. Elizabeth Johnson, "Naming God She: The Theological Implications," *Boardman Lecture in Christian Ethics, Scholarly Commons*, University of Pennsylvania, October 19, 2000, 1.

49. Ibid.

50. Filemoni-Tofaeono and Johnson, *Reweaving the Relational Mat*, 81.

51. Helen Hood, "Speaking Out and Doing Justice: It's No Longer a Secret but What are the Churches Doing about Overcoming Violence Against Women?," *Feminist Theology* 11, no. 2 (2003): 220.

52. These passages have been analyzed in some depth in Filemoni-Tofaeono and Johnson, *Reweaving the Relational Mat*, 97–101.

53. Elsa Tamez, "Women's Re-Reading of the Bible," in *With Passion and Compassion: Third World Women Doing Theology*, ed. Virginia Fabella and Mercy Amba Oduyoye (Maryknoll, NY: Orbis Books, 1988), 176. See also her more recent "Feminist Biblical Studies in Latin America and the Caribbean," in *Feminist Biblical Studies in the Twentieth Century: Scholarship and Movement*, The Bible and Women, ed. Elisabeth Schüssler Fiorenza (Atlanta, GA: Society of Biblical Literature, 2014), 35–52. Similar voices in non-Western feminist biblical scholarship include women

such as Kwok Pui-Lan, Dora Mbuwayesango, Nambalirwa Helen Nkabala, Muriel Orevillo-Montenegro, and Jacqueline Hidalgo.

54. Filemoni-Tofaeono and Johnson, *Reweaving the Relational Mat*, 96.

55. Maretha M. Jacobs, "The 'Sense' of Feminist Biblical Scholarship for Church and Society," *Scriptura* 80 (2002): 174. Italics in original.

56. Letty M. Russell, "Introduction: Liberating the Word," in *Feminist Interpretation of the Bible*, ed. Letty M. Russell (Philadelphia, PA: Westminster Press, 1985), 11.

57. See Penny Martin, "Implementing Women's and Children's Rights: The Case of Domestic Violence in Samoa," *Alternative Law Journal* 27, no. 5 (October 2002): 227, Attachment 12.

58. Sio, "O Le Tofa Mamao," 37.

59. AusAID, *Annual Report 2007–2008* (Canberra: Australia Department of Foreign Affairs and Trade, 2008), 18. See also Atunaisa Laqeretabua, Vijay Naidu, and Sharon Bhagwan-Rolls, *Pacific Perspectives on the Commercial Sexual Exploitation and Sexual Abuse of Children and Youth* (Bangkok: United Nations Economic and Social Commission for Asia and the Pacific, 2009), 97.

60. Filemoni-Tofaeono and Johnson, *Reweaving the Relational Mat*, 106.

61. Ibid.

62. Ibid., 120.

63. Seyla Benhabib, *The Claims of Culture: Equality and Diversity in the Global Era* (Princeton, NJ: Princeton University Press, 2002), 1.

64. Ibid.

65. Mulitalo-Lauta, *Fa'asamoa and Social Work*, 22.

66. Tavita Maliko, *O Le Soga'imiti: The Embodiment of God in the Samoan Male Body* (PhD Thesis, University of Auckland, 2012), 217.

67. Mulitalo-Lauta, *Fa'asamoa and Social Work*, 21.

68. Filemoni-Tofaeono and Johnson, *Reweaving the Relational Mat*, 89. Aruna Gnanadasen describes this pastoral counseling for abused women this way: "Christ suffered on the cross; can't you bear a little suffering too?" See Aruna Gnanadasen, *No Longer a Secret: The Church and Violence Against Women*, rev. ed. (Geneva: WCC Publications, 1997), 49.

69. Huffer and So'o, "Consensus Versus Dissent," 249.

70. Nicholas Wolsterstorff, *Until Justice and Peace Embrace* (Grand Rapids, MI: William B. Eerdmans, 1994).

71. Maiava Iulai Toma, "Churches Need to Bear Witness to Domestic Violence," *Samoa Observer*, December 12, 2013.

72. Ibid.

Epilogue

I end with a summary of the findings of this work regarding a proposed values-centered public theology, as well as recommendations for future reflection and action. As noted in the Prologue, my effort to do research on public theology in Samoa was met initially with a discovery of the dearth of published information on my topic. Although the literature on public theology in the Western world is extensive, the absence of materials on the concept of public theology in the Samoan or Oceanian context made this research particularly challenging. This necessitated a commitment to move with deliberation, and some risk-taking, toward my own response to the absence of a public theology in Samoa and the broader Pacific.

SUMMARY

This study argues for the need to develop a Samoan public theology premised on the conviction that theological discourse in the Samoan public square, if it is to have relevance for society as a whole, must reflect values that are central to the Samoan collective identity. In the process of constructing a Samoan public theology, the main focus has been on responding to central questions such as: What might a Samoan public theology look like? What are its constitutive elements? How might we go about doing public theology in Samoa? Who would be its agents? What avenues might they pursue to enact public theology?

On that basis, the study focused on the "why, what, who and how" of a relevant public theology for Samoan society. This began with a survey of the literature on public theology emanating largely from the West, followed by an introduction to the Samoan context in terms of its core cultural and Christian values. The study then examined in greater depth the significance of the *fa'asamoa* and its value system, including the ways in which *aganu'u*, *agaifanua*, and *fa'akerisiano* have shaped Samoan identity. I have argued that what we now perceive as the *fa'asamoa* is enacted through the interplay of these three core social constructs.

I next examined the contextual nature of public theology, with an eye toward establishing a deeper understanding of the Samoan context, both in terms of its cultural beliefs and customs and its incorporation and synthesis of Christian beliefs and values within its cultural worldview. Because of the thoroughgoing fusion of Samoan and Christian values, I proceeded on the premise that any authentic public theology for Samoa must engage with the core Samoan-Christian values of *alofa, fa'aaloalo, tautua, soalaupule*, and *amiotonu*. This contextual approach was aided by insights gleaned from Stephen Bevans' synthetic model of contextual theology, which insists on a balance between the experiential starting point of all theological reflection (context) and the enduring foundation of Christian beliefs and traditions.

Because the subjects of public theology are "the public" in whose interest theology exists, a crucial element of this research was the incorporation of knowledge from representative voices within contemporary Samoan society. Using constructivist grounded theory and *talanoa* as research methodologies to gather useful information, I conducted seventy-five interviews with the Samoan public, within the four spheres of government, churches, villages, and civil society. These interviews garnered valuable information on the participants' core values and their understanding of public theology. Their views proved to be critical to the process of constructing a public theology for Samoa; indeed, their contributions revealed that public theology is already being practiced by some of "the public." Acknowledging the importance of Pacific Indigenous Research, the *talanoa* dialogical approach was used in the process of acquiring information in a way that honored the participants' self-understanding and that sought at all times to achieve authenticity in describing their perspectives.

The conclusion of this research is that the core values articulated in this study, and the ways in which they can be brought to bear on social issues such as the problem of domestic violence, can contribute significantly to theological discourse in the Samoan public sphere. *Alofa, fa'aaloalo, tautua, soalaupule*, and *amiotonu* suggest concrete ways of shaping such discourse and the moral actions and public policies that can flow from this discourse. Samoa's core values have everything to do with both personal morality and social ethics. And, as this research has revealed consistently, these core values are always interrelated.

Findings from this study also demonstrate the complexity of the Samoan self. Such complexity complicates the difficult task of interrogating one's core values in public—difficult because Samoans' personal values are connected to the values of their parents, extended family, village, church, and Samoan society as a whole. Questioning how these core values are (or are not) being adequately lived out in Samoan society today necessarily involves questioning the efficacy of the agents of socialization (family, village, and church). This means asking these agents, "How well are we applying our commonly held core values to the social problems with which we are confronted?"

Given the increasing influence of globalization in Samoa, the Samoan "relational self" is also being challenged by an alien worldview—a foreign value system that is impinging on Samoan society in many ways. The absence of an effective public theology in the Samoan public sphere in the face of this onslaught of globalization has contributed to the fraying of the social fabric. It has contributed to the perils of growing violence and abuse, corruption, crime, environmental destruction, growing economic disparities, and so on. Although not a subject for research in this study, it is incumbent upon Samoan public theologians to grapple with the societal, cultural, and religious ramifications of the globalized world in which we live.

This study culminated in a contextual application of the principles of public theology, demonstrating how a Samoan public theology of values might be applied to the social problem of domestic violence. In this as in other examples, theologians, lay people, and the general Samoan public must be continually reminded of their underlying objective, which is to work for the common good and flourishing of all.

It is also important to stress that this study is ultimately not simply for Samoans. Every society has its own core values, created, cultivated, and sustained over countless generations. Although typically taken for granted, every society is capable of revisiting, reflecting on, and revitalizing its core values in relation to contemporary realities. Every society confronts social problems in the public sphere, including the problem addressed in this study, domestic violence. In this sense, my proposal to "do" public theology by means of a re-examination of core values is an invitation to other cultural and religious communities to do the same.

RECOMMENDATIONS

This work would not be complete without recommendations related to how the proposed public theology of values might best take shape in the Samoan public square. The following suggestions are offered as a way to initiate the practice of public theology, beginning with a broadening of people's understanding of its significance for the well-being of all Samoans. My hope is that the concerns that undergird these recommendations might also suggest applicability in other contexts, particularly in other Oceanian societies.

1. An initial period of orientation is needed, initiated by the churches, so that people can respond to the following questions through the process of *talanoa*:
   What is public theology?
   Where does it happen?
   Who is involved?
   Why do we need a public theology?
   How do we do public theology?
2. After addressing the above questions, representatives of the churches, villages, civil society, and government should intentionally search for ways to ensure that the contributions of public theology are well publicized and well received in deliberations on social policies and issues. This will entail the inclusion of public theology in the curriculum of theological schools, and their hosting of forums on social issues to which representatives of all sectors of society are invited—clergy, laity, government, and civil society.
3. Lay Christians, theologians, and clergy are challenged to work in a collaborative manner to create awareness of the importance of public theology in their everyday lives. This can be implemented through ongoing *talanoa*, workshops, forums, or informal gatherings hosted by villages and churches.
4. The churches, through the National Council of Churches, should include in their ecumenical programs a focus on social issues that people encounter in the public sphere. Such initiatives must address the relationship between church and state. This includes issues relating to public policies, laws, and constitutional frameworks. The issue of domestic violence could be used as a starting point for such programs, drawing on the framework outlined in this study.
5. Samoan public theology must work in an interdisciplinary manner that involves seeking assistance from experts on particular public issues being addressed. Theological schools are encouraged to collaborate with academics at the National University of Samoa and professionals in the public and private sectors to promote greater public awareness of particular social issues.
6. The vision and language of Samoan public theology must at all times be rooted in Samoan core values and Jesus's life-giving vision and ministry. This requires both serious theological reflection and social analysis, at all levels of church and society.

These recommendations are presented in the hope that they will become avenues to enhance better communication and collaboration between church and society, but most of all to recover the common good. The proposed Samoan public theology of values will not achieve its practical embodiment if people depend only on their own wisdom and understanding, without the power and guidance of the Holy Spirit. It is with this foundation in mind that I humbly offer this work as a potential springboard for a much broader *talanoa* on the gift of public theology to the people of Samoa, to other Oceanian communities, and beyond.

Bibliography

Afamasaga, Toleafoa. "Of Sacred Cows and Cash Cows and Violence in God's Own." *Samoa Observer*, October 7, 2007, 2.
Afamasaga, Toleafoa, and Kuineselani Tago. "Family Health and Safety Study of Violence Against Women in Oceania." Report prepared for the Samoan Ministry of Women, the South Pacific Commission, and the UN Development Program, Presented at the *Pacific Regional Workshop on Strengthening Partnerships for Eliminating Violence Against Women*, Suva, Fiji, February 17–19, 2003.
Ahdar, Rex Tauati. "Is Samoa a Christian State?" *Public Lecture*, National University of Samoa, Le Papaigalagala, October 6, 2011.
———. "Samoa and the Christian State Ideal." *International Journal for the Study of the Christian Church* 13, no. 1 (2013): 59–72.
Ah Siu-Maliko, Mercy. "Conscientization and Pacific Women." *Pacific Journal of Theology* II, no. 40 (2008): 64–84.
———. "Women in Acts and in Oceania." In *A Commentary on Acts*, edited by Yon Gyong Kwon, 160–168. London: SPCK, 2012.
Aiono-Le Tagaloa, Fanaafi. *O La Ta Gagana*. Alafua, WS: Lamepa Press, 1996.
———. "Samoan Culture: Language and Communication." Paper Presented, *South Pacific Association of Theological Schools*, Piula Theological College, Samoa, 1994.
———. "The Samoan Culture and Government." In *Culture and Democracy in the South Pacific*, edited by Ron Crocombe, Uentabo Neemia, Asesela Ravuvu, and Werner Von Busch, 117–138. Suva, FJ: University of the South Pacific, 1992.
———. *Tupuai: Samoan Worship*. BA Hons Thesis, University of Otago, 2001.
Alatini, Moses N. *Housing and Related Social Conditions of the Tongan Community Living in Otara (Ko e Fale Nofo'anga pea mo 'ene Fekau'aki mo e Mo'ui 'a e Kainga Tonga Nofo 'i Otara)*. MA Thesis, University of Auckland, 2004.
"American Samoa Population." *Worldometers*. Accessed November 21, 2019. https://www.worldometers.info/world-population/american-samoa-population/.

Anae, Melanie. *Fofoa-i-vao-ese: The Identity Journeys of New Zealand Born Samoans*. PhD Thesis, University of Auckland, 1998.
———. "Nafanua and Reflections on Samoan Female Sexual Personhood." In *The Relational Self: Decolonising Personhood in the Pacific*, edited by Upolu L. Vaai and Unaisi Nabobo-Baba, 203–219. Suva, FJ: Pacific Theological College and University of the South Pacific, 2017.
Andre, Claire, Manuel Velasquez, Thomas Shanks, and Michael J. Meyer. "The Common Good." Last modified August 2, 2014. http://www.scu.edu/ethics/practicing/decision/commongood.html.
Annells, Merilyn. *The Impact of Flatus upon the Nursed*. PhD Thesis, Flinders University of South Australia, 1997.
Atherton, John. "Marginalization, Manchester and the Scope of Public Theology." *Studies in Christian Ethics* 17, no. 2 (2004): 20–36.
AusAID. *Annual Report 2007–2008*. Canberra: Australia Department of Foreign Affairs and Trade, 2008.
Barber, William. "America's Moral Malady and a New Poor People's Campaign." *The Atlantic*, February 2018. https://www.theatlantic.com/magazine/archive/2018/02/a-new-poor-peoples-campaign/552503/.
Bedford-Strohm, Heinrich. *Liberation Theology for a Democratic Society: Essays in Public Theology*. Zurich: Lit Verlag GmbH & Co., 2018.
———. "Poverty and Public Theology: Advocacy of the Church in a Pluralistic Society." *International Journal of Public Theology* 1, no. 2 (2008): 230–248.
———. "Public Theology and Political Ethics." *International Journal of Public Theology* 6, no. 3 (2012): 273–291.
Bellah, Robert N. "Civil Religion in America." *Daedulus* 90, no. 1 (1967): 1–21.
———, Richard Madsen, William M. Sullivan, Ann Swindler, and Steven M. Tipton. *Habits of the Heart: Individualism and Commitment in American Life*. Berkeley, CA: University of California Press, 1985.
Benhabib, Seyla. "Models of Public Space: Hannah Arendt, the Liberal Tradition, and Jürgen Habermas." In *Habermas and the Public Sphere*, edited by Craig Calhoun, 73–98. Cambridge, MA: MIT Press, 1992.
———. *Situating the Self: Gender, Community and Postmodernism in Contemporary Ethics*. Cambridge, MA: Polity Press, 1992.
———. *The Claims of Culture: Equality and Diversity in the Global Era*. Princeton, NJ: Princeton University Press, 2002.
Benne, Robert. *The Paradoxical Vision: A Public Theology for the Twenty-First Century*. Minneapolis, MN: Fortress Press, 1995.
Berger, Peter. *The Desecularization of the World: Resurgent Religion and World Politics*. Grand Rapids, MI: William B. Eerdmans, 1999.
———. *The Sacred Canopy: Elements of a Sociological Theory of Religion*. New York, NY: Anchor, 1990.
Bevans, Stephen. *An Introduction to Theology in Global Perspective*. Maryknoll, NY: Orbis Books, 2009.
———. *Models of Contextual Theology*. Revised and expanded. Maryknoll, NY: Orbis Books, 2002 [1997] [1992].

———. "Models of Contextual Theology." *Missiology: An International Review* 13, no. 2 (April 1985): 185–202.
———. "What Has Contextual Theology to Offer to the Church of the 21st Century?" *Mission in Context Lecture*, Church Mission Society, Oxford, UK, October 15, 2009.
Boff, Leonardo, and Clodovis Boff. *Introducing Liberation Theology*. Maryknoll, NY: Orbis Books, 1987.
Bond, L. Susan. "What is Public Theology?" *Encounter* 70, no. 4 (2009): 33–52.
Bonhoeffer, Dietrich. *Ethics*. New York, NY: Touchstone, 1995.
———. *Letters and Papers from Prison*. Abridged edition. Edited by Eberhard Bethge. London: SCM Press, 1953.
Bonino, José Miguez. *Toward a Christian Political Ethics*. Minneapolis, MN: Fortress Press, 1983.
Bosch, David J. *Transforming Mission: Paradigm Shifts in Theology of Mission*. Maryknoll, NY: Orbis Books, 1991.
Boston, Jonathan. "Christianity in the Public Square." In *Voices for Justice: Church, Law and State in New Zealand*, edited by Alan Cameron and Jonathan Boston, 11–35. Palmerston North, NZ: The Dunmore Press, 1998.
Bradstock, Andrew. "Doing God, Doing Good: The Role of Theology in the Public Square." *Public Lecture*, Centre for Theology and Public Issues, University of Otago, Dunedin, NZ, July 2008.
———. "In Search of a Good Society: Theology, Secularism and the Importance of Vision." *Public Lecture*, Ephesus Centre, Timaru, NZ, July 14, 2013.
———. "Public Theology? No Thanks, I'll Stick with the Normal Kind." *Public Lecture*, Centre for Theology and Public Issues, University of Otago, Dunedin, NZ, June 2, 2010.
———. "Recovering the Common Good: The Key to Truly Prosperous Society?" *Public Lecture*, Centre for Theology and Public Issues, University of Otago, Dunedin, NZ, January 21, 2013.
———. "Seeking the Welfare of the City: Public Theology as Radical Action." In *Radical Christian Voices and Practice: Essays in Honour of Christopher Rowland*, edited by Zoe Bennett and David B. Gowler, 225–240. Oxford: Oxford University Press, 2012.
———. "The Bible in the Public Square." Paper Presented, *Great and Manifold Conference: A Celebration of the Publication of the King James Bible in 1611*, Wellington, NZ, August 27, 2011.
———. "Theology and Values in Secular Society." Paper Presented, *Sea of Faith Network (NZ) Conference*, Auckland, NZ, October 5–7, 2012.
Breckenridge, Jenna P. "Choosing a Methodological Path: Reflections on the Constructivist Turn." *Grounded Theory Review: An International Journal* 11, no. 1 (2012): 1–13.
Breitenberg, Eugene Harold. "To Tell the Truth: Will the Real Public Theology Please Stand Up?" *Journal of the Society of Christian Ethics* 23, no. 2 (2003): 55–96.
———. "What Is Public Theology?" In *Public Theology for a Global Society: Essays in Honor of Max L. Stackhouse*, edited by Deidre King Hainsworth and Scott R. Paeth, 3–17. Grand Rapids, MI: William B. Eerdmans, 2010.

Brown, Malcolm, Stephen Pattison, and Graeme Smith. "The Possibility of Citizen Theology: Public Theology after Christendom and the Enlightenment." *International Journal of Public Theology* 6, no. 2 (2012): 183–204.

Browning, Don S., and Francis S. Fiorenza. *Habermas, Modernity, and Public Theology*. New York, NY: Crossroad Publishing, 1992.

Brueggemann, Walter. *Journey to the Common Good*. Louisville, KY: Westminster John Knox Press, 2010.

Budvietas, Sophie. "Enough is Enough." *Samoa Observer*, December 18, 2013.

———. "Lemalu Sina Retzlaff Breaking the Silence." *Samoa Observer*, January 1, 2014.

Burr, Vivien. *Social Constructionism*. 2nd edition. London: Routledge, 2003.

Cady, Linell, and Elizabeth S. Hurd. *Comparative Secularisms in a Global Age*. London: Palgrave Macmillan, 2013.

Calhoun, Craig J. *Habermas and the Public Sphere*. Cambridge, MA: MIT Press, 1992.

Calvin, John. *Calvin's New Testament Commentaries: Romans and Thessalonians*, edited by Thomas F. Torrance and David W. Torrance, translated by Ross Mackenzie. Milton Keynes, UK: Paternoster Press, 1960.

Cantor, Emma. "Violence Against Women." In *In God's Image: Human Rights and Human Dignity*, edited by Hope Antone, Irene Chan, James Isbister, and Aida Jean Manipon, 31–36. Hong Kong: Christian Conference of Asia, 1996.

Carter, Stephen L. *The Culture of Disbelief: How American Law and Politics Trivialize Religious Devotion*. New York, NY: Basic Books, 1993.

Casimira, Aisake, and Anna Anisi. "An Historical Overview of Ecumenical Formation and Development." In *Navigating Troubled Waters: The Ecumenical Movement in the Pacific Islands Since the 1980s*, edited by Manfred Ernst and Lydia Johnson, 13–50. Suva, FJ: Pacific Theological College, 2017.

Chan Mow, Ioana. *The Effectiveness of Cognitive Apprenticeship Based Learning Environment (CABLE) in Teaching Computer Programming*. PhD Thesis, University of South Australia, 2006.

Chaplin, Jonathan. *Talking God: The Legitimacy of Religious Public Reasoning*. London: Theos, 2008.

Charmaz, Kathy. "Between Positivism and Postmodernism: Implications for Methods." *Studies in Symbolic Interaction* 17 (1995): 43–72.

———. *Constructing Grounded Theory: A Practical Guide through Qualitative Analysis*. London: Sage Publications, 2006.

———. "Grounded Theory: Objectivist and Constructivist Methods." In *Strategies of Qualitative Inquiry*, edited by Norman K. Denzin and Yvonna S. Lincoln, 249–291. London: Sage Publications, 2006.

Chopp, Rebecca S. *The Power to Speak: Feminism, Language, God*. New York, NY: Crossroad Publishing, 1991.

Chung, Paul S. *Public Theology in an Age of World Christianity: God's Mission as World Event*. New York, NY: Palgrave Macmillan, 2010.

Conn, Harvie M. "Contextualization: Where Do We Begin?" In *Evangelicals and Liberation*, edited by Carl E. Amerding, 90–119. Phillipsburg, NJ: Presbyterian and Reformed Publishing, 1977.

Corbin, Juliet, and Anselm Strauss. *Basics of Qualitative Research: Grounded Theory Procedures and Techniques.* 2nd edition. Thousand Oaks, CA: SAGE Publications, 1990.

Cortez, Marc. *Models, Metaphors, and Multivalent Contextualizations: Religious Language and the Nature of Contextual Theology.* MTh Thesis, Western Theological Seminary, 2004.

Corvino, John. "Drawing a Line in the 'Gay Wedding Cake' Case." *New York Times,* November 27, 2017. https://www.nytimes.com/2017/11/27/opinion/gay-wedding-cake.html.

Crawford, Ronald James. *The Lotu and the Fa'asamoa: Church and Society in Samoa, 1830–1880.* PhD Thesis, University of Otago, 1977.

Cronshaw, Darren. "The Shaping of Public Theology in Emerging Churches." Paper Presented, *Australian Association of Mission Studies & Public and Contextual Theology Conference,* Australian Centre for Christianity and Culture, Canberra, October 4, 2008.

Darragh, Neil. "Doing Theology in Public: An Engagement with Economic Rationalism." *International Journal of Public Theology* 4, no. 4 (2010): 391–409.

Davies, Brian, and G. R. Evans, eds. *Anselm of Canterbury: The Major Works.* Oxford: Oxford University Press, 1998.

Davis, Charles. *Religion and the Making of Society: Essays in Social Theology.* Cambridge: Cambridge University Press, 1994.

Day, Katie. "The Construction of Public Theology: An Ethnographic Study of the Relationship between the Theological Academy and Local Clergy in South Africa." *International Journal of Public Theology* 2, no. 3 (2008): 354–378.

de Gruchy, John W. "From Political to Public Theologies: The Role of Theology in Public Life in South Africa." In *Public Theology for the Twenty-first Century: Essays in Honour of Duncan B. Forrester,* edited by William F. Storrar and Andrew R. Morton, 45–62. London and New York, NY: T&T Clark, 2004.

———. "Public Theology as Christian Witness: Exploring the Genre." *International Journal of Public Theology* 1, no. 1 (2007): 26–41.

de Gruchy, John W., and Steven Martin, eds. *Religion and the Reconstruction of Civil Society.* Pretoria, SA: UNISA, 1995.

Deist, Ferdinand. *A Concise Dictionary of Theological Terms, with an English-Afrikaans and Afrikaans-English List.* Pretoria, SA: Van Schalk, 1984.

de Lange, Frits. "Against Escapism: Dietrich Bonhoeffer's Contribution to Public Theology." In *Christians in Public: Aims, Methodologies and Issues in Public Theology,* edited by Len Hansen, 141–152. Beyers Naudé Centre Series on Public Theology #3. Stellenbosch, SA: Sun Press, 2008.

Derrida, Jacques. *Acts of Religion.* London: Routledge, 2001.

———. *Sovereignties in Question: The Poetics of Paul Celan.* New York, NY: Fordham University Press, 2005.

Dewey, John. *The Public and its Problems: An Essay in Political Inquiry.* Revised edition. Edited and with an Introduction by Melvin L. Rogers. University Park, PA: Penn State University Press, 2012.

Doak, Mary. *Reclaiming Narrative for Public Theology*. Albany, NY: SUNY Press, 2004.
Dorrien, Gary J. *Reconstructing the Common Good: Theology and the Social Order*. Maryknoll, NY: Orbis Books, 1990.
Drozdow-St. Christian, Douglas. *Elusive Fragments: Making Power, Propriety and Health in Samoa*. Durham, NC: Carolina Academic Press, 2002.
Duranti, Alessandro. "Intentions, Language, and Social Action in a Samoan Context." *Journal of Pragmatics* 12 (1988): 13–33.
———. "Language and Bodies in Social Space: Samoan Ceremonial Greetings." *American Anthropologist, New Series* 94, no. 3 (1992): 657–691.
Ebeling, Gerhard. *s v Theologie: Begriffgeschichtlich*. Religion in Geschichte und Gegenwart, Vol. 1. Edited by Kurt Galling. Tubingen: Mohr (Paul Siebeck), 1957.
Edwards, Alan, and Susan Sharpe. *Restorative Justice in the Context of Domestic Violence: A Literature Review*. Edmonton, AB: Mediation and Restorative Justice Center, 2004.
Efi, Tui Atua Tupua Tamasese Taisi. "A Wedding, A Party and Samoan Funerals: Pacific Leadership and Cultural Competence." In *Su'esu'e Manogi: In Search of Fragrance*, edited by I'uogafa Tuagalu, Tamasa'ilau Sualii-Sauni, Tofilau Nina Kirifi-Alai, and Naomi Fuamatu, 123–126. Le Papaigalagala, WS: Centre for Samoan Studies, National University of Samoa, 2008.
———. "*Fa'asamoa* Speaks to my Heart and my Soul." In *Su'esu'e Manogi: In Search of Fragrance*, edited by I'uogafa Tuagalu, Tamasa'ilau Sualii-Sauni, Tofilau Nina Kirifi-Alai, and Naomi Fuamatu, 52–69. Le Papaigalagala, WS: Centre for Samoan Studies, National University of Samoa, 2008.
———. "More on Meaning, Nuance and Metaphor." In *Su'esu'e Manogi: In Search of Fragrance*, edited by I'uogafa Tuagalu, Tamasa'ilau Sualii-Sauni, Tofilau Nina Kirifi-Alai, and Naomi Fuamatu, 70–103. Le Papaigalagala, WS: Centre for Samoan Studies, National University of Samoa, 2008.
———. "Navigating Our Future Together." Paper Presented, *Emerging Pacific Leaders Dialogue Conference*, Brisbane, Australia, June 28, 2006.
———. "*O Le e Lave i Tiga, O le Ivi, le Toto, ma le Aano*: He Who Rallies in my Hour of Need is my Kin." Paper Presented, *New Zealand Families Commission, Pasifika Families Fono*, Wellington, NZ, November 3, 2009.
———. "*Sufiga o le Tuaoi*: Negotiating Boundaries—from Beethoven to Tupac, the Pope to the Dalai Lama." Paper Presented, *Samoa Conference II*, National University of Samoa, Le Papaigalagala, July 5, 2011.
———. *Tau Mai Na O Le Pua Ula: Fragrancing Samoan Thought*. Dunedin, NZ: University of Otago Press, 2009.
———. "*Tupualegase*: The Eternal Riddle." In *Su'esu'e Manogi: In Search of Fragrance*, edited by I'uogafa Tuagalu, Tamasa'ilau Sualii-Sauni, Tofilau Nina Kirifi-Alai, and Naomi Fuamatu, 207–213. Le Papaigalagala, WS: Centre for Samoan Studies, National University of Samoa, 2008.
———. "Whispers of Vanities in Samoan Indigenous Religious Culture." *Public Lecture*, World Parliament of Religions, Melbourne, Australia, December 3, 2009.

Elliott, Alison. "Doing Theology: Engaging the Public." *International Journal of Public Theology* 1, nos. 3 and 4 (2007): 290–305.

Ernst, Manfred. "Ecumenism in the Pacific Islands: A Stocktaking at the Beginning of the 21st Century—Global Developments in Christianity." In *Navigating Troubled Waters: The Ecumenical Movement in the Pacific Since the 1980s*, edited by Manfred Ernst and Lydia Johnson, 497–543. Suva, FJ: Pacific Theological College, 2017.

———, ed. *Globalization and the Re-shaping of Christianity in the Pacific Islands.* Suva, FJ: Pacific Theological College, 2006.

Fa'alafi, Fineaso T. S. *Carrying the Faith: Samoan Methodism, 1828–1928.* Apia, WS: Piula Theological College, 2006.

Fa'atauva'a, Roina. "Precedents for Samoan Women's Ministry: Samoan Women—Caught in Culture Change." *Pacific Journal of Theology* II, no. 7 (1992): 15–30.

Fairbairn-Dunlop, Peggy. *Tamaitai Samoa: Their Stories.* Suva, FJ: Institute of Pacific Studies, University of the South Pacific, 1998.

Fala, Alexander, and Katie Fala. "Bio-ethics and the Samoan Indigenous Reference." In *Su'esu'e Manogi: In Search of Fragrance*, edited by I'uogafa Tuagalu, Tamasa'ilau Sualii-Sauni, Tofilau Nina Kirifi-Alai, and Naomi Fuamatu, 354–362. Le Papaigalagala, WS: Centre for Samoan Studies, National University of Samoa, 2008.

Farley, Edward. "Worship as Public Theology." *New Theology Review* 22, no. 1 (February 2009): 70–90.

Farrelly, Tricia, and Unaisi Nabobo-Baba. "*Talanoa* as Empathic Research." Paper Presented, *International Development Conference*, Auckland, NZ, December 3–5, 2012.

Field, Michael J. *Black Saturday: New Zealand's Tragic Blunders in Samoa.* Auckland: Reed Books, 2006.

Filemoni-Tofaeono, Joan A., and Lydia F. Johnson. *Reweaving the Relational Mat: A Christian Response to Violence Against Women from Oceania.* London: Equinox Press, 2006.

Fiorenza, Elisabeth Schüssler. "The Will to Choose or Reject: Continuing our Critical Work." In *Feminist Interpretation of the Bible*, edited by Letty Russell, 123–135. Philadelphia, PA: Westminster Press, 1985.

Fleming, Bruce. *Contextualization of Theology: An Evangelical Assessment.* Pasadena, CA: William Carey Library, 1980.

Ford, David F. "God and Our Public Life: A Scriptural Wisdom." *International Journal of Public Theology* 1, no. 1 (2007): 63–81.

Forrester, Duncan B. *Beliefs, Values and Policies.* Oxford: Clarendon Press, 1989.

———. *On Human Worth: A Christian Vindication of Equality.* London: SCM Press, 2001.

———. *Theology and Politics.* Oxford: Blackwell Publishers, 1988.

———. "The Scope of Public Theology." *Studies in Christian Ethics* 17, no. 2 (2004): 5–19.

———. "The Scope of Public Theology: What is Public Theology?" In *Forrester on Christian Ethics and Practical Theology: Collected Writings on Christianity,*

India, and the Social Order, edited by John R. Hinnells, 441–448. Ashgate Contemporary Thinkers on Religion: Collected Works. Farnham, UK: Ashgate Publishing Ltd., 2010.

———. *Truthful Action: Explorations in Practical Theology*. Edinburgh: T&T Clark, 2000.

———. "Violence and Non-Violence in Conflict Resolution: Some Theological Reflections." *Studies in Christian Ethics* 16, no. 2 (2003): 64–79.

———. "Working in the Quarry: A Response to the Colloquium." In *Public Theology for the Twenty-first Century: Essays in Honour of Duncan B. Forrester*, edited by William F. Storrar and Andrew R. Morton, 431–438. London and New York, NY: T&T Clark, 2004.

Forster, Greg. *The Contested Public Square*. Downers Grove, IL: InterVarsity Press, 2008.

Freeman, Derek. *Margaret Mead and Samoa: The Making and Unmaking of an Anthropological Myth*. Cambridge, MA: Harvard University Press, 1983.

Freire, Paulo. *Cultural Action for Freedom*. Cambridge, MA: Harvard University Press, 1972.

———. *Education for Critical Consciousness*. New York, NY: Continuum, 2005.

———. *Pedagogy of the Oppressed*. 30th anniversary edition. New York, NY: Continuum, 2000.

———. *The Politics of Education: Culture, Power and Liberation*. Translated by Donaldo Macedo. Westport, CT: Bergin & Garvey Publishers, 1985.

Garrett, John. "The Conflict between the London Missionary Society and the Wesleyan Methodists in 19th Century Samoa." *The Journal of Pacific History* 9, no. 1 (1974): 65–80.

Gerson, Samantha. "Feminist Biblical Interpretation." *Capstone Project* (Spring 2014): 1–12. Accessed August 2018. https://www.artsci.uc.edu/content/dam/artsci/departments/judaic%20studies/Docs/Capstone_Final.pdf.

Giddens, Anthony. *The Consequences of Modernity*. Cambridge, MA: Polity Press, 1990.

Gilson, Richard P. *Samoa 1830–1900: The Politics of a Multi-Cultural Community*. Melbourne: Oxford University Press, 1970.

Glaser, Barney G. "Constructivist Grounded Theory?" *Forum: Qualitative Social Research* 3, no. 3 (September 2002). Accessed September 2014. http://www.qualitative-research.net/index.php/fqs/article/view/825/1792.

———. *Theoretical Sensitivity: Advances in the Methodology of Grounded Theory*. Vol. 2. Mill Valley, CA: Sociology Press, 1978.

Gnanadasen, Aruna. *No Longer a Secret: The Church and Violence Against Women*. Revised edition. Geneva: WCC Publications, 1997.

Government of Samoa. *Constitution Amendment Act (No. 2)*. Apia, WS: Government Printing Office, 1997.

———. Section 17. *Public Service Act 2004 (No. 14)*. Accessed July 2015. https://www.mof.gov.ws/LinkClick.aspx?fileticket=XgYGI2Kivls%3D.

Graeb, Wilhelm. "The Influence of Communications Technology and Mass Media in Modern Society: A Challenge for Public Theology." In *Pathways to the Public*

Square: Practical Theology in an Age of Pluralism, edited by Elaine L. Rowlands and Anna Graham, 129–138. Piscataway, NJ: Transaction Publishers, 2005.

Graham, Elaine. *Between a Rock and a Hard Place: Public Theology in a Post-Secular Age*. London: SCM Press, 2013.

———. "Power, Knowledge and Authority in Public Theology." *International Journal of Public Theology* 1, no. 1 (2007): 42–62.

Grattan, F. J. H. *An Introduction to Samoan Custom*. Apia, WS: Samoa Printing and Publishing Company, 1948.

Green, Clifford J. "Bonhoeffer's 'Non-Religious Christianity' as Public Theology." *Dialog* 26 (Fall 1987): 275–280.

Guba, Egon G., and Yvonna S. Lincoln. "Competing Paradigms in Qualitative Research." In *Handbook of Qualitative Research*, edited by Norman K. Denzin and Yvonna S. Lincoln, 105–117. Thousand Oaks, CA: Sage Publications, 1994.

Gutierrez, Gustavo. *A Theology of Liberation: History, Politics, and Salvation*. 15th anniversary edition with new Introduction by author. Translated by Caridad Inda and John Eagleson. Maryknoll, NY: Orbis Books, 1988.

Habermas, Jürgen. *Moral Consciousness and Communicative Action*. Cambridge, MA: Polity Press, 1990.

———. *The Structural Transformation of the Public Sphere: An Inquiry into a Category of Bourgeois Society*. 2nd edition. Cambridge, MA: MIT Press, 1991.

Haire, James. "The Gospel and Globalization." In *Church and Civil Society: A Theology of Engagement*, edited by Francis Sullivan and Sue Leppert, 52–60. Adelaide: ATF Press, 2004.

Halapua, Sitiveni. "Talanoa—Talking from the Heart." Interview. *SGI Quarterly* (January 2007): 9–10.

Halapua, Winston. *Living on the Fringe: Melanesians in Fiji*. Suva, FJ: Institute of Pacific Studies, University of the South Pacific, 2001.

———. *The Role of Militarism in the Politics of Fiji*. Saarbrucken: VDM Verlag Dr. Müller, 2010.

Hallman, David G. *Spiritual Values for Earth Community*. Risk Book Series. Geneva: WCC Publications, 2000.

Hannay, Alastair. *On the Public (Thinking in Action)*. New York, NY: Routledge, 2005.

Hansen, Len D., ed. *Christians in Public: Aims, Methodologies and Issues in Public Theology*. Beyers Naudé Centre Series on Public Theology #3. Stellenbosch, SA: Sun Press, 2008.

Hanson, Paul. *Political Engagement as Biblical Mandate*. Eugene, OR: Cascade Books, 2010.

Harasta, Eva. "Karl Barth, a Public Theologian? The One Word and Theological 'Bilinguality'." *International Journal of Public Theology* 3, no. 2 (2009): 188–203.

Havea, Jione, ed. *Talanoa Ripples: Across Borders, Cultures, Disciplines*. Auckland and Albany, NZ: Masilamea Press and Office of the Directorate Pasifika, Massey University, 2010.

Hayes, Kelly. "Standing Rock and the Power and Determination of Indigenous Americans." *Pacific Standard*, March 13, 2018. https://psmag.com/magazine/standing-rock-still-rising.

Hazelman, Nicola Marie. "PM: Church Warning on Casinos a Joke." *Samoa News*, July 16, 2012, 3.
Hearn, Jeff. "The Sociological Significance of Domestic Violence: Tensions, Paradoxes and Implications." *Current Sociology* 61, no. 2 (February 2013): 152–170.
Heitzenrater, Richard P. *Wesley and the People Called Methodists*. 2nd edition. Nashville, TN: Abingdon Press, 2013.
Hereniko, Vilsoni, and David Hanlon. "Interview with Albert Wendt." In *Inside Out: Literature, Cultural Politics, and Identity in the New Pacific*, edited by Vilsoni Hereniko and Rob Wilson, 85–94. Lanham, MD: Rowman and Littlefield Publishers, 1999.
Himes, Michael J., and Kenneth R. Himes. *Fullness of Faith: The Public Significance of Theology*. New York, NY: Paulist Press, 1993.
Hobson, John. *The Eurocentric Conception of World Politics: Western International Theory, 1760–2010*. New York, NY: Cambridge University Press, 2012.
Hochschild, Adam. *Bury the Chains: Prophets and Rebels in the Fight to Free an Empire's Slaves*. Wilmington, DE: Mariner Books, 2006.
Hollenbach, David. "Public Theology in America: Some Questions for Catholicism after John Courtney Murray." *Theological Studies* 37, no. 2 (June 1976): 290–303.
Holmes, Lowell D. "Samoan Oratory." *The Journal of American Folklore* 82 (1969): 342–352.
Honneth, Axel. *The Struggle for Recognition: The Moral Grammar of Social Conflict*. Cambridge, MA: Polity Press, 1995.
Hood, Helen. "Speaking Out and Doing Justice: It's No Longer a Secret but What are the Churches Doing about Overcoming Violence Against Women?" *Feminist Theology* 11, no. 2 (2003): 261–275.
Hooper, Steven. "'Supreme Among Our Valuables': Whale Teeth (Tabua), Chiefship and Power in Eastern Fiji." *The Journal of the Polynesian Society* 122, no. 2 (June 2013): 103–160.
Horsley, Richard A. "Jesus and the Politics of Roman Palestine." *Journal for the Study of the Historical Jesus* 8, no. 2 (2010): 99–145.
"How 'Pray for our Pacific' is Strengthening the Pacific Climate Movement." *350 Pacific*, September 30, 2016. https://350pacific.org/.
Huffer, Elise, and Asofou So'o. "Consensus versus Dissent: Democracy, Pluralism and Governance in Samoa." *Asia Pacific Viewpoint* 44, no. 3 (2001): 281–304.
Iati, Iati. "The Good Governance Agenda for Civil Society: Implications for the Fa'asamoa." In *Governance in Samoa: Pulega i Samoa*, edited by Elise Huffer and Asofou So'o, 67–78. Suva, FJ and Canberra: Institute of Pacific Studies, University of the South Pacific and Asia Pacific Press, 2000.
Iofi, Fa'afouina. *Samoan Cultural Values and Christian Thought: An Attempt to Relate Samoan Traditional Values to Christian Understanding*. PhD Diss., School of Theology at Claremont, 1980.
Ivara, Tofilau Lupematasila Nanai Misa Faamanu. "School Brawls and Fights Exasperating." *Samoa Observer*, August 5, 2012.

Jacobs, Maretha M. "The 'Sense' of Feminist Biblical Scholarship for Church and Society." *Scriptura* 80 (2002): 173–185.

Jacobs, Pierre. "The Social Gospel Movement Revisited: Consequences for the Church." *HTS Teologiese Studies/Theological Studies* 71, no. 3 (2015): 1–8.

"*Jesus and the Politics of Roman Palestine*, by Richard A. Horsley." *Press Release*, University of South Carolina Press. Last modified July 2018. https://www.sc.edu/uscpress/books/2013/ 7293.html.

"Jesus Is My Boyfriend, and Other Things You Should Keep to Yourself." *The Pocket Scroll*, August 13, 2013. https://thepocketscroll.wordpress.com/2013/08/07/.

Johnson, Elizabeth. "Naming God She: The Theological Implications." *Boardman Lecture in Christian Ethics, Scholarly Commons*, University of Pennsylvania, October 19, 2000.

Johnson, Lydia F. *Drinking from the Same Well: Cross-Cultural Concerns in Pastoral Care and Counseling.* Eugene, OR: Wipf & Stock Publications, 2011.

Johnson, Lydia F., and Joan A. Filemoni-Tofaeono, eds. *Weavings: Women Doing Theology in Oceania.* Suva, FJ: Institute of Pacific Studies, University of the South Pacific and South Pacific Association of Theological Schools, 2003.

Joldersma, Clarence. "Shared Praxis: A Pedagogy of Hope for Public Theology." *Journal for Peace and Justice Studies* 10, no. 1 (1999): 67–93.

Kamu, Lalomilu. *The Samoan Culture and the Christian Gospel.* Suva, FJ: Donna Lou Kamu, 1996.

Kelly, James R. "Sociology and Public Theology: A Case Study of Pro-Choice/Profile Common Ground." *Sociology of Religion* 60, no. 2 (1999): 99–124.

Kelly, Liz. "The VIP Guide: Vision, Innovation and Professionalism in Policing Violence against Women and Children." *Report Produced for the Council of Europe, Police and Human Rights Program*, 2000.

Kelly, Robert A. "Public Theology and the Modern Social Imaginary." *Dialog: A Journal of Theology* 50, no. 2 (2011): 162–173.

Kerslake, Maria. *Maloafua: Structural Adjustment Programs—The Case of Samoa.* PhD Thesis, Massey University, 2007.

Kim, Sebastian. *Theology in the Public Sphere: Public Theology as a Catalyst for Open Debate.* London: SCM Press, 2011.

Kluckholm, Clyde. *Mirror for Man: The Relation of Anthropology to Modern Life.* New York, NY: Books on Demand, 1985.

Kocan, Gurcan. *Models of the Public Sphere in Political Philosophy.* Eurosphere Online Working Paper Series #2. Istanbul: Technical University, 2008.

Kohn, Melvin. *Class and Conformity: A Study in Values.* Chicago, IL: University of Chicago Press, 1989.

Kolia, Fepa'i Fiu. "The Church and Development." In *Samoa National Human Development Report: Sustainable Livelihoods in a Changing Samoa*, edited by Unasa Felise Va'a, Le'apai Lau, Asofou So'o, and Telesia Lafotanoa, 137–148. Le Papaigalagala, WS: Centre for Samoan Studies, National University of Samoa, 2006.

Koopman, Nico. "A Public Theology of Global Transformation in Challenging Times." *Unpublished Paper*, Beyers Naudé Centre for Public Theology, Stellenbosch University, South Africa, 2012.

———. "Churches and Public Policy Discourse in South Africa." Accessed June 2015. http://www.csu.edu.au/faculty/arts/theology/pact/documents/Churches.

———. "Public Theology as Prophetic Theology: More than Utopianism and Criticism." *Journal of Theology for Southern Africa* 134 (July 2009): 117–130.

———. "Some Contours for Public Theology in South Africa." *International Journal of Practical Theology* 14, no. 1 (2010): 123–138.

Koya-Vaka'uta, Cresantia Frances. "Rethinking Research as Relational Space in the Pacific: Pedagogy and Praxis." In *Relational Hermeneutics: Decolonising the Mindset and the Pacific Itulagi*, edited by Upolu L. Vaai and Aisake Casimira, 65–84. Suva, FJ: Pacific Theological College and University of the South Pacific, 2017.

———. "The Digital *Va*: Negotiating Socio-spatial Relations in Cyberspace, Place and Time." In *The Relational Self: Decolonising Personhood in the Pacific*, edited by Upolu L. Vaai and Unaisi Nabobo-Baba, 79–101. Suva, FJ: Pacific Theological College and University of the South Pacific, 2017.

Lange, Raeburn. *The Origins of the Christian Ministry in the Cook Islands and Samoa*. Christchurch: Macmillan Brown Centre for Pacific Studies, University of Canterbury, 2006.

Laqeretabua, Atunaisa, Vijay Naidu, and Sharon Bhagwan-Rolls. *Pacific Perspectives on the Commercial Sexual Exploitation and Sexual Abuse of Children and Youth*. Bangkok: United Nations Economic and Social Commission for Asia and the Pacific, 2009.

Latu, Latuivai. *Fetausia'i: A Servant Leadership Paradigm for the Mission of the Methodist Church in Samoa*. MTh Thesis, University of Otago, 2017.

Lawson, Stephanie. *Tradition Versus Democracy in the South Pacific: Fiji, Tonga, and Western Samoa*. Cambridge: Cambridge University Press, 1996.

Lee, Jung Young. *Marginality: The Key to Multicultural Theology*. Minneapolis, MN: Augsburg Fortress Press, 1995.

Lefaoseu, Iosefa. "*Faaaloalo* as a Model for the Church Ministry." *Class Presentation*, Piula Theological College, November 11, 2001.

Leiataua, Tolofuaivalelei Falemoe. "Commission for the Status of Women in Samoa." *Public Statement, 57th Session of the United Nations Commission on the Status of Women*, on behalf of the Ministry of Women, Community and Social Development, New York, NY, March 5, 2013.

Lesa, Mataafa Keni. "Domestic Violence, a Coward and Speaking Up." *Samoa Observer*, February 18, 2014.

———. "Those Evils are Already Here." *Samoa Observer*, March 8, 2013.

"Liberation Theology." Accessed June 1, 2015. http://www.theopedia.com/Liberation_theology.

Lichtman, Marilyn. *Qualitative Research in Education*. London: SAGE Publications, 2006.

Lilomaiava-Doktor, Sailiemanu. "Beyond Migration: Samoan Population Movement (*Malaga*) and the Geography of Social Space (*Va*)." *The Contemporary Pacific* 21, no. 1 (2009): 1–32.

Luhmann, Niklas. *Modern Society Shocked by its Risks*. Hong Kong: University of Hong Kong, 1996.

Luther, Martin. *Lectures on Romans. Luther's Works*. Vol. 25. Edited by Hilton C. Oswald. Translated by Jacob A. O. Preus. St. Louis, MO: Concordia Publishing House, 1972.

———. *Martin Luther's Basic Theological Writings*. Edited by Timothy F. Lull. Minneapolis, MN: Fortress Press, 1989.

———. *On the Jews and Their Lies. Luther's Works*. Vol. 47. Edited by Helmut T. Lehmann. Translated by Martin H. Bertram. Philadelphia, PA: Fortress Press, 1971.

MacIntyre, Alasdair. *After Virtue: A Study in Moral Theory*. London: Duckworth, 1981.

Macpherson, Cluny, and La'avasa Macpherson. "Churches and the Economy of Samoa." *The Contemporary Pacific* 23, no. 2 (2011): 303–338.

———. *The Warm Winds of Change: Globalisation in Contemporary Samoa*. Auckland: University of Auckland Press, 2010.

———. "When Theory Meets Practice: The Limits of the Good Governance Program." In *Governance in Samoa: Pulega i Samoa*, edited by Elise Huffer and Asofou So'o, 17–40. Canberra and Suva, FJ: Asia Pacific Press and Institute of Pacific Studies, University of the South Pacific, 2000.

Macquarrie, John. *Principles of Christian Theology*. London: SCM Press, 1997.

Maddox, Marion. "A Case for Public Theology in Secular Contexts." *Annual Lecture in Public Theology*, School of Theology, University of Auckland, July 2006.

———. "Religion, Secularism and the Promise of Public Theology." *International Journal of Public Theology* 1, no. 1 (2007): 82–100.

Mageo, Jeannette M. "*Aga/Amio* and the *Lotu*: Perspectives on the Structure of the Self in Samoa." *Oceania* 59 (1989): 181–199.

———. *Theorizing Self in Samoa: Emotions, Genders, and Sexualities*. Ann Arbor, MI: University of Michigan Press, 1998.

Maliko, Selota. *Restorative Justice: A Pastoral Care Response to the Issue of Fa'ate'a Ma Le Nu'u (Banishment) in Samoan Society*. PhD Thesis, University of Otago, 2016.

Maliko, Tavita. *O Le Soga'imiti: The Embodiment of God in the Samoan Male Body*. PhD Thesis, University of Auckland, 2012.

Marshall, Christopher D. *Beyond Retribution: A New Testament Vision for Justice, Crime and Punishment*. Grand Rapids, MI: William B. Eerdmans, 2001.

———. *Crowned with Glory and Honour: Human Rights in the Biblical Tradition*. Kitchener, ON: Pandora Press, 2011.

———. "What Language Shall I Borrow? The Bilingual Dilemma of Public Theology." *Stimulus: The New Zealand Journal of Christian Thought and Practice* 13, no. 3 (2005): 11–18.

Martin, Penny. "Implementing Women's and Children's Rights: The Case of Domestic Violence in Samoa." *Alternative Law Journal* 27, no. 5 (October 2002): 227–232.

Marty, Martin. "Reinhold Niebuhr: Public Theology and the American Experience." *The Journal of Religion* 54, no. 4 (October 1974): 332–345.
———. *The Public Church.* New York, NY: Crossroad Publishing, 1981.
Matheny, Paul Duane. *Contextual Theology: The Drama of Our Times.* Eugene, OR: Pickwick Publications, 2011.
Mathewes, Charles. *A Theology of Public Life.* Cambridge: Cambridge University Press, 2007.
Maude, Harry E. "Beachcombers and Castaways." *Journal of the Polynesian Society* 73, no. 3 (1964): 254–293.
McDonald, James Ian H. *Christian Values: Theory and Practice in Christian Ethics Today.* Edinburgh: T&T Clark, 1995.
McFall-McCaffery, Judy T. "Getting Started with Pacific Research: Finding Resources and Information on Pacific Research Models and Methodologies." *MAI Review* 1, no. 8 (2010): 1–5.
Mead, Margaret. *Coming of Age in Samoa: A Psychological Study of Primitive Youth for Western Civilization.* New York, NY: Harper Perennial Modern Classics, 2001.
Medhurst, Kenneth, and James Sweeney. "Public Theology and Changing Social Values." *Studies in Christian Ethics* 17, no. 2 (2004): 118–133.
Meleisea, Malama. *Change and Adaptation in Western Samoa.* Christchurch: University of Canterbury, 1992.
———. *Lagaga: A Short History of Western Samoa.* Suva, FJ: Institute of Pacific Studies, University of the South Pacific, 1987.
———. *The Making of Modern Samoa: Traditional Authority and Colonial Administration in the History of Western Samoa.* Suva, FJ: Institute of Pacific Studies, University of the South Pacific, 1987.
Michael, Robert. "Luther, Luther Scholars, and the Jews." *Encounter* 46, no. 4 (Autumn 1985): 339–370.
Micklethwait, John, and Adrian Wooldridge. *God Is Back: How the Global Revival of Faith is Changing the World.* New York, NY: Penguin, 2009.
Migliore, Daniel L. *Faith Seeking Understanding: An Introduction to Christian Theology.* 2nd edition. Grand Rapids, MI: William B. Eerdmans, 2004.
Mills, Jane, Ann Bonner, and Karen Francis. "Adopting a Constructivist Approach to Grounded Theory: Implications for Research Design." *International Journal of Nursing Practice* 12, no. 1 (2006): 8–13.
———. "The Development of Constructivist Grounded Theory." *International Journal of Qualitative Method* 5, no. 1 (2006): 25–35.
Milner, G. B. *Samoan Dictionary.* London: Oxford University Press, 1966.
Ministry of Education, Sports and Culture, Government of Samoa. *Strategic Policies and Plans: July 2006–June 2015.* Apia, WS: MESC, 2006.
Ministry of Women, Community and Social Development, Government of Samoa. *Samoa Family Safety Study.* Apia, WS: MWCSD, 2017.
Moghaddam, Fathali M. "Domestic Violence." *Report Prepared for the Australian Institute of Criminology*, 1998.
———. *Social Psychology: Exploring Universals Across Cultures.* New York, NY: W. H. Freeman, 1998.

Moltmann, Jürgen. *Experiences in Theology: Ways and Forms of Christian Theology*. Minneapolis, MN: Fortress Press, 2000.

———. *God for a Secular Society: The Public Relevance of Theology*. Minneapolis, MN: Fortress Press, 1999.

———. "Political Theology in Germany After Auschwitz." In *Public Theology for the Twenty-first Century*, edited by William F. Storrar and Andrew R. Morton, 37–43. London and New York, NY: T&T Clark, 2004.

———. *Spirit of Hope: Theology for a World in Peril*. Louisville, KY: Westminster John Knox Press, 2019.

———. *Theology of Hope*. Translated by J. W. Leitch. London: SCM Press, 1967.

———. *Theology of Hope*. Philadelphia, PA: Fortress Press, 1993.

Mooney, Margarita. "The Catholic Bishops Conferences of the United States and France: Engaging Immigration as a Public Issue." *American Behavioral Scientist* 49, no. 11 (2006): 145–170.

Moyle, Richard M., ed. *The Samoan Journals of John Williams, 1830 and 1832*. Canberra: Australian National University Press, 1984.

Mulitalo-Lauta, Pa'u T. *Fa'asamoa and Social Work within the New Zealand Context*. Palmerston North, NZ: The Dunmore Press, 2000.

Mullender, Audrey, and Catherine Humphreys. *Domestic Violence and Child Abuse: Policy and Practice Issues for Local Authorities and Other Agencies*. London: Local Government Association, 1998.

Müller-Fahrenholz, Geiko. *The Kingdom and the Power: The Theology of Jürgen Moltmann*. Philadelphia, PA: Augsburg Fortress Press, 2001.

Nepo, Gataivai. *A Theological Study of 'Tautua' (Service) in the Light of the Christian Faith: With Special Reference to the Ministry of the Congregational Church in Samoa*. BD Thesis, Pacific Theological College, 1990.

Netzler, Jasmine. "Life of Fear." *Samoa Observer*, November 3, 2012.

———. "Student in Samoa Charged with Murder." *Samoa Observer*, September 14, 2012.

Neville, David. "Christian Scripture and Public Theology: Ruminations on their Ambiguous Relationship." *International Journal of Public Theology* 7, no. 1 (2013): 5–23.

———. "Dialectic as Method in Public Theology: Recalling Jacques Ellul." *International Journal of Public Theology* 2, no. 2 (2008): 163–181.

———. "Justice and Divine Judgment: Scriptural Perspectives for Public Theology." *International Journal of Public Theology* 3, no. 3 (2009): 339–356.

Nicholls, Bruce. *Contextualization: A Theology of Gospel and Culture*. Downers Grove, IL: InterVarsity Press, 1979.

Niebuhr, Reinhold. *Faith and Politics*. Edited by Ronald H. Stone. New York, NY: George Braziller, 1968.

Nikora, Linda Waimarie. "Pacific Indigenous Psychologies—Starting Points." In *Relational Hermeneutics: Decolonising the Mindset and the Pacific Itulagi*, edited by Upolu L. Vaai and Aisake Casimira, 143–150. Suva, FJ: Pacific Theological College and University of the South Pacific, 2017.

Nokise, Feleterika. "Ecumenism in the Navigators' Archipelago—An Elusive Reality: Samoa and American Samoa." In *Navigating Troubled Waters: The Ecumenical Movement in the Pacific Islands Since the 1980s*, edited by Manfred Ernst and Lydia Johnson, 253–330. Suva, FJ: Pacific Theological College, 2017.

Nürnberger, Klaus. *Martin Luther's Message for Us Today: A Perspective from the South.* Pietermaritzburg, SA: Cluster Publications, 2005.

O'Donovan, Oliver. "A Theology of Public Life." *Political Theology* 12, no. 4 (2011): 616–620.

"Overview of Efforts to Eliminate Violence Against Women in the Pacific." In *Strengthening Pacific Partnerships for Eliminating Violence Against Women: A Pacific Regional Workshop Report*, 81–90. London and Suva, FJ: Commonwealth Secretariat, UNDP, UNIFEM and Pacific Islands Forum Secretariat, 2003.

Oyserman, Daphna. "Values, Psychology of." In *International Encyclopedia of the Social and Behavioral Sciences*, Vol. 25, edited by James D. Wright, 16150–16153. Oxford: Pergamon/Elsevier Press, 2015.

Pace, Bradley. "Public Reason and Public Theology: How the Church Should Interfere." *Anglican Theological Review* 91, no. 2 (2007): 273–291.

Pacific Conference of Churches. *Towards a Relevant Pacific Theology: The Role of the Churches and Theological Education.* Report of a Theological Consultation held at Bergengren House, Suva, Fiji, July 8–12, 1985. Suva, FJ: Lotu Pasifika Productions, 1986.

Paeth, Scott R. "Jürgen Moltmann's Public Theology." *Political Theology* 6, no. 2 (2005): 215–234.

Pears, Angie. *Doing Contextual Theology.* Abingdon, UK: Routledge, 2009.

Pearson, Clive. "The Public Comeback of God." In *Reimagining God and Mission: Perspectives from Australia*, edited by Ross Langmead, 83–98. Adelaide: ATF Press, 2007.

———. "The Purpose and Practice of a Public Theology in a Time of Climate Change." *International Journal of Public Theology* 4, no. 3 (2010): 356–372.

———. "The Quest for a Glocal Public Theology." *International Journal of Public Theology* 1, no. 2 (2007): 151–172.

———. "What Is Public Theology?" *The Council of Societies for the Study of Religion Bulletin* 47, no. 2 (2008): 92–95. Accessed November 2015. www.csu.edu.au/faculty/arts/theology/pact/documents/what_is_public_theology.pdf.

Pence, Ellen, and Michael Paymar. *Educating Groups for Men Who Batter: The Duluth Model.* 2nd edition. New York, NY: Springer, 1996.

Pereira, Janet Aileen. *The Decision to Lotu.* BA Hons Diss., University of Otago, 1978.

Petersen, Rodney L., ed. *Christianity and Civil Society: Theological Education for Public Life.* Cambridge, MA: Boston Theological Institute, 1995.

Peterson, Paul S. *The Decline of Christianity in the Western World.* Studies in World Christianity and Interreligious Relations. London: Routledge, 2017.

Peteru, Maiava Carmel. *Falevitu: A Literature Review on Culture and Family Violence in Seven Pacific Communities in New Zealand.* Auckland: Ministry of Social Development, 2012.

———. *O Le Tofa Mamao: A Samoan Conceptual Framework for Addressing Family Violence*. Wellington: Samoan Working Group, NZ Family and Community Services, 2012.

Peteru, Maiava Carmel, and Teuila Percival. *O Aiga O Le Anofale O Afioaga Ma Le Fatu O Le Aganuu: Samoan Pathways to the Prevention of Sexual Violence*. Auckland: School of Population Health, University of Auckland, 2000.

Piper, John. "Peculiar Doctrines, Public Morals, and the Political Welfare." *Public Lecture*, Bethlehem Conference for Pastors, Bethlehem, PA, February 2, 2002. https://www.desiringgod.org/messages/peculiar-doctrines-public-morals-and-the-political-welfare.

"Practical Theology." Accessed May 10, 2016. http//:theoblogy.blogspot.co.nz/2005/02/what-is-practical-theology-part-1.html.

Pratt, George. *Pratt's Grammar and Dictionary of the Samoan Language*. Apia, WS: Malua Printing Press, 1977 [1911].

"Preamble." *Constitution of the Independent State of Samoa, 1960: Consolidated Acts of Samoa, 2008*. Edited by Legislative Drafting Division. Apia, WS: Government Printing Office, 2008.

Prescott, James. "Using Talanoa in Pacific Business Research in New Zealand: Experiences with Tongan Entrepreneurs." *Alternative, Special Edition* 1 (2008): 127–148.

Price, Vincent. "The Public and Public Opinion in Political Theories." In *The Sage Handbook of Public Opinion Research*, edited by Wolfgang Donsbach and Michael W. Traugott, 11–24. London: Sage Publications, 2008.

Pryke, Julie, and Martin Thomas. *Domestic Violence and Social Work*. Aldershot, UK: Ashgate Publishing, 1998.

Ramesh, Abhinaya. "Why is Domestic Violence a Human Rights Concern?" *Journal of Association for Women's Rights in Development* 110 (December 2008). Accessed June 2014. http://www.eurowrc.org/06.contributions/1.contrib.en/51 cor.

Rauschenbusch, Walter. *A Theology for the Social Gospel*. New York, NY: Abingdon Press, 1917.

Rawls, John. *Political Liberalism*. New York, NY: The Free Press, 1973.

Ripine, Sarai. "60 Year Old Father Jailed for Raping Daughter." *Samoa Observer*, March 20, 2013.

Robson, Andrew. "Factors in the Conversion of Samoa, Then and Now." *Pacific-Credo Publications*, 49–56. Accessed September 2018. https://books.openedition.org/pacific/126?lang=en.

———. "Malietoa, Williams, and Samoa's Embrace of Christianity." *The Journal of Pacific History* 44, no. 1 (June 2009): 21–39.

Rokeach, Milton. *The Nature of Human Values*. New York, NY: Free Press, 1973.

———. *Understanding Human Values*. New York, NY: Free Press, 2000.

Ropeti-Iupeli, Marie. "A Biblical Basis for the Ordination of Women in the Pacific Churches." In *Weavings: Women Doing Theology in Oceania*, edited by Lydia Johnson and Joan A. Filemoni-Tofaeono, 133–140. Suva, FJ: Institute of Pacific Studies, University of the South Pacific and SPATS, 2003.

———. "A Pacific Woman's Journey in Ministry." *Pacific Journal of Theology* II, no. 7 (1992): 33–38.
Ruether, Rosemary. *Women-Church: Theology and Practice*. San Francisco, CA: Harper & Row, 1985.
Russell, Letty M. "Introduction: Liberating the Word." In *Feminist Interpretation of the Bible*, edited by Letty M. Russell, 1–21. Philadelphia, PA: Westminster Press, 1985.
"Samoa Population 2019." *World Population Review*. Accessed March 11, 2019. http://world populationreview.com/countries/samoa-population/.
Samoa Victim Support Group. "Stop the Violence Against Women." Accessed August 2018. http://www.victim support.ws/stop-the-violence-against-women.
"Samoans Urged to Return to Origins of *Fa'asamo*a." *News Release, Radio New Zealand*, January 19, 2009.
Sanga, Kabini F. "Making Philosophical Sense of Indigenous Pacific Research." In *Researching the Pacific and Indigenous Peoples*, edited by Tupeni M. Baba, Nuhisifa Williams, and Unaisi Nabobo-Baba, 41–52. Auckland: University of Auckland, 2004.
Sauoaiga, Laufai. *O le Mavaega i le Tai: The Will by the Sea*. Apia, WS: Methodist Printing Press, 2000.
Sauter, Gerhard. *Protestant Theology at the Crossroads: How to Face the Crucial Tasks for Theology in the Twenty-first Century*. Grand Rapids, MI: William B. Eerdmans, 2007.
Sauvy, Alfred. "Trois Mondes, Une Planète (Three Worlds, One Planet)." *L'Observateur* (August 1952): 14–17.
Scheler, Max. *Formalism in Ethics and Non-Formal Ethics of Values*. Translated by Manfred Frings and Robert Funk. Evanston, IL: Northwestern University Press, 1973.
Schmidt, Kaydee. *The Aitu Nafanua and the History of Samoa: A Study in the Relationship between Spiritual and Temporal Power*. PhD Thesis, Australian National University, 2011.
Schoeffel, Penelope. "Rank, Gender and Politics in Ancient Samoa: The Genealogy of Salamāsina O Le Tafaifā." *The Journal of Pacific History* 22, no. 4 (1987): 174–193.
———. "The Ladies' Row of Thatch: Women and Rural Development in Western Samoa." *Pacific Perspective* 8, no. 2 (1979): 1–11.
Schreiter, Robert J. *Constructing Local Theologies*. Maryknoll, NY: Orbis Books, 1985.
Schultz, Erich. *Proverbial Expressions of the Samoans*. Wellington: The Polynesian Society, 1965.
Secretariat for Pacific Community. *Annual Report*. Noumea, NCL: SPC, 2007.
Shore, Brad. "Human Ambivalence and the Structuring of Moral Values." *Ethos* 18, no. 2 (1990): 165–179.
———. *Sala'ilua: A Samoan Mystery*. New York, NY: Columbia University Press, 1982.
Sio, Peseta Betty. "O Le Tofa Mamao: A Samoan Conceptual Framework for Addressing Family Violence." Paper Presented, *Auckland Regional Network*

Meeting—Family and Sexual Violence, Western Springs, Auckland, NZ, September 10, 2012.
Smith, Frank. *The Johannine Jesus from a Samoan Perspective: Toward an Intercultural Reading of the Fourth Gospel*. PhD Thesis, University of Auckland, 2010.
Smith, Peter. *An Introduction to the Baha'i Faith*. Cambridge: Cambridge University Press, 2008.
"Social Gospel Movement." Accessed June 1, 2015. http://www.theopedia.com/SocialGospel.
So'o, Asofou, Le'apai Lau, and Rob Laking. "Samoan Public Sector Reform: Views from Apia and the Villages." *Policy Quarterly* 4, no. 3 (September 2008): 30–36.
St Augustine. *The Trinity (De Trinitate)*. 2nd edition. Edited by John E. Rotelle. Translated by Edmund Hill. Works of Saint Augustine Book 5. Hyde Park, NY: New City Press, 2012.
Stackhouse, Max L. "Civil Religion, Political Theology, and Public Theology: What's the Difference?" *Journal of Political Theology* 5, no. 3 (2004): 275–293.
———. "From the Social Gospel to Public Theology." In *Being Christian Today: An American Conversation*, edited by Richard J. Neuhaus and George Weigel, 33–58. Washington, DC: Ethics and Public Policy Center, 1992.
———. "Public Theology and Political Economy in a Globalizing Era." In *Public Theology for the Twenty-first Century*, edited by William F. Storrar and Andrew R. Morton, 179–194. London and New York, NY: T&T Clark, 2004.
———. "Public Theology and the Future of Democratic Societies." In *The Church's Public Role*, edited by David Hessel, 63–83. Grand Rapids, MI: William B. Eerdmans, 1993.
Stair, John B. *Old Samoa: Or, Flotsam and Jetsam from the Pacific Ocean*. London: Religious Tract Society, 1956 [1897].
Stone, Howard D., and James O. Duke. *How to Think Theologically*. 3rd edition. Minneapolis, MN: Fortress Press, 2013.
Storrar, William F., and Andrew R. Morton. "Introduction." In *Public Theology for the Twenty-first Century*, edited by William F. Storrar and Andrew R. Morton, 1–21. London and New York, NY: T&T Clark, 2004.
———, eds. *Public Theology for the Twenty-first Century*. London and New York, NY: T&T Clark, 2004.
Strauss, Anselm, and Juliet Corbin. *Basics of Qualitative Research: Grounded Theory Procedures and Techniques*. 2nd edition. Thousand Oaks, CA: Sage Publications, 1990.
Suaali'i-Sauni, Tamasailau M. "*E Faigata le Alofa*—The Samoan *Fa'amatai*: Reflections from Afar." In *Changes in the Matai System: O Suiga i le Fa'amatai*, edited by Asofou So'o, 33–60. Le Papaigalagala, WS: Centre for Samoan Studies, National University of Samoa, 2007.
———. *Le Matuamoepo: Competing 'Spirits of Governing' and the Management of New Zealand-based Samoan Youth Offender Cases*. PhD Thesis, University of Auckland, 2006.

———. "To *Talanoa, Fa'afaletui*, or Not? Reflections on the Development of Pacific Research Methods." Paper Presented, *Vaaomanu Pasifika Units VASA Seminar Series*, Victoria University, Wellington, NZ, June 20, 2012.

Suaali'i-Sauni, Tamasailau M., and M. Fulu-Aiolupotea. "Decolonizing Pacific Research, Building Pacific Research Communities and Developing Pacific Research Tools: The Case of the 'Talanoa' and the 'Faafaletui' in Samoa." *Asia Pacific Viewpoint* 16 (May 2013): 3–15.

"Suicide Rate in Pacific Islands Among Highest in the World." *Pacific Islands Report*, August 15, 2015. http://www.pireport.org/articles/2015/08/15/suicide-rate-pacific-islands-among-highest-world.

Sunia, Fofo Iosefa F. *Lupe o le Foaga Vaega Muamua*. Tafuna, AS: Matagaluega o A'oga, 1997.

Ta'ase, Elia. *A Study of the Siovili Cult and the Problems Facing the Church in Samoa Today*. BD Thesis, Pacific Theological College, 1971.

Tamasese, Kiwi, Carmel Peteru, Charles Waldegrave, and Allister Bush. "*O Le Taeao Afua*—the New Morning: A Qualitative Investigation into Samoan Perspectives on Mental Health and Culturally Appropriate Services." *Australian and New Zealand Journal of Psychiatry* 39, no. 4 (1997): 300–309.

Tamez, Elsa. "Feminist Biblical Studies in Latin America and the Caribbean." In *Feminist Biblical Studies in the Twentieth Century: Scholarship and Movement*, edited by Elisabeth Schüssler Fiorenza, 35–52. Atlanta, GA: Society of Biblical Literature, 2014.

———. "Women's Re-reading of the Bible." In *With Passion and Compassion: Third World Women Doing Theology*, edited by Virginia Fabella and Mercy Amba Oduyoye, 163–176. Maryknoll, NY: Orbis Books, 1988.

Tamua, Evotia, Graeme Lay, Tony Murrow, and Malama Meleisea. *Samoa: Pacific Pride (Peoples of the Pacific)*. Auckland: Polynesian Press, 2000.

Tanner, Kathryn. "Public Theology and the Character of Public Debate: Observations on the Ramifications of Christian Beliefs, Symbols and Doctrines for Socio-economic and Political Issues." *Annual of the Society of Christian Ethics* 16 (1996): 77–89.

———. *Theories of Culture: A New Agenda for Theology*. Minneapolis, MN: Fortress Press, 1997.

Taulealeausumai, Feiloaiga. "Herstory: The Struggle of Pacific Women in Ministry." *Pacific Journal of Theology* II, no. 7 (1992): 31–34.

———. "The Word Made Flesh: A Samoan Theology of Pastoral Care." In *Counselling Issues and South Pacific Communities*, edited by Philip Culbertson, 161–188. Auckland: Accent Publications, 1997.

Tavana, G. V. "Cultural Values and Education in Western Samoa: Tensions between Colonial Roots and Influences and Contemporary Indigenous Needs." *International Journal of Educational Reform* 6, no. 1 (1997): 11–19.

Taylor, Charles. *A Secular Age*. Cambridge, MA: Belknap Press, 2007.

———. *Modern Social Imaginaries*. Durham, NC: Duke University Press, 2004.

Taylor, Rachel Ann. *Professional Perceptions of Domestic Violence: The Relationship between Causal Explanations and Views on Prevention and Intervention*. MCJ Thesis, Edith Cowan University, 2006.

Tcherkezoff, Serge. "Are the Matai Out of Time? Tradition and Democracy: Contemporary Ambiguities and Historical Transformations of the Concept of Chief." In *Governance in Samoa: Pulega i Samoa*, edited by Elise Huffer and Asofou So'o, 113–132. Canberra and Suva, FJ: Asia Pacific Press and Institute of Pacific Studies, University of the South Pacific, 2000.

———. *'First Contacts' in Polynesia—The Samoan Case (1772–1848): Western Misunderstandings about Sexuality and Divinity*. Christchurch and Canberra: Macmillan Brown Centre for Pacific Studies and *Journal of Pacific History*, 2004.

Thiemann, Ronald F. *Constructing a Public Theology: The Church in a Pluralistic Culture*. Louisville, KY: Westminster John Knox Press, 1991.

Thomas, Michael. "Treatment of Family Violence: A Systemic Perspective." In *Family Intervention in Domestic Violence: A Handbook of Gender-inclusive Theory and Treatment*, edited by John Hamel and Tonia L. Nicholls, 417–438. New York, NY: Springer, 2007.

Thomson, Heather. "Stars and Compasses: Hermeneutical Guides for Public Theology." *International Journal of Public Theology* 2, no. 1 (2008): 258–276.

Thornton, Alec, Maria T. Kerslake, and Tony Binns. "Alienation and Obligation: Religion and Social Change in Samoa." *Asia Pacific Viewpoint* 51, no. 1 (2010): 1–16.

Tiatia-Seath, Jemaima. "Negotiating Personhood in Light of Pacific Suicide Prevention." In *The Relational Self: Decolonising Personhood in the Pacific*, edited by Upolu L. Vaai and Unaisi Nabobo-Baba, 79–101. Suva, FJ: Pacific Theological College and University of the South Pacific, 2017.

Tiffany, Sharon W. "The Politics of Denominational Organization in Samoa." In *Mission, Church and Sect in Oceania*, edited by James A. Boutilier, Daniel T. Hughes, and Sharon W. Tiffany, 423–456. Lanham, MD: University Press of America, 1978.

Tillich, Paul. *Love, Power and Justice: Ontological Analysis and Ethical Applications*. Oxford: Oxford University Press, 1954.

Tipton, Steven. "Public Theology." In *The Encyclopedia of Politics and Religion*, Vol. 2, edited by Robert Wuthnow, 164. New York, NY: Routledge, 2013.

Tofaeono, Amaamalele. *Eco-Theology: Aiga—The Household of Life: A Perspective from Living Myths and Traditions of Samoa*. Erlanger: Verlag fur Mission and Oikumene, 2000.

Toma, Maiava Iulai. "Churches Need to Bear Witness to Domestic Violence." *Samoa Observer*, December 12, 2013.

Tomlinson, Matt, and Ty P. Kāwika Tengan, eds. *New Mana: Transformations of a Classic Concept in Pacific Languages and Cultures*. Canberra: ANU Press, 2016.

Tracy, David. *The Analogical Imagination: Christian Theology and the Culture of Pluralism*. New York, NY: Crossroad Publishing, 1981.

Tuala, Falelua. *A Theological Reflection on Tuaoi in the Search for Peace and Harmony in the Samoan Society*. BD Thesis, Piula Theological College, 2008.

Tuhiwai-Smith, Linda. *Decolonizing Methodologies: Research and Indigenous People*. London and New York, NY: Zed Books, 1999.

Tui'hai, Sione, Yvette Guttenbeil-Po'uhila, Jennifer Hand, and Tim Htay. "Gambling Issues for Tongan People in Auckland, Aotearoa-New Zealand." *Journal of Gambling Issues* 12 (December 2004): 43–49.

Tuisuga, Fa'alepo A. *O Le Tofa Liliu a Samoa: A Hermeneutical Critical Analysis of the Cultural-Theological Praxis of the Samoan Context*. PhD Thesis, Melbourne University of Divinity, 2011.

Tupuola, Anne-Marie. "Raising Consciousness: The *Fa'a Samoa* Way." *New Zealand Annual Review of Education* 3 (2007): 175–189.

Turan, Omer. *The Triangle of Publicness, Communication and Democracy*. MSc. Thesis, Middle East Technical University, 2004.

Tuvale, Teo. *An Account of Samoan History Up to 1918*. New Zealand Electronic Text Center. Accessed September 14, 2018. www.nzetc.org.

Uasike, Lousiale. *Women in Transforming Mission: The Wesleyan Authority of Experience and Women Doing Theology in Tonga*. DMin Diss., San Francisco Theological Seminary, 2014.

Va'a, Unasa F. "Samoan Custom and Human Rights: An Indigenous View." *Victoria University Wellington Law Review* 40 (2009): 237–249.

Vaai, Emma Kruse. *Producing the Text of Culture: The Appropriaton of English in Contemporary Samoa*. Le Papaigalagala, WS: Centre for Samoan Studies, National University of Samoa, 2011.

———. "Religion." In *Samoa's Journey 1962–2012: Aspects of History*, edited by Leasiolagi Malama Meleisea, Penelope Schoeffel, and Ellie Meleisea, 77–96. Wellington: Victoria University Press, 2012.

Vaai, Saleimoa. *Samoa: Fa'afetai and the Rule of Law*. Le Papaigalagala, WS: Centre for Samoan Studies, National University of Samoa, 1999.

Vaai, Upolu L. *A Theology of Giving*. BD Thesis, Piula Theological College, 2001.

———. *Faaaloalo: A Theological Reinterpretation of the Doctrine of the Trinity from a Samoan Perspective*. PhD Thesis, Griffith University, 2006.

———. "Relational Hermeneutics: A Return to the Relationality of the Pacific Itulagi as a Lens for Understanding and Interpreting Life." In *Relational Hermeneutics: Decolonising the Mindset and the Pacific Itulagi*, edited by Upolu Lumā Vaai and Aisake Casimira, 17–41. Suva, FJ: University of the South Pacific and Pacific Theological College, 2017.

———. "Tino Theology." In *The Relational Self*, edited by Upolu Lumā Vaai and Unaisi Nabobo-Baba, 223–241. Suva, FJ: University of the South Pacific and Pacific Theological College, 2017.

Vaaimamao, Seresese Tapu. *Justice and Righteousness: A Comparative Study of the Word Pair in Amos with its Application to the Life of Communalism in Samoa*. MTh Thesis, University of Otago, 1998.

Vaioleti, Timote Masima. "Talanoa Research Methodology: A Developing Position on Pacific Research." *Waikato Journal of Education* 12 (2006): 21–34.

———. "Talanoa Research Methodology: A Perspective on Pacific Research." Paper Presented, *Pasifika Nations Educators Association Conference*, Wellington, NZ, April 15–17, 2003.

Vaka'uta, Nasili. *Talanoa Rhythms: Voices from Oceania*. Albany, NZ: Office of the Directorate Pasifika, Massey University, 2013.

Van Aarde, Andries. "What is 'Theology' in 'Public Theology' and What is 'Public' about 'Public Theology'?" *Hervormde Teologiese/Theological Studies* 64, no. 3 (2008): 123–134.

Vasquez, Gabriel M., and Maureen Taylor. "Research Perspectives on 'the Public'." In *Handbook of Public Relations*, edited by Robert Lawrence Heath and Gabriel M. Vasquez, 139–154. London: Sage Publications, 2000.

Vassiliadis, Petros Von. "Orthodoxie und Kontextuele Theologie." *Okumenische Rundschau* 42 (October 1993): 407–541.

Velasquez, Manuel, Claire Andre, Thomas Shanks, and Michael J. Meyer. "The Common Good." Markkula Center for Applied Ethics. Last modified August 2, 2014. http://www.scu.edu/ethics/practicing/decision/commongood.html.

von Sinner, Rudolf. "Brazil: From Liberation Theology to a Theology of Citizenship as Public Theology." *International Journal of Public Theology* 1, nos. 3–4 (2007): 338–363.

Ward, Kevin. *Losing Our Religion? Changing Patterns of Believing and Belonging in Secular Western Societies.* Eugene, OR: Wipf & Stock Publishers, 2013.

Weavers. *VAW: A Theological Education Coursebook.* Suva, FJ: SPATS, 2006.

Wesley, John. *Personal Journal*, June 11, 1739. Last modified June 1, 2005. http://www.ccel.org/ccel/wesley/journal.vi.iii.v.html.

Wete, Tamara. *Women and Ministry in Melanesia: A Kanak Perspective.* Dunedin, NZ: Manahine Press, 2007.

Williams, Rowan. "Secularism, Faith and Freedom." *Keynote Address*, Pontifical Academy of Social Sciences, Rome, November 23, 2006.

Winn, Christian T., Christopher Gehrz, G. William Carlson, and Eric Holst, eds. *The Pietist Impulse in Christianity.* Eugene, OR: Wipf & Stock Publishers, 2012.

Wolsterstorff, Nicholas. *Until Justice and Peace Embrace.* Grand Rapids, MI: William B. Eerdmans, 1994.

Wren, Brian. *What Language Shall I Borrow? God-Talk in Worship: A Male Response to Feminist Theology.* London: SCM Press, 1989.

Wuthnow, Robert. *Christianity and Civil Society: The Contemporary Debate.* Valley Forge, PA: Trinity Press, 1996.

———. *Christianity in the Twenty-first Century.* New York, NY: Oxford University Press, 1993.

———. *Producing the Sacred: An Essay on Public Religion.* Urbana, IL: University of Chicago Press, 1994.

Yabaki, Akuila. Paper Presented, *Pacific Regional Workshop on Strengthening Partnerships for Eliminating Violence Against Women*, Pacific Forum Secretariat, Suva, Fiji, February 17–19, 2003.

Yates, Melissa. "Rawls and Habermas on Religion in the Public Sphere." *Philosophy and Social Criticism* 33, no. 7 (2007): 880–891.

Young, Iris Marion. "Five Faces of Oppression." In *Justice and Politics of Difference*, 39–65. Princeton, NJ: Princeton University Press, 1990.

———. *Inclusion and Democracy.* Oxford: Oxford University Press, 2000.

Zafirovski, Milan. *The Enlightenment and its Effects on Modern Society.* New York, NY: Springer-Verlag, 2011.

Index

Afamasaga, Toleafoa, 49
afitunu, 66
agaifanua, 16, 64–66, 87
aganu'u, 63–64, 87
agape, 58, 208
aga tausili, 15–16, 111, 121
Ahdar, Rex, 49
aiga, 53–54, 68, 75, 81–82, 85, 96, 182, 208; *aiga potopoto*, 57, 117, 134; *puiaiga*, 82
Aiono-Le Tagaloa, Fanaafi, 16–17, 52, 57, 64, 70–71, 75–78
alofa, 16, 57–58, 112–13, 120–21, 128, 208–9; as center of interlinked values, 134–36, *135*; as gift, 121; as unconditional sacrifice, 120
alo mai, alo atu, 54. *See also fa'aaloaalo*
Ambrose, 27
American Samoa, 48, 59n3, 82
amiotunu, 16, 55–56, 119; and biblical justice, 56; and honesty, 119; and leadership, 119
Anae, Melanie, 62, 98. *See also* Indigenous Pacific Research
Annells, Merilyn, 101
Anselm, 11
application of core values to Samoan public theology, 207–14. *See also* Samoan public theology; *alofa* (love), 208–9; *amiotonu* (justice), 213–14; *fa'aaloalo* (respect), 209–10; *soalaupule* (consensual dialogue), 212–13; *tautua* (service), 210–11
Aquinas, Thomas, 10
Aristotle, 10
Augustine, 10, 60n35
ava ceremony, 75; origins of, 114–16
avenues for Samoans to participate in public theology, 151–61. *See also* Samoan public theology; education, 155; *fa'asamoa*, 156–57; mass media, 152–53; preaching, 153–54; public awareness, 155–56; public policy, 159–61; village councils, 157–59. *See also fono*

Barber, William, 36; Poor Peoples' Campaign, 36, 45n81
Barth, Karl, 28; Barmen Declaration, 28
beachcombers, 90n24
Becket, Thomas á, 27
Bedford-Strohm, Heinrich, 28
Bellah, Robert, 25–26, 182
Benhabib, Seyla, 8–9
Benne, Robert, 33–34

Bevans, Stephen, 12–14, 48; contextual theology, models of, 12–14; relevance for Samoan contextual theology, 14
Bonhoeffer, Dietrich, 27–29; *Letters and Papers from Prison*, 29
Bradstock, Andrew, 19n15, 21n49
Breitenberg, Harold, 25–26, 31
Brown, Malcolm, 35
Browning, Don, 10
Brueggemann, Walter, 10–11

Calvin, John, 27–28
Carter, Stephen, 4
Casas, Bartolomé de las, 27
Casimira, Aisake, 136–37
casino bill, 50–51
CGT. *See* constructivist grounded theory
Chaplin, Jonathan, 4
Charmaz, Kathy, 101–2
Christian Right, 1–2
Chrysostom, John, 10
church group core values, 129–32, *129*; interweaving of values, 129–31; *lotomaualalo* (humility), 131–32
civil religion, 25–26. *See also* Bellah, Robert
common good, 2, 10–11; in Christian tradition, 10; erosion of, 10–11
Congregational Church of Jesus Theological School, 161
conscientization, 5–6. *See also* Freire; critical consciousness, 51; naïve transivity, 51; semi-intransivity, 51
Constitution of Samoa, 49, 185
constructivist grounded theory (CGT), 101–2, *106*
context, definition of, 47
contextual considerations in Samoan public theology, 183–89. *See also* Samoan public theology; church and social policies, 187; church and state, 184; *fa'asamoa* and Christianity, 185; media, churches' use of, 188–89; theological training, flaws in, 187; vision, churches' lack of, 185–87
contextual theology, 12–14, 48. *See also* Bevans, Stephen
Council for World Mission (CWM), 201–2. *See also* London Missionary Society
Crawford, Ronald, 82
CWM. *See* Council for World Mission

Darragh, Neil, 14, 172
Day, Katie, 180–81
de Gruchy, John, 31–32, 47
de Lange, Fritz, 28–29
Dewey, John, 7
Doak, Mary, 30
domestic violence, definitions of, 193–97. *See also* violence against women; feminist theory, 195; human rights theory, 197; psychological theory, 196; social learning theory, 195–96; sociological theory, 194–95
domestic violence, Samoan context, 198–201. *See also* power imbalance, Samoan culture; case studies of, 199–200; in the church, 206–7; statistics for, 198–99
Domestic Violence Prevention Unit, 196
Drozdow-St. Christian, Douglas, 62
Duke, James, 11
Duranti, Alessandro, 78

enacting theology in Samoan public life, 168–75. *See also* Samoan public theology; clergy, enactment by, 172–75; communicating values effectively, 170–71; core values, enactment of, 169–70; laity, enactment by, 171–72
Enlightenment, the, 3, 92n60
Ernst, Manfred, 1, 18n5, 18n7, 18n8, 48, 136, 142n40
Eurocentrism, 30, 33, 42n43, 52–53, 71, 97

fa'aaloalo, 15, 53–54, 58, 111–13, 165, 209–10; *alo mai, alo atu*, 112–13, 165; *osiaiga*, 111–12
fa'akerisiano, 16, 53, 61, 73, 87
fa'alavelave, 112, 121. *See also fa'aaloalo; alofa*
fa'alupega, 80
fa'amatai, 50, 64, 86–87, 188
fa'asamoa, 5, 15–17, 48, 52–55, 58, 61–65, 68–74, 77–87, 122, 130, 170, 189, 196, 207; definitions of, 61–63; fusion with Christianity, 86–87; governing principles, 86–87. *See also fa'amatai;* institutions of, 81–86; language, importance of, 77–78. *See also* Duranti, Alessandro; missionary influence on, 70–71, 73; oratory in, 78–79; signs in, 78
fa'asinomaga, 78
fa'avavau, 74
faifeau, 54, 72–73, 95. *See also feagaiga*
Fairbairn-Dunlop, Peggy, 206
Fala, Alexander, 118
Fala, Katie, 118
faletua, 84, 95. *See also nu'u*
Farley, Edward, 26–27
Farrelly, Trisia, 100–101
feagaiga, 70, 83. *See also faifeau*
fesagaiga o paolo, 65
Filemoni-Tofaeono, Joan A., 198, 201, 207
Fiorenza, Elizabeth Schüssler, 203
Fiorenza, Francis Schüssler, 10
fono, 57, 72, 81, 85, 118
Forrester, Duncan, 4, 25, 29, 32–33, 35, 37
Freeman, Derek, 62
Freire, Paulo, 5–6, 51, 100, 155. *See also* conscientization

Gerson, Samantha, 203
Giddens, Anthony, 136
Gilson, Richard, 68

globalization, 4, 136–38; Samoan values, influence on, 136–38
Global South, 11, 20n24. *See also* Third World
government workers and politicians group core values, 132–34, *132*; Samoa public service values, 132–33; *tuaoi* (boundaries), 134
Graham, Elaine, 3, 30
Grattan, F. J. H., 61, 67, 84
grounded theory (GT), 101
GT. *See also* grounded theory

Habermas, Jürgen, 8, 78, 170
Halapua, Sitiveni, 98–100. *See also* Indigenous Pacific Research
Halapua, Winston, 35, 44n71
Hannay, Alastair, 7–9
Havea, Jione, 100
Himes, Kenneth, 10
Himes, Michael, 10
Hollenbach, David, 11, 24
Horsley, Richard, 26
Howell, Lowell, 72
Huffer, Elise, 57, 111, 117, 212
Humphreys, Catherine, 193

'ie tōga, 89n19
Indigenous Pacific Research (IPR), 97–99, 220; *fonofale*, 98; *iluvatu*, 98; *kakala*, 98; *ta-va*, 98; *teu le va*, 98; *vanua*, 98
Inside Out, 201–2. *See also* Council for World Mission
Iofi, Fa'afouina, 181
IPR. *See also* Indigenous Pacific Research

Jacobs, Maretha, 205
Johnson, Elizabeth, 204
Johnson, Lydia, 198, 201, 207
Joldersma, Clarence, 3

Kamu, Lalomilo, 67, 73, 186–87
Keesing, Felix, 61

Kelly, Liz, 194
Kim, Sebastian, 36–39
King, Martin Luther Jr. *See also* Barber, William
Kluckholm, Clyde, 15
Kocan, Gurcan, 8
Kohn, Melvin, 15
Kolia, Fepa'i, 184
Koopman, Nico, 37
Koya-Vaka'uta, Cresantia, 97–98, 176n3

Lands and Titles Court, 77, 87
lauga fa'asamoa, 78–81. *See also fa'asamoa*, oratory in; preaching as, 80–81
Le'aupepe, Kasiano, 51
Lesa, Mata'afa Keni, 181
liberation theology, 29, 33, 180
Lichtman, Marilyn, 100
Lilomaiava-Doktor, Sa'iliemanu, 81–82
Lini, Walter, 44n72
London Missionary Society, 67, 90n35; Samoa, Congregationalists in, 68
lotu, 66–68, 73, 182
Luther, Martin, 27–28

MacIntyre, Alasdair, 32–33
Macpherson, Cluny, 117, 137, 184
Macpherson, La'avasa, 117, 137, 184
Macquarrie, John, 11
Maddox, Marion, 34
Mageo, Jeannette, 52, 62, 80
Mahina, Okustino, 98. *See also* Indigenous Pacific Research
Maliko, Selota, 68–70, 93n83
Malua Theological College, 161
mamalu, 113
mana, 99, 109n14
Marshall, Christopher, 197
Marty, Martin, 24; public church, 24
Marx, Karl, 174
matai, 9, 49–50, 54, 65–66, 69–70, 77, 82–85, 114, 118–19, 127, 213; *alii*, 84, 145, 158, 198–99; missionary influence on, 69–70, 77; *tulafale*, 71, 79–80
Mathewes, Charles, 31; theology of public life, 31
Medhurst, Kenneth, 15
Melanesian Brotherhood, 35, 44n73
Meleisea, Malama, 68, 82, 87
Methodist Church in Samoa, 96
Micklethwait, John, 1
Migliore, Daniel, 11
Milner, G. B, 55. *See also Samoan Dictionary*
Moamoa Theological College, 161
Moghaddam, F. M., 195
Moltman, Jürgen, 3, 11, 29, 37
Mulitalo-Lauta, Pa'u, 63, 208
Mullender, Audrey, 193

Nabobo-Baba, Unaisi, 100–101
Nafanua, 67, 90n28; Malietoa, conversion of, 67, 90n30; Tamafaiga, assassination of, 67, 90n30
Naisilisili, Sereima, 98. *See also* Indigenous Pacific Research
National University of Samoa (NUS), 96
Nepo, Gataivai, 54–55
New Religious Movements (NRMs), 2
Newell, James, 75–76. *See also Papers and Diaries on Samoan Tapuaiga*
NGO group core values, 128–29, *128*; *alofa* and *tautua*, 128; honesty, team work, sharing, 128–29
NGOs. *See* nongovernmental organizations
Nicholls, Bruce, 12
Nokise, Feleterika, 64
nongovernmental organizations (NGOs), 128
NRMs. *See* New Religious Movements
NUS. *See* National University of Samoa
nu'u, 80–86, 182; *aualuma*, 85; *aumaga*, 83; *faletua ma tausi*, 83–84, 95; *tama'ita'i*, 83; *tamaiti*, 84; *taule'ale'a*, 83, 127

O Le Siosiomaga (OLSSI), 156
OLSSI. *See O Le Siosiomaga*

Pacific Theological College, 5, 202
Paeth, Scott, 37
Papers and Diaries on Samoan Tapuaiga, 75–76. *See also* Newell, James
patriarchy, 201–6. *See also* power imbalance, Samoan culture; use of Bible to reinforce, 203–6
Paymar, Michael, 193
Pearson, Clive, 14, 34
Pence, Michael, 193
Piula Theological College, 96, 161. *See also* Methodist Church in Samoa
Polynesia, 48, 58–59n2
power imbalance, Samoan culture, 201–2. *See also* domestic violence, Samoan context
practical theology, 43n48
Pratt, George, 112, 117
Pray For Our Pacific movement, 36
Prescott, Semisi, 99–100
Proslogium, 11
public, 7, 9–10; origins of, 7; in public theology, 9–10
public ethics, 26
public sphere, 4, 8, 20, 175, 180; according to Habermas, 20n33; in Samoa, 9, 180; origins of, 8
public theology, 14–15, 24–27, 30, 32–36; biblical roots of, 26–27; central claims of, 36–38; Christian in, 32–35; definitions of, 24–26; historical precursors of, 27–29; public theologians, definition of, 35–36; Western construct, 30
Pulotu-Endermann, Fuimaono Karl, 98. *See also* Indigenous Pacific Research

Ramesh, Abhinaya, 196–97
Rauschenbush, Walter, 29. *See also* social gospel movement
Rawls, John, 10

The Relational Self, 63. *See also* Vaai, Upolu
res publica, 24
Retzlaff, Lemalu Sina, 200
Rhema Bible Training Centre, 161
Rokeach, Milton, 15
role of public theology in Samoa, 166–68. *See also* Samoan public theology; connecting church and society, 168; embodying core values, 166–67; providing solutions to problems, 167
Roman Catholic social teachings, 10

sailor cults, 89n23
Samoa National Council of Churches, 51, 222
Samoan Dictionary, 55. *See also* Milner
Samoan public theology, 14–15, 144–51, 180–83. *See also* avenues for Samoans to participate in public theology; contextual considerations in Samoan public theology; biblical basis for, 144–45; importance of addressing social problems in, 147–48; importance of connecting sacred and secular in, 148–49; praxis orientation of, 145–46; relationality as core of, 145; role of core values in, 149–51; Samoan translation of, 14–15
Samoa Observer, The, 152, 173–74, 181, 200; *Sunday Observer*, 173–74
Samoa Victim Support Group (SVSG), 199, 207
Sanga, Kabini, 98–99. *See also* Indigenous Pacific Research
Sauoaiga, Laufai, 113
Scheler, Max, 135
Schoeffel, Penelope, 62, 73–74
Schreiter, Robert, 20n63
Secretariat of the Pacific Community (SPC), 198
Shore, Brad, 62, 125
si'ialofa, 65–66, 121. *See also alofa*
Sio, Peseta, 198–99, 201

Smith, Frank, 111
soalaupule, 16, 56–57, 117–18, 212–13; and *pule*, 117; and *tofa*, 118
social gospel movement, 29. *See also* Rauschenbush, Walter
So'o, Asofou, 57, 111, 117, 212
South Pacific Association of Theological Schools (SPATS), 6–7
South Pacific Nazarene Theological School, 161
SPATS. *See* South Pacific Association of Theological Schools
SPC. *See* Secretariat of the Pacific Community
Stackhouse, Max, 32
Stone, Howard, 11
Suaalii-Sauni, Tamasailau, 100–101
suicide rate in Samoa, 190n11
Sunia, Fofo Iosefa, 112
SVSG. *See* Samoa Victim Support Group
Sweeney, James, 15

tabua, 140n13
Tagaloa, 71, 73–74
talanoa, 17, 35, 211–12, 222
talanoa-CGT synthesis, 102–7, *106*. *See also* constructivist grounded theory; data analysis, 105–6; evaluation, 107; format, 103–4; interviews, 103; participants, 102–3
talanoa research methodology, 97–101, *105*
tala o le vavau, 73–74
tama'ita'i, 70
Tamez, Elsa, 205
Tanner, Kathryn, 10
tapuaiga, 74–77
taula-aitu, 77, 91n37
Taulealeausumai, Feiloaiga, 113
tautua, 15, 54–55, 58, 112–17, 128; and blessings, 114–16; *tautua i le lotu*, 116–17; *tautua matavela*, 114; *tautua tuavae*, 114
Taylor, Maureen, 7

Taylor, Rachel, 195
teu le va, 52, 64. *See also* Indigenous Pacific Research
Thaman, Konai Helu, 98. *See also* Indigenous Pacific Research
theology, definition of, 11
Thiemann, Ronald, 37–38
Third World, 19n24. *See also* Global South
Tofaeono, Amaamalele, 64
tofaloloto, 162
tofamamao, 162
Toma, Maiava, 214
Tracy, David, 24–25, 36–37, 180–81
training of Samoan public theologians, 161–66. *See also* Samoan public theology; authoritarianism, problem of, 164–66; conservatism, problem of, 161–63; gender inequality, problem of, 163–64
TRC. *See* Truth and Reconciliation Commission
trivialization of Christianity, 4
Truth and Reconciliation Commission (TRC), 34
tufanua, 113
Tui Atua, T. T. T. E., 58, 62, 66, 76–77, 108n2, 111, 115–16, 120, 125
Tuilaepa, Aiono, 51
Tuisuga, Fa'alepo, 118, 183
Tupuola, Anne-Marie, 98. *See also* Indigenous Pacific Research
Tutu, Desmond, 34
Tuwere, Ilaitia Sevati, 98. *See also* Indigenous Pacific Research

Va, 51–53, 86, 118, 125; Samoan self, 52–53
Va'a, Felise, 114
Vaai, Emma Kruse, 72, 87
Vaai, Upolu L., 53, 63, 113; tino theology, 63
VAGST. *See* Value Added to Goods and Services Tax

Vaioleti, Timote, 99–100
Vaka'uta, Nasili, 100
Value Added to Goods and Services Tax (VAGST), 186
values, definition of, 15–16; Samoan definition of, 15–16
van Aarde, Andries, 35
Vasquez, Gabriel, 7
Victorian era, 71; English Protestantism in, 71
village group core values, 123–27, *124*; *tausa'afia* (well-bred), 124–25. *See also fa'aaloalo; tautua fa'amaoni* (loyal servant), 125–27; values flowing from *alofa*, 123–24
violence against women, 6–7. *See also* domestic violence, definitions of; in Oceania, 7

Ward, Kevin, 2
Water Protectors, 36, 45n80

WCC. *See* World Council of Churches
Weavers. *See* South Pacific Association of Theological Schools
Wendt, Albert, 52
Wesley, John, 4, 19n14
Wesleyan Methodist Missionary Society, 67–68, 90n35; Samoa, Methodists in, 68
Westminster parliamentary system, 50
Wilberforce, William, 3–4, 19n13
Williams, John, 67–68
Williams, Rowan, 4
Wolterstorff, Nicholas, 214
Wooldrige, Adrian, 1
World Council of Churches (WCC), 12
World Health Organization, 198
Wuthnow, Robert, 10

Yabaki, Akuila, 201
Yates, Melissa, 4
Young, Iris Marion, 8

About the Author

Mercy Ah Siu-Maliko is a lecturer in Theology at Piula Theological College in Samoa and a research affiliate at the Centre for Theology and Public Issues of the University of Otago in New Zealand. She earned her PhD in public theology at the University of Otago, and was previously the director of *Weavers*, the women's advocacy arm of the South Pacific Association of Theological Schools based in Fiji. She is the author of numerous journal articles and conference papers, and, in 2018, *Tatala le Ta'ui a le Atua: Rolling out the Fine Mat of Scripture*, published by the Centre for Theology and Public Issues at Otago University.

www.ingramcontent.com/pod-product-compliance
Lightning Source LLC
Chambersburg PA
CBHW050901300426
44111CB00010B/1331